FAMILY WEALTH COUNSELING

Getting to the Heart of the Matter

A revolution in estate planning for wealthy families

Jay Link

Clare Price

In this book, the editors and contributors are not engaged in rendering legal, tax, accounting, financial planning, investment or similar professional advice or services for any specific individual or situation. Examples in this text are used for illustrative purposes only and do not represent recommendations. All stories in this book including the supplement are based on actual experiences. In some cases, the names and details have been changed to protect the privacy of the people involved. Some material may be affected by changes in the laws or in the interpretations of such laws since the manuscript for this book was completed. For that reason, the accuracy and completeness of such information and the opinions based thereon are not guaranteed. In addition, state or local tax laws or procedural rules may have a material impact on the general recommendations made by the contributing authors, and the strategies outlined in this book and its supplement may not be suitable for every individual. Anyone planning to take action in any of the areas this book describes should, of course, seek professional advice from Family Wealth Counselors, accountants, lawyers, tax and other advisors, as would be prudent and advisable under their given circumstances.

ISBN 0-9674023-0-1
Library of Congress Catalog Card Number 99-066550

Project Editor: Judy Kenninger
Assisting Editor: Paul H. Brock
Technical Editor: William R. Muench JD, CPA
Project Assistant: Wendy N. Curry
Print Manager: Don Carnagua, MetroGraphics Printing
Managing Editor: Sonya Baker-Hallett

PROFESSIONAL MENTORING PROGRAM
P.O. Box 697
Franklin, Indiana 46131
1-888-736-7201
www.fwc9dots.com

Clare Price is President of Family Wealth Consultants, Ltd. a firm specializing in intergenerational planning for families. For 25 years she has worked with families enabling them to maximize the impact of their wealth as it relates to their lifestyle choices and sense of purpose. Her sincerity and ability to inspire individuals makes her an integral member of the family's advisory team.

Clare is a Family Wealth Counselor and a Chartered Financial Consultant. She conducts educational workshops for attorneys, CPAs and nonprofit institutions. Clare is an advisor to the Beaumont Foundation, Judson Center, Inc. and the Detroit Symphony Orchestra Planned Giving Advisory Councils.

INTRODUCTION

When I was first introduced to Family Wealth Counseling in June 1996 I didn't realize the profound impact it would have not only on the lives of my clients but my life as well.

For the previous sixteen years I had focused most of my attention in the areas of business succession and traditional estate planning. The driving force for many of the plans that were developed during this period of time was the elimination of transfer (federal estate tax) taxes. Yet, when I presented a completed plan that substantially reduced the tax consequences to the family often times little if any action was taken. There was hesitancy, an uncertainty that seemed to keep the family from moving forward. How could a family ignore such tremendous tax savings available to them? As many families have done and continue to do, they would purchase life insurance as a means to pay transfer taxes. But in the end who still receives 100% of the tax dollars? That's right, the federal government. Assets leaving our control and our community.

It was Family Wealth Counseling that helped me understand that the numbers - no matter how compelling - were often not enough by themselves to motivate an individual to adopt a sophisticated strategy or implement a comprehensive plan. Instead, what I came to understand was that until an individual addresses the deeper personal issues in their life, issues that center on their values and beliefs, they are often unable to implement an effective estate plan. Through the Family

Wealth Counseling Process individuals are able to gain clarity and thus an enhanced sense of purpose.

In the last four years I have totally devoted my practice to Family Wealth Counseling. During this time I have had the opportunity to take several families through this process. A few individuals thought their estate plans were well in place. In every situation the family was able to increase their philanthropic capacity, and substantially reduce federal estate taxes without impacting their current lifestyle or the legacy they wished to leave their children. Especially meaningful for many of these families was the creation of their own family charitable fund or family foundation. It gave them a very tangible way to allow future generations to actively participate in philanthropy. Further, it helped them understand the importance of giving back to the community.

Each time a family or individual engages in the Family Wealth Counseling Process they achieve increased clarity concerning personal issues, which often allows them to discover their unique ability to make a significant difference—a difference beyond their imagination.

For those clients and myself who choose to engage in Family Wealth Counseling, estate planning has transcended to Legacy Planning. Helping families move from a position of success to one of significance.

What advisors are saying about Family Wealth Counseling . . .

"Speaking from my more than twenty-five years of experience as an estate planning professional, I am very impressed with the dimensions that have been added through Family Wealth Counseling. It has been very refreshing to work with Clare simply because the combination of technical skills and broad planning insights that can be developed as a team can provide the client with more than just a paper product. I have witnessed first hand the great fulfillment that clients experience when the planning process is expanded to a comprehensive development of vision, objectives and wealth preservation. I am pleased that this book has been developed to show real life examples of the success of the Family Wealth Counseling approach."

Douglas J. Rasmussen, Esq.
Clark-Hill, Detroit, MI

"The Family Wealth Counseling process, along with Clare Price has taken one of my best clients and helped them become acclimated to the sudden infusion of liquidity they received from the sale of their family business. Clare has helped them broaden their view of who they are themselves, their family and the community. In addition to teaching these clients how to monitor and manage their own wealth, her work with them has allowed them to see themselves as full members of that small group of society that can shape and guide the future. In the process, they provide a role model for their own family, a true legacy of self worth in addition to a financially secure future. Through a Family Foundation, they will be able to make meaningful financial contributions to causes which they embrace."

Melvyn S. Goldstein, Esq., Birmingham, MI

"Most of my clients are filled with anxiety over the subject of estate planning, particularly when significant wealth is involved and/or family issues make decisions difficult. The Family Wealth Counseling process has eased that anxiety, and actually helped my clients resolve many of the conflicting emotions that troubled them when deciding who should inherit their wealth and how. I have been extremely pleased with the results of the work Clare has done for my clients."

Linda J. Russell, CPA, West Bloomfield, MI

Preface

Family Wealth Counseling
A Paradigm Shift in Estate Planning

Family Wealth Counseling is a revolutionary approach to working with wealthy families that has swept our country over the past several years. Articles about Family Wealth Counseling have appeared in the *LA Times, Denver Post, Detroit Free Press, Indianapolis Star, Chicago Tribune and Forbes Magazine,* just to name a few. Family Wealth Counseling has been written about and expounded upon in numerous professional journals as well. The press, professional advisors and the affluent have been impressed with the uniqueness and the power of this human approach to planning. Imagine a virtues-based, purpose-driven, life planning process. Contrast that with the traditional estate planning process that many times is unfulfilling and often only serves to minimize the damage. What a fresh alternative!

Financial planners, attorneys, accountants, money managers and life underwriters from all over the U.S. have witnessed the remarkable power and phenomenal success of the Family Wealth Counseling process. As a result, hundreds of them have decided to join this revolution. They have spent substantial amounts of money and undertaken hundreds of hours of comprehensive classroom and field training all to help move them from traditional estate planners to Family Wealth Counselors.

A Common Problem

The most frequent comment from America's financial and legal advisors is that everybody is talking about this kind of planning, but nobody is actually doing it. Sadly, they are absolutely correct. There are many advisors out there selling some piece of the puzzle—some inventive tool, powerful trust, clever strategy or hot financial product—but they are not doing much comprehensive planning.

Consider this illustration. You have some interest in buying an airplane. After three minutes of conversation with a salesman, he makes arrangements for you to meet him at the airstrip where he can show you the "perfect" plane for you.

The plane he shows you happens to be the very one that the salesman owns himself. To the salesman, his plane is the plane everyone should own. He believes this plane has it all. In fact, he has led the company in sales for the past three years, selling this same model.

After arriving at the airport, he shows you the plane and describes the tensile strength of the metal alloy in the wings. He shows you page after page of test results. He opens up the hood and shows you the engine. He produces the specs. He tells you it has the most powerful engine in its class. He tells you of the thrust this engine can produce, the speed the plane can fly and how fast it can climb. He is excited and tells you to look at those numbers. He tries to engage you, "Impressive, isn't it?" You are not sure what all those numbers mean, but you act impressed, because he is so impressed.

He takes you inside and asks you to note the quality of the upholstery. He shows you the control panel—the finest IFR equipment manufactured. He shows you the warranties and the accuracy tests on each piece of equipment. You are beginning to feel somewhat overwhelmed. You feel a tugging on your sleeve and hear words whispered softly in your ear, "Let's go, Honey." You do not want to be rude, so you endure the sales pitch a little longer.

You are now back in the cargo area—most cargo space of any plane in its class by a full three cubic feet. Once you crawl out of the cabin area, he takes you under the wings to show you the landing gear. This is no ordinary landing gear. It is the most expensive hydraulic landing gear made. Stronger than any other on the market. He again produces pages of statistics.

The fuel capacity of this plane is the largest in its class. He shows you the charts. Look how far you can fly before needing to refuel. By this time you are completely overwhelmed and more than a little ready to bring this plane tour to an end. Your enthusiasm for flying has been squelched by the data-dump of all the details. You politely excuse yourself in spite of his insistence that you go back to his office to see what kind of price can be negotiated.

You agree that you have never seen a more impressive airplane in your life but tell him that you need to think about it some more before you make a decision. The reality is that you will never call him back.

He tries one final close by reminding you that there is no time like the present and warns you that things happen. You agree, but still resist. You retreat to your car and give up on the idea of flying —at least for now.

There is just too much about flying that you do not understand. You cannot make an informed decision. You feel it would be better to wait and think about it some more.

⟺◆⟺

One year later, you meet with a Family Wealth Counselor. He explains that the first step in the Family Wealth Counseling process is to spend a day, talking about and answering some very important questions. He needs to get to know you. He wants to understand what it is that you want out of life and what is important to you. Finally, he wants to know exactly where you want your life to go.

After spending the day together, you clarify that spending time with your spouse, children and grandchildren is extremely important to you. Your business requires you to do a great amount of traveling, and you do not enjoy being gone overnight. But, because your work requires you to fly to many small towns with limited scheduled flights, you often end up spending the night away from home. Driving to the airport, parking your car, checking your luggage and waiting for your flight to take off all add up to weeks away from your family time each year.

In your discussions, you tell him that you logged several hours flying planes when you were in college. But, with a new family and the financial demands of business, you had put buying your own plane on the back burner for over thirty years.

He also learns that there is a private airport just two miles from your home. So he explores the option of you buying a plane. With the tax benefits and depreciation, he discovers that it might make sense. Your interest in buying a plane has returned. You always loved flying. The thrill of piloting a multi-ton piece of machinery into thin air is beyond description. You love to soar above the clouds. You remember the breathtaking view of landing in a major city at night with its sea of lights dotting the darkness. You recall the sensation of breaking through the cloud-cover on a cold winter day and soaking up the warm sunlight that the world below could not see or enjoy.

You decide you do want to fly again. You want to have more time with your family and flying will make that possible. It is perfect.

You ask, "What kind of a plane should I get?" After considerable research on your behalf, the Family Wealth Counselor determines that a single engine turbo-prop would be ideal.

Your spouse asks, "Is it safe? I want him in a safe plane! If he's going to fly, I want him in a safe plane!"

"Oh yes," he tells you. "It is not only the safest plane made but also the most efficient. There is no plane on the market that is any better for what you want to do," he reassures them.

You enthusiastically get out your checkbook to write a check to purchase the exact plane that he has recommended. You are so excited that you have trouble sleeping that night.

By the way, the plane you just bought was the exact plane the airplane salesman was trying to sell you earlier. So, what was the difference? The Family Wealth Counselor was not selling airplanes. In fact, he was not selling anything. He was simply asking you important questions in an attempt to help you discover what you wanted to do.

In this case, it just so happened an airplane was an excellent decision. But now you can see that decision within the larger context of a total life-plan. You understand the "why." Once you know why, you can be excited again about buying and flying a plane. It is hard to be impressed with the majesty of a picture of Michaelangelo's Sistine Chapel on a jigsaw puzzle if you see only six pieces of the puzzle. The same is true when someone is promoting only a certain trust, innovative transaction or a hot new product.

You might ask, "How does it all fit together? Does it all fit together? If we can get it all to fit together, what kind of monstrosity might it look like when it is done? What if I don't like it after it's done? Is it irrevocable?" Understanding how a piece fits within the context of the whole life-plan brings about the clarity a client needs in order to be excited—and not overwhelmed.

The Common Question

Professional advisors in the financial and legal industries continue to ask us one question whenever they see the work we do with our clients—How are you getting clients to do all this?

Some years ago, we received a call from an attorney who was the head of planned giving for a major religious charity. He was a brilliant technician and was committed to his organization. During the past year, through referrals, several of his wealthiest donors had retained us to take them through the Family Wealth Counseling process. The results we achieved were beyond the wildest dreams of these families. We recovered millions of dollars that would otherwise have been lost to the IRS, and most of that money was now on its way to this planned giving officer's organization. After each report of a major unsolicited planned gift, he would ask the donor, "Who has helped you do this?"

He got the same answer each time. The donor would tell him about us. He could no longer contain himself. He called and asked if we would meet with him the next time we were in town. The day arrived when we were to meet. We sat down in his office and asked him what he wanted to ask us.

He said he did not have any questions about

the planning tools we use. The one question he did have was how we were getting his donors to make all of these major planned gifts. He told us that he had been talking with these people for decades about doing something like this but had never been able to get them "off the dime." He asked us what we were doing that prompted his donors to make such substantial planned gifts.

—————≥·◇·≤—————

In a similar experience, we were meeting with one of the largest law firms in America. The firm had more than fifty estate planning attorneys in the trust-and-estate department. Our clients' net worth in this case was forty million dollars. We were meeting with the clients and all the advisors at the law firm to begin implementing the master plan we had designed for them. The advisors and the couple had approved the plan beforehand. This meeting was to delegate implementation tasks.

After the meeting, a senior partner of the law firm took us aside to his personal office. He told us that he had to ask us one question that had been gnawing at him. He asked us how we were getting this family to do all this planning all at one time. He said that it would have taken his firm twenty years of meetings, talking and presenting ideas to get this couple to implement all the strategies and techniques we had incorporated into their master plan—*if* his firm could have done it at all. He further asked us what we had done to get the couple so excited and so motivated to action.

The Answer

The answers to the questions posed by the planned giving officer and the attorney are exactly the same. It is the process that we take our clients through that motivates them to implement these sophisticated plans and empowers them to take control of the process and enjoy the fulfilling results the plans produce.

In the chapters to follow, we outline the Family Wealth Counseling process. Time and time again, this process leads to plan implementation instead of the never-ending period of evaluation, hesitation and uncertainty that is common with traditional planning.

With traditional planning, clients often recognize the process has left them with a tax, inheritance or business-continuation plan, but clients are not always sure what has been done. Further, the traditional planning process does not generate any degree of excitement for clients. Once our clients complete the Family Wealth Counseling process, they understand how everything fits together into one big picture. They have built a master *life*-plan that they indeed understand and find exciting, fulfilling and motivating.

Through our counseling process, our clients become absolutely clear about what they want. Enhanced clarity produces greater confidence, and that greater confidence empowers them to effectively take control of the entire planning process. The *clients* are able to tell their advisors what they want done instead of wholly relying upon their advisors. With this enhanced clarity and greater confidence, they discover substantially increased leverage for their remaining time, unique talents and accumulated treasures. This discovery will motivate and fulfill them for the rest of their days.

A Unified Team

In order for wealthy people to discover such increased leverage, they need to have a team of advisors who trust one another. Clients need a team that can work together, think and plan creatively, and know the hard technical issues as well as the soft central issues of life and planning. They need a team that can effectively integrate all three aspects of each family's wealth into a client's plan design. If all the players on the planning team are not working in concert, respecting each other's expertise, listening more than talking, and working toward consensus, the process will be sabotaged, and the client will not act.

———⊰◆⊱———

We recently heard back from one of our potential clients. He had called one of his other advisors after our initial meeting. He had explained to his advisor what we were offering to do for him. His advisor had told him that what we were telling him could not be done. As a result, he would not retain us.

This wealthy man, who had been so excited about the new possibilities for his life and his wealth, became emotionally paralyzed. Because one of his advisors was still operating under an old planning paradigm—because of a categorical rejection of a new planning process—this wealthy man was emotionally immobilized. We knew what this wealthy man could have done with what he had. We knew what joy he could have experienced and the good he could have accomplished.

This kind of disregard for other advisors, caused either by *paradigm paralysis or the all-other-advisors-are-the-enemy syndrome,* is far too common and very unfortunate. It confuses, frustrates and even irritates clients to such an extent that they become unsure of themselves or fearful that they might be making a mistake. They frequently abandon the entire planning process, or they end up abandoning their current advisors to look for others. Either way, no one is well served.

A Family Wealth Counselor is specifically trained in how to build effective planning teams and how to build unity and consensus among the team members. This allows everyone to be a winner. We do not come to replace any current advisor on the planning team, nor are we coming with any preset plan, hidden agenda, pet-planning tool or favorite product. We come to counsel the family. We come to help them discover where they really want to go. Then, through sophisticated, creative planning and effective teamwork with the other advisors, we design a plan that helps clients get to where they want to go.

Whether you are a wealthy individual, a professional advisor or a charity, we believe you will find this book to be a fascinating insight into

Family Wealth Counseling, a process whose time has come. For those of you who are ready to embrace a powerful new planning paradigm, this book will give you both the rationale and the methodology to break free like a butterfly from its cocoon, seeing both life and the world from an exhilarating new perspective. It will open your eyes. It will open your heart. It will allow you to begin thinking beyond . . .

E.G. "Jay" Link

Contents

SECTION II

The Unique Counseling Process of Family Wealth Counseling

SECTION III

The Unique Family Planning Issues
Addressed in Family Wealth Counseling

Chapter 9 –
Understanding the Psychological
Pyramid of Priorities
129

Chapter 10 –
Planning with Your Heart as
Well as Your Head
143

Chapter 11 –
Resolving Family Conflicts
and Repairing Broken Relationships
159

Chapter 12 –
Preparing Your Heirs for
Their Inheritance
185

Chapter 13 –
Building a Strong Family Tree:
A Lasting Legacy for Future Generations
207

ADDENDA

TECHNICAL SUPPLEMENT

The common planning tools and techniques of our profession

Sample Case Studies

SECTION I

THE UNIQUE CRITICAL MENTAL ANGLE OF FAMILY WEALTH COUNSELING

CHAPTER 1

What Makes the Family Wealth Counseling Approach Unique?

Because Family Wealth Counselors are relatively new to the planning scene, one of the first questions we are asked by both potential clients and professional advisors is, What makes the Family Wealth Counseling approach unique?

Family Wealth Counseling is considerably more than simply looking at a financial statement and an estate tax table and then "running the numbers." Family Wealth Counselors recognize that there are actually three distinct aspects to each family's wealth. Only by fully exploring and incorporating all three aspects into the overall planning process can we hope to achieve maximum planning results and maximum benefits to the family.

#1 – The Financial Aspect
of a Family's Wealth

The financial aspect of a family's wealth is the most commonly understood and addressed of the three. The financial aspect includes all the "stuff" you have accumulated over the years—stocks, bonds, mutual funds, buildings, businesses, personal property, etc. These are the things that in a real sense you have traded your life for, by trading major blocks of your time and energy to accumulate them. But they are still just *stuff*.

Of the three aspects of a family's wealth, the financial aspect is the most shallow. It is shallow because looking at a financial statement, listing in detail all the things you possess, tells us nothing about you—the person behind the property. Of course, we will know that you own a manufacturing business, or you like Microsoft stock, or that you live in a very exclusive neighborhood. But we will not know much, if anything, about you as a person.

You can see that this makes the financial aspect the most impersonal. If we were to line up ten wealthy people and provide you with a balance sheet, could you pick out the owner of that balance sheet? If you could, it would have been nothing more than a lucky guess. Assets and liabilities are not about people. They are about things owned by people.

A very wealthy man, who had heard about what we do, mailed us a "hypothetical" balance sheet and asked us to give him some ideas on "if this were his situation" what planning steps he

4

might take. He hinted that if we gave him answers he liked he might retain us. We told him his request was akin to calling up a doctor and asking, "I am sick. What drug or surgery would you recommend for me?"

As you know, the doctor would refuse to prescribe any drug or recommend any surgery without a comprehensive examination. It would be malpractice to do otherwise. Similarly, simply looking at a financial balance sheet in no way provides us enough information about a couple or a family to do anything but the most superficial planning. As you will learn in this book, we are not in the business of doing superficial planning.

The financial aspect is also extremely well defined. Most affluent people have a very accurate idea of their net worth. Much of their net worth can be determined by looking in the financial section of the newspaper on any given day. Harder-to-value assets such as real estate and businesses can be accurately valued through detailed appraisals. We rarely come across clients who have no real idea of their net worth.

Because the financial aspect of a family's wealth is so shallow, so impersonal and so well defined, it is easy to discuss. When you go to one of your advisors, what is the first piece of information they want to see or talk with you about? Your current financial information. This is almost universal.

Do you remember the old television show *Dragnet?* Joe Friday always requested witnesses to give him, "Just the facts, ma'am. Just the facts." This is the same approach taken by many traditional advisors. They are not particularly interested in getting into matters that cannot be explained or illustrated by a legal document, cash-flow ledger or balance sheet. This does not make them uncaring or incompetent professionals. They are simply doing the job for which they have been trained and for which you have hired them. They are experts in "just the facts." To expect more is unrealistic.

It is for this reason that we suggest that the financial aspect is the least important of all three aspects of a family's wealth. We are not saying it is not important, because it is. In fact, it is very important. But, in comparison to the other two aspects of a family's wealth, we strongly believe it is the least important.

Yet, as we have worked with thousands of wealthy clients all over the United States, we have observed that more than ninety percent of all estate planning currently being done begins and ends with the financial aspect. The other two aspects are never even discussed, much less integrated into their plans.

We have observed that traditional estate planning is nothing more than a series of unpleasant business decisions that must be made in order to minimize the damage.

We have not met many people who get enthusiastic over minimizing the damage. That is why no one gets excited about going to the dentist. The best news you can possibly get from your dentist is that nothing new has gone wrong. That is the best news. The worst news could be a need for fillings, root canals, plates, bridges or teeth pulling—all of these procedures have the singular goal of minimizing the damage.

Imagine that you went on a trip and received a phone call from your local fire chief. "Mr. Jones," he begins, "I have some good news and some bad news."

"Oh, wonderful," you think. You cannot wait to hear this!

"Well, Sir, the bad news is . . . your house burned down last night."

"So what's the good news?" you ask anxiously.

"Well, Sir, we were able to save your garage."

Somehow, we think you would not be enthusiastic over the good news. Likewise, most people are less than enthusiastic when told that the federal government is going to take half of their estate in taxes. That is the bad news. The good news, your advisors tell you, is that, if you buy a life insurance policy, you can minimize the damage to your estate.

"Oh, now that is exciting," you moan. "We get to choose between reducing our current cash flow now to pay for the insurance, so we can minimize the damage once we are dead. Or, we can preserve our current cash flow but have our family's wealth devastated by taxes when we die. It seems our only decision is which way do we want to lose.

People do not get excited about minimizing the damage. What people do get excited about, however, is maximizing their potential! That is what Family Wealth Counseling is all about—helping families maximize their potential.

However, addressing exclusively the financial aspects of a family's wealth cannot do this. The other two aspects must be addressed fully and carefully incorporated into the planning process.

#2 – The Social Aspect of a Family's Wealth

The social aspect of family wealth may be the most misunderstood of the three aspects. We find that this aspect has been completely overlooked in almost every current plan we review for our clients. This is tragic. But, before we explain the power of the social aspect, let us explain what it is. The federal government has passed laws requiring all wealthy Americans to donate a considerable portion of their families' wealth to the general welfare of this country. It is the law. No one can be born in this country, grow rich in this country or die rich in this country without contributing a substantial portion of his or her accumulated wealth to others. This is how wealth is redistributed.

However, what very few wealthy families know is that the federal government gives you a choice in how you support the general welfare of our country. You can do so as an involuntary philanthropist or you can do so as a voluntary philanthropist.

Involuntary Philanthropy
vs. Voluntary Philanthropy

Involuntary philanthropists agree by default simply to relinquish that portion of their accumulated wealth going to support others to the federal government, giving the government the authority to distribute those funds as it sees fit. We call the portion of a family's wealth required to be distributed to others *Social Capital.* The overwhelming majority of Americans select the default option of involuntary philanthropy, even though they may fiscally, morally or ethically oppose how our government will use their Social Capital contributions.

In contrast, voluntary philanthropists choose to self-direct their Social Capital to the causes and organizations they wish to support—those that they believe are doing the most good for the most people—instead of simply turning that wealth over to the IRS in the form of estate taxes. Being proactive in this decision-making process produces surprising and exciting results, which we will outline in chapter 2. We ask you, If you wrote a check for one million dollars to the IRS or wrote that same million-dollar check to your favorite local charity, where would it do the most good?

We have asked that question of thousands of wealthy families around this country, and we hear the same response. The most efficient use of that one million dollars would be to give it to charity. Yet, if everyone agrees making gifts directly to charity is far more efficient than funneling those same funds through the federal bureaucracy, there is a profound question that must be asked. The question is:

If we all agree that self-directed Social Capital is more efficient than paying taxes, why isn't every wealthy family in America doing it?

We think there is only one answer to this question, and it must not be taken lightly. That answer is:

Not every wealthy family in America knows they have a choice!

Since many families do not know they have this powerful and compelling choice—a vastly superior alternative—it is not surprising they do not take advantage of it.

A New World of Opportunities

Once you choose to be a voluntary philanthropist instead of an involuntary one, a new world of opportunities opens up. But with this new world come options few have considered seriously.

As you can see, this social aspect is more complex than the financial aspect. It also gets moderately personal. We need to know more about you than simply what stuff you own. We need to learn what you care about, whom you care about, and which communities you want to help outside your own family. For our clients, this social aspect is typically not well defined before they meet us. They simply have never had anyone help them understand and then act upon this understanding in a meaningful and fulfilling way.

As we explore the social aspects of our clients' wealth, we ask them: "If we gave you a million dollars right now and told you not to spend it on yourself or give it to your children, but you had to give it away to charity, where would you give it?" Can you guess how the overwhelming majority of our clients reply? What would you say?

Often, a client's response is, "I am not really sure. I would have to give that some thought."

Do you know why they have to give it some thought? Because they have never considered the possibility that they might give one million dollars away to charity at some point in time, much less ten, fifty, or perhaps one hundred million dollars.

If a wealthy family has never contemplated making any major charitable gifts, they often will find this topic very difficult to discuss. They do not know what the options are. They do not even know what questions to ask. They do not know how to engage the entire family in this process. Therefore, we find ourselves gladly assisting in exploring all the exciting possibilities and opportunities this new world has to offer.

This social aspect is very important in the Family Wealth Counseling process. The following chart shows the considerable impact including the social aspect has in the planning results we achieve.

	Traditional Planning *Ignoring* Social Aspect	Family Wealth Counseling *Including* Social Aspect
Family Social Capital Distribution Controlled by	Government	Family
Effectiveness of Social Capital Use	Low	High
Personal Fulfillment	Low	High
Motivation to Implement Plan	Low	High

With the Family Wealth Counseling approach, the family can decide where their Social Capital will be directed instead of the government making those choices for them. Wealthy families believe they can more efficiently direct their Social Capital than the government can. When they know they have a choice, they choose to do so.

Asserting that writing a check to the IRS is less fulfilling than writing a check to your favorite charity may be a gross understatement. No one gets excited on April 15 each year. No one feels he or she is making a substantial donation to the government. You will likely never hear anyone say, "Oh, I love writing checks to the IRS. I get such a blessing out of it. It is such a thrill to do it!" It could be said that sending your family's Social Capital to the IRS is not low fulfillment, it is no fulfillment.

In fact, if you write a one-million-dollar check to the IRS for taxes, you will not even get a "thank you" note. But, if you send that same million-dollar check to a charity, they will have a banquet for you, put a plaque on the wall and treat you like the nearest thing to divinity this side of heaven. Which distribution option would give you the greatest sense of personal fulfillment?

Similarly, traditional estate planning with its "just the facts" and "minimize the damage" approach produces very little personal motivation to implement the plan. Many traditional advisors share with us their high level of frustration. They are not able to get their clients to do needed planning. This is no surprise. Nobody gets excited about doing damage control. However, when a family includes the Social Capital aspect, they cannot wait to get it done.

Leonard and Phyllis Lyon

Some years ago, Leonard and Phyllis retained us to take them through the Family Wealth Counseling process. The team of advisors met in early November for a final review of the plan.

All estate taxes will be eliminated. Check. Their income will increase by twenty percent. Check. The business will pass to their one son, tax-free. Check. He will be giving three million dollars to a world-renowned museum he deeply cares about. Check. Everyone was on the same page.

The Lyons then issued a directive to the planning team. They wanted this plan completely implemented before the end of the year. They were leaving January 4th on a ninety-four-day world cruise, and they wanted the new plan implemented before they left.

The various assignments were given. The attorneys were drafting the legal documents. The accountants were handling the appraisal of the business. The insurance broker would order the Life Expectancy Reports. We were to supervise the overall implementation process to make sure it was all done in a timely manner and in the proper order. The plan was completed on schedule.

On January 4th, they left on their world cruise. Six weeks later, we got a postcard from India. To our surprise, it was from Leonard and Phyllis. We were amazed they had our address with them. Turning the postcard over, we read the following:

> For six weeks now, we have been trying to get you out of our minds, and we cannot. We are so excited about what we are doing with you.
>
> —Love, Leonard and Phyllis

How many times has a client sent a postcard like that to an advisor? We had changed more than their finances. We had changed their lives!

It is the introduction of these social variables into the traditional estate-planning equation that produces such exciting new planning options.

#3 – The Spiritual/Emotional Aspect of a Family's Wealth

If the financial aspect is the most shallow of the three aspects, and the social aspect is the least defined, the spiritual/emotional aspect is undoubtedly the most intimate. Just as the financial aspect appeals to the head, the spiritual/emotional aspect appeals to the heart. Here, the deepest and most profound issues of life are confronted and addressed. Here is where we come to grips with what life is really all about.

This is where we ask the questions that cannot be answered by looking at a financial statement, balance sheet or legal document. Life is more than the accumulation of money or the avoidance of taxes. Life is about influence, relationships and making a difference. It is about being fondly remembered by those whose lives we touch along the way.

There is a moving scene in the movie, *Little Lord Fauntleroy*. The young Lord Fauntleroy is talking with his mother about when he will become the earl of Dorincourt. His mother tells him of all the wonderful good that he will be able to do for others with the incredible wealth that will someday be under his control. She makes a profoundly powerful statement. She looks tenderly into his eyes and says, "Son, the world should always be a better place because a man has lived." This mother is transferring her beliefs and molding them into values that will guide her son for the rest of his life. What kind of an earl will this son be?—likely a kind and generous one.

Even though we seldom consciously think so deeply upon such things, it would be safe to say that all of us would like to make the world a better place because we have lived. But how does that happen? How can we make the world a better place because we have lived? How can we "cast a shadow beyond the grave?"

We must first accept that we are mortal. Our Creator has granted us a certain number of days to dwell upon this earth. For some, it may be only a few. For others, it may be tens of thousands of days. No matter how many days we receive, all of us will reach our last day. Then this life, as we now know it, will be over.

At this point, who we were and what we did with our lives will be permanently fixed in the minds of those who knew us. There will be no more additions to those memories. No corrections. Our relationships with people, our actions, what was important to us, how we lived our lives and how we used our resources will be etched in the memories of all who knew us. The final paragraph of the final chapter of our book will have been written, and the indelible ink will have dried.

How fondly will you be remembered by those who knew you? Most of us hope that once our days have played out and we are gone someone will remember us with gratitude and affection. We hope something of what we have done in our lives will survive us and serve to one degree or another as a meaningful monument to our brief time on this planet.

Do you remember the powerful story of Ebenezer Scrooge? He was a tight-fisted, cold-blooded, calculating business man, who had amassed an incredible fortune yet continued to squeeze every penny he could out of everyone with whom he dealt. His goal was to become rich—to be happy. He had achieved his financial goals several times over. Yet it was not enough. He continued to amass ever-greater piles of gold. The means (gaining wealth) to happiness had actually shifted from being a means to being the end itself.

One cold Christmas Eve, Ebenezer is given a gift by his deceased business partner, Jacob Marley. The gift was a chance to see his life from a different perspective. After the three spirits' visitations, Ebenezer sees himself as a broken shell of a man.

The most gripping scene in the story is when he kneels over his own gravestone after seeing everyone's disdain and disrespect for him after his death. Ebenezer appeals to the Spirit of Christmas Future to assure him that what he has seen is not fixed for eternity, but can be changed—if he changes. He asks if the outcome of his life might be different from the horrors he has witnessed. After seeing beyond his days, he desperately regretted the way he had lived and pleaded with the spirit to give him a chance to go back and do things differently. With indescribable gratitude, he awakens Christmas morning in his own bed— alive!

In one short night, this miserable, stingy, odious man is radically transformed into one of the most caring, generous, self-sacrificing men ever known by the people of London. Not only did he use his wealth and his life to bless the lives of countless people, he also found the true happiness that had eluded him. He finally understood the ancient truth, "It is more blessed to give than to receive."

Although none of us will be given the super-natural opportunity to go beyond our grave and see how our life impacted others, we really do not need to do so to grasp the full scope of the shadow we cast with our lives (chap. 17). If we are totally honest with ourselves, it is not too difficult to get some idea of the size and length of the shadow we are casting.

Ernest Becker, the Pulitzer Prize-winning author, said it well:

> This is mankind's age-old dilemma in the face of death: What man really fears is not so much extinction, but extinction *with insignificance*. Man wants to know that his life has somehow counted, that it has left a trace, a trace that has meaning. And in order for anything once alive to have meaning, its effects must remain alive in eternity some way.

We have seen that this aspect, more than any of the three in our counseling process, takes most professional, financial and legal advisors way out of their comfort zones. This discomfort should be no surprise. Advisors have not been trained to discuss these intimate and personal aspects of people's lives. They do not know the questions to ask, and even if they did, they likely would not know what to do with the answers. But a Family Wealth Counselor *has* been trained. That is why, no matter how many other advisors clients may have on their current planning team, there will always be a chair at the advisors' table for a Family Wealth Counselor.

Finding a vision and a purpose in life that provides both the desired motivation and needed emotional energy is essential. Once these two are mobilized, they allow our clients to actually find and participate in something that will indeed cast a shadow both now and beyond their graves. Getting to the heart of the matter is not something that can be done quickly or casually over lunch or during an afternoon meeting around a conference table. It takes time—lots of time. We block off an entire day with our clients at the beginning of our relationship, so we can explore fully the social, spiritual and emotional issues of life. We will explain our Client Retreat in chapter 5. We will discuss discovering your life purpose and finding your "fire within" in much greater detail in chapter 7.

So we return to our question at this chapter's beginning, What makes the Family Wealth Counseling approach unique? It is the Family Wealth Counselor's ability to successfully understand and skillfully blend the financial, social and spiritual/emotional aspects of each family's life into a master life-plan that makes our approach unique.

CHAPTER 2

Understanding Your Family's Wealth
Avoiding the Two Greatest Misconceptions

It seems presumptuous to suggest that people who have accumulated large amounts of wealth might not fully understand their wealth. But after years of working with many wealthy families, we are convinced that this is often the case.

For an affluent family to make optimal choices regarding their wealth, they must be clear in their understanding of all their possible planning options—what can and cannot be done. Assume the box below represents your family's accumulated wealth. It does not matter whether you are worth two million, twenty million, two hundred million or even two billion dollars. Let this box symbolize your wealth.

MY MULTIMILLION DOLLAR WEALTH

21

This is how most wealthy people we meet see their wealth while they are alive. They see their wealth as one block of wealth—owned and controlled by them. It may surprise you to know, however, that this is not the case. Your wealth is actually divided into two distinct categories as shown in the box below.

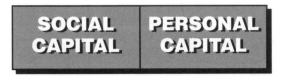

| SOCIAL CAPITAL | PERSONAL CAPITAL |

Your Personal Capital is the portion of your wealth over which you have unrestricted control and ownership. You may sell it, consume it or pass it on to your heirs. You may do whatever you like with it. It is yours.

Your Social Capital is the portion of your accumulated wealth that does not belong to you, even though you temporarily have control over it. This is the portion of your wealth that according to our laws you must allocate to provide benefits to the general welfare of this country.

When first received, this revelation usually comes as somewhat of an unpleasant surprise to wealthy families. The idea that the Internal Revenue Service already has a "lien" on their wealth of up to fifty-five percent of their net worth and up to seventy-five percent of their qualified retirement plan is often something they have not grasped fully. The IRS is merely waiting for you to die, or even just sell an appreciated asset, to collect its share of your wealth. The IRS particularly likes the sale option, because you get to make two contributions to its cause—once when you sell it, and then again when you die.

While you are alive, you may see your accumulated wealth like the first box above. Once you die, everyone who survives you—your children, your attorney, your accountant, and the IRS—will see your wealth like the set of boxes.

It serves no one's best interest to refuse to face this fact. It is true, whether you like it or not. However, this revelation is relatively easy to deal with once you get, as Paul Harvey would say, "the rest of the story."

The rest of the story begins with an understanding of the two major misconceptions that cause many wealthy families to make less than optimal decisions concerning their wealth.

Misconception #1:
All My Social Capital Must Go to the IRS

Almost every wealthy person we have spoken with over the past two decades has been under this unfortunate misconception. Nearly everyone, when asked to complete the following statement, knows exactly how it ends. "There are only two things in life that are inevitable: _____ and _____." Do you know how it ends? Of course you do. "There are only two things in life that are inevitable, <u>death</u> and <u>taxes</u>."

The saying goes back to our nation's beginning. Our own Benjamin Franklin first made this statement. It seems as American as apple pie. However, while the saying is very old and comes from a well-respected man, it is not necessarily true—at least the part about taxes.

The figure below depicts the way a typical wealthy family views the passing of the family's wealth after death.

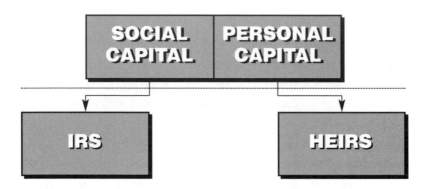

At first blush, one might think, "What is so disastrous about that misconception?" You will see as we explain the second misconception.

Misconception #2:
Anything I Give to Charity Will Reduce My Children's Inheritance

This second misconception is also pervasive and leads some wealthy families to draw false conclusions and make inferior choices. The prevailing attitude among wealthy families is, "If I give any of my wealth to charity, it will reduce the amount going to my children, and I love my children more than I do charity. After all, the IRS is going to take half of what we have when we die. We at least want our children to get the other half."

Because of this misconception, few parents plan for major gifts to charity at their deaths. We have observed that this is the primary reason parents decide not to give to charity. We have not conducted a formal study, but our experience tells us that very few wealthy parents have included some type of major transfer to charity in their current plans. It seems contrary to their objectives of maintaining their own lifestyles and providing an adequate inheritance to their children. This is how they see the results of including gifts to charity in their planning.

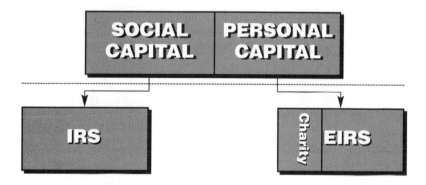

We often hear parents express an overriding affection for their children that precludes any gifts to charity. They say, "Well, you know charity begins at home." Actually, this statement is not exactly true. Charity does not begin at home—*responsibility* begins at home. When we feed and clothe our children, we are not being charitable; we are being responsible. When we make sure they get a good education, we are not being charitable; we are being responsible. The fact of the matter is charity begins outside the home—when you start doing these things for others.

Fortunately, what wealthy people mean when they make this statement is that they love their children more than they love charity.

Debunking the Misconceptions

What if, instead of relinquishing all your Social Capital to the IRS, it could somehow be possible to disinherit the IRS? What if you could choose to self-direct that same Social Capital to worthwhile charitable causes and organizations you gen- uinely care about and want to help—to charities you believe do important work? Now, wouldn't that make for some interesting planning options? Consider this scenario as an alternative:

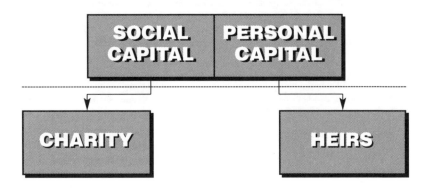

If charity must compete with heirs for Personal Capital, charity will almost always lose. However, when charity is put in competition with the IRS for the family's Social Capital, charity will always win. If charities and wealthy families understood this, the amount of wealth flowing to worthwhile charitable organizations would stagger the imagination.

In our initial meetings, we sometimes hear a wealthy person say something like, "I'm not charitably inclined."

Our response is always the same, "You are not charitably inclined? Based upon your current plan, you seem to be very charitable. What surprises us is just how philanthropic you will be."

Everyone with wealth is going to be a philanthropist in one form or another. In fact, many of America's affluent donate more than half of their collective wealth to a nonprofit organization with headquarters in Washington, D.C. and fundraising offices in every major city in America. However, you can have charitable organizations, other than the federal government, be the beneficiary of your Social Capital.

Something significant often results when a family chooses to self-direct their Social Capital to their chosen charities instead of the IRS. In many situations, the parents actually end up with an increase in their net spendable income for the rest of their lives. They make a profit by giving it away.

This increase in the parents' income can translate to a larger inheritance for the heirs. In fact, if the parents believe it is in their family's best interest, we can show them how to pass the full value of their wealth on to their heirs with no shrinkage whatsoever. So, the distribution plan often looks like this:

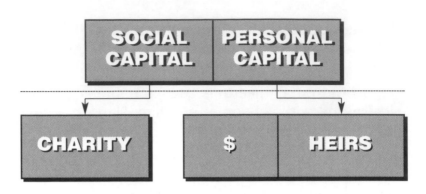

But we are not finished. There is still one final exciting benefit to this unique planning approach. When you self-direct your Social Capital to your chosen charities instead of making tax payments to the IRS, the charities you support actually receive more dollars than you would have otherwise paid to the IRS in taxes. This is the "cherry on top of the cake." It is truly a win-win-win situation. You win. Your heirs win. America wins. Everyone ends up with more. It is almost like magic. Of course, it is not magic; it is just responsible planning.

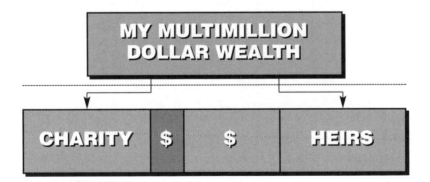

What we are doing here is taking your multi-million-dollar wealth and exploding it, allowing you and your family to maintain maximum control over not only all your Personal Capital but also all of your Social Capital.

The overwhelming majority of our clients are people who like to remain in control. This type of plan really excites them. They and their family actually control more.

Every wealthy person knows the power and influence of wealth is not in how much of it you own; it is in how much of it you control.

It may seem counter-intuitive to you that even with a fifty-five percent estate tax in force your family can actually grow wealthier as each generation passes its wealth to the next. But welcome to the world of Family Wealth Counseling.

After seeing one of our presentations, a man looked at us in surprise and asked, "Does the government know about this?"

Of course—not only does the government know about this—it wrote the laws upon which all of this planning is based.

Do not mistake creativity for illegality. We do not deal in tax loopholes and questionable planning practices that seem like great deals until the IRS finds out about them and attacks them. These planning strategies have been around for years. They come from the heart of the tax code. Why this unique approach to planning produces such powerful, almost unbelievable, results is due to our multi-disciplined training in more than half a dozen fields. Each discipline in and of itself is a full-time career. Each area is full of professionals who do nothing but specialize in that one field. This planning depends on depth and breadth of knowledge. Therein lies the power of the Family Wealth Counseling process.

Once the two misconceptions we have just discussed are exposed and the alternatives examined, most wealthy people become excited about their new and far more interesting planning options.

How do you want to be remembered when you are gone? As a taxpayer who had it involuntarily taken away? Or as a philanthropist who voluntarily gave it away? The choice is yours.

CHAPTER 3

Processing Critical Mental Angles
Learning to Think Beyond . . .

"Critical Mental Angle" – a statement or assertion that is contrary to a person's current knowledge, or understanding, yet is something that person wants to believe is true

In the previous two chapters, we introduced you to a couple of Critical Mental Angles about our Family Wealth Counseling approach. The idea that you could "give your estate taxes away to charity" is a Critical Mental Angle for virtually everyone we meet. Giving estate taxes away to charity is contrary to their current knowledge or understanding about estate planning, but it is certainly something they would want to be true.

We also presented the Critical Mental Angle that "giving to charity actually can be financially profitable to you and your family." This contradicts the common notion that giving always means giving up.

The Critical Mental Angle that giving can actually mean gaining is a statement people are very pleased to discover is true. These are only two of the dozens of Critical Mental Angles you will discover if you go through the Family Wealth Counseling process.

Look at the definition again. You first must recognize a Critical Mental Angle when you hear one. Then you must effectively process it, so you can maximize its impact and benefit to you and your family. Before discussing how to effectively process Critical Mental Angles, let us outline how not to process them.

The Wrong Way to Process Critical Mental Angles

Rule #1
Do Not Reject a Critical Mental Angle Simply Because It Seems Too Good to be True

Sometimes, we deal with Critical Mental Angles in unproductive ways. One way is illustrated by a common statement you have likely heard hundreds of times and probably even have said on more than one occasion: "If it sounds too good to be true, it probably is!"

This method of processing Critical Mental Angles is to simply refuse to believe that something could be true because it sounds so good. We dismiss it out-of-hand, categorically. The fact is that not everything in life that seems too good to be true is. But, because we struggle to process Critical Mental Angles effectively, we often miss legitimate opportunities during our lives that could be material and emotional blessings to our families and us.

Rule #2
Do Not Reject a Critical Mental Angle Simply Because You Did Not Think of It

There are those who process Critical Mental Angles based upon the assumption that they already know everything they need to know.

This attitude is presumptuous. No one can know everything about anything, much less everything about everything. When you meet people who either state or imply that they "know it all," we suggest that you run—not walk—away. We believe these people are obviously dangerous to your well-being.

One attitude we find refreshing among top professionals is the open acknowledgment that they have not heard it all or know it all. Working with these professional advisors is a joy. We get tremendous amounts of worthwhile work done with them.

However, other advisors are professionally insecure. They convey their insecurity by being critical of any creative idea or strategy (Critical Mental Angle) they did not think of or do not know enough about to be recommending to their clients. They are afraid to admit they do not know it all. They have trouble saying—I don't know the answer, I don't have a solution, or I don't know how to do that. They fear they may lose their clients' respect and maybe even their business.

This is not how we feel. We believe a person's credibility is greatly enhanced when they can freely admit that other professionals may actually have some Critical Mental Angles they have not heard of or skill sets that are different and possibly even better than theirs.

We are attracted to the Critical Mental Angles of other professionals. We thrive on them. We learned many of our most powerful planning strategies from other professionals. We accept that *learning is not a destination, it is a journey.* We will never fully get there—no one can. We believe that this acknowledgment of our limitations gives us a decided advantage in our work with clients. We are never afraid to be taught by others. We are never unwilling to be shown a better way. We are never hesitant to say, "I don't know."

Rule #3
Do Not Reject a Critical Mental Angle by Passing the Decision-Making Responsibility to Someone Else

Another way to process a Critical Mental Angle improperly is to delegate that responsibility to someone else. This occasionally happens when we first meet a client who has been referred to us by an advisor or wealthy friend. Sometimes it even happens as we are trying to set an appointment to meet them.

They might say something like, "You need to talk to my attorney or my accountant first. If they like it, then I will talk with you."

For whatever the reason, they simply do not want to take the time or make the effort to process personally these powerful Critical Mental Angles. We wholeheartedly agree and even insist that all the client's advisors be actively involved in the planning process. However, what these potential clients are usually saying is, "I want my advisors to tell me if this is what I want to do."

This shift of decision-making responsibility is not appropriate. An attorney can tell you if a certain strategy is legal. An accountant can advise you whether the cash flow is adequate. But it is not their job to tell you what you want to do. That is your job. You need to decide what you want to do and then tell them your desire, not vice versa. In order to know what you want to do, you must be personally ready and willing to hear and evaluate Critical Mental Angles when they are presented to you.

If it is not something you want to do, why bother your attorney or accountant with a meaningless meeting? If these Critical Mental Angles do not challenge and motivate you or will not get you where you want to go, why waste their time evaluating something you are not personally interested in doing? If you discover a new and powerful Critical Mental Angle that will allow you to do what you really want to do, bring your advisors into a meeting. We will discuss all the Critical Mental Angles and then turn your advisors loose to make it happen for you. But the ultimate destination is your decision, not theirs. You cannot delegate destination planning to others.

The Best Way to Process
Critical Mental Angles

In order to process Critical Mental Angles effectively in your life, you need two basic skills: unhindered imagination and open-minded listening. These skills can be learned by anyone.

Unhindered Imagination

Creative planning begins with creative thinking, and creative thinking begins with thinking beyond. But, as we grow into adulthood, we have a tendency to get locked into routines, paradigms and habits that inhibit if not completely destroy our ability to dream dreams, to imagine how what is not might become what is.

Our nation's history is full of people who were not afraid to dream, who did what could not be done.

The Wright brothers had this foolish notion that man could fly like the birds. "Impossible! Cannot be done." But they did it.

Alexander Graham Bell had this ridiculous idea that a person could talk to someone else using a metal wire. "Impossible! Cannot be done." But he did it.

Thomas Edison had this hair-brained idea about turning electricity into light. "Impossible! Cannot be done." But he did it.

Properly processing Critical Mental Angles requires you to imagine that things could be different than they currently are and that current perception is not ultimate reality.

There is a brainteaser that illustrates our point very effectively. Within the box below are nine dots. In order to make the game more practical, you need to imagine each dot represents one of your major personal or financial goals.

- One dot may represent your desire to have an adequate retirement income.

- Another may represent your desire to leave your children an adequate inheritance.

- Another is your desire to minimize taxes both now and at your death.

- Another may be to make a major gift to some charities you care about.

Your task is to connect all nine of these dots using four straight lines all connected at one end. See if you can connect all nine dots.

As simple as this task seems, it can become infuriating. No matter how you apply the lines, you always seem to fall one dot short of completing the task. After multiple attempts, you might finally give up and conclude that it simply cannot be done. I cannot accomplish all of my goals and objectives. I cannot connect all nine dots. You might be willing to go through the rest of your life accepting the fact that everything you want to do with your life and your wealth "cannot be done."

The following are some examples of how people typically attempt to solve this puzzle.

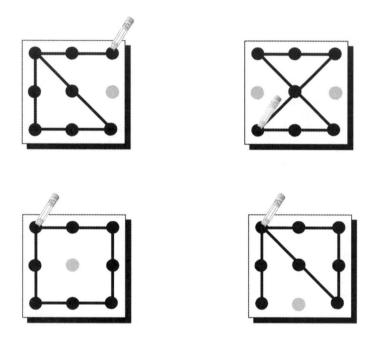

Contrary to what your current understanding and knowledge would tell you, there is a solution to this puzzle. It can be done! But you will not solve this puzzle with traditional thinking. You can only solve this puzzle by thinking beyond . . . beyond the nine dots.

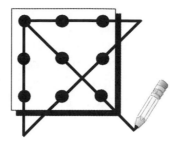

Did anyone tell you that you could not go out-side the box? You voluntarily "boxed yourself in" mentally and, as a result, did not consider all the possible solutions. If you want different results, you must think differently. Thinking beyond . . . Unhindered imagination.

Open-minded Listening

Once you break free from traditional assump-tions, beliefs and preconceptions in favor of open-minded listening, you will find a host of exciting new alternatives and possibilities.

Years ago, we were holding one of our Max-imum Wealth Control Strategies private briefings in a major city. Mark Hail, a professional in one of the local businesses, had seen our presentation earlier and was extremely excited about the possi-bilities our process could generate for his wealthy boss, Larry Jamison. Larry and Mark had become good friends over the years. Mark was determined to get Larry to our presentation no matter what it took.

When Mark first approached Larry about attending the briefing, he got the cool reception he expected. Larry stated with confidence that he had the finest advisors money could buy, and they reviewed his plan annually. He told Mark that he had already done everything that could be done and that, if there were other great strategies out there, his advisors would have already brought them to him for consideration. Thanks, but no thanks.

Mark, fortunately, would not give up. He told Larry that this briefing would not be like any he had ever attended. He offered to buy Larry's dinner beforehand. He even went so far as to personally guarantee that this would be "the best presentation on estate planning" he had heard.

It was only after several weeks of relentless pursuit—and as a personal favor to his key employee and friend—that Larry finally agreed to attend the meeting. Here is "the rest of the story" from the personal pen of Larry after attending our presentation:

> I was absolutely shocked. The presentation was incredibly stimulating. It presented wealth planning tools and techniques that had never been explained to me by any of my professional advisors. All of a sudden, I realized this was definitely a whole new level of wealth planning

> A couple months later, I began the Family Wealth Counseling process by having my current situation evaluated and a Family Wealth Plan developed using tools and techniques similar to those presented in the seminar I attended. The plan that was created was beyond anything I had imagined possible. It

outlined how to avoid all estate taxes yet pass more on to my heirs. It showed me how to avoid all capital gains taxes on the sale of my highly appreciated assets. It also showed me how to multiply my charitable will bequest to fifty times more than the amount I had planned to give to charity at my death. And, to my amazement, my accountant was in the presentation meeting continually nodding agreement and approval with what was being presented.

This all sounded too good to be true. I knew when my estate-planning attorney got his turn to speak at the meeting he would dismantle this plan completely. Instead, my attorney told me that he was familiar with all these tools, had researched the techniques and not only agreed that everything in the plan was completely legal, he went on to recommend that we put the plan into effect. Absolutely amazing!

I came to understand that, even though accountants and attorneys know about these methods, they are not necessarily expert in presenting the concepts to their clients so that the client can understand the benefits of utilizing these tools. Advisors seldom motivate their clients to use them. Consequently, they rarely discuss or recommend these tools. As you can see, it takes a Family Wealth Counselor to actually get people like me to do these things.

So, guess what? I have implemented the plan upon the recommendation and approval of my accountant and my attorney. I am eliminating very substantial income, capital gains and estate taxes, increasing my heirs' inheritance and giving major dollars away to the charities I really want to help. Amazingly enough, it is not costing me one penny from my current cash flow. I must tell you, my understanding of estate planning has been changed radically.

We could fill this book with other examples of how wealthy people have processed successfully the Critical Mental Angles that Family Wealth Counseling presents and how the financial, social, and spiritual/emotional aspects of their lives have been impacted profoundly.

Here is how an entire law firm's concept of estate planning was changed through open-minded listening to the Critical Mental Angles found in our planning process.

We explained the process of Family Wealth Counseling to the head of the law firm's estate tax section and two of his top estate planning attorneys. Initially, the attorneys responded negatively. However, as they continued to listen to what we were saying, our message began to appeal to them.

These lawyers had all been frustrated with the estate planning process at one time or another. Although the firm is extremely successful, they knew that more often than not clients did not go far enough in the estate planning process because they were confused. Charitable planning was never brought up, or if it was, the clients typically viewed it as adding more expense and diminishing the inheritance to their heirs. This situation is very common among estate planning attorneys.

Our answer to this dilemma is to work exclusively with clients who know what they want to achieve. A client who has a clear set of objectives as well as a thorough understanding of their true wealth potential is truly prepared for the estate planning process. The attorney's job of giving counsel to a well-educated, well-motivated client is a completely different task than the typical situation in which the client has only one or two objectives in mind and has not yet developed a master plan.

As we explained this problem, the lawyers were all nodding in agreement. They were very aware of the common perception of estate planning as a "necessary evil." Their only question now was, How do you only work with clients who know what they want to achieve?

The answer is to work with families who are willing to go through the Family Wealth Counseling process. After completing the counseling phase of the process, our clients come away with the needed motivation to implement a plan that reflects their true desires. Through the Client Retreat and subsequent meetings, the family gains a deeper understanding of all aspects of their wealth: financial, social, spiritual and emotional. More importantly, they develop a vision for their wealth, a vision that carries them through the complexities of the planning process to the completion of their goals.

After we reviewed with them a couple of our sample cases and answered more questions about the process and particularly the roles of the various professionals in that process, they asked us to hold a private briefing for their current clients. In this presentation, we would jointly explain the benefits of the Family Wealth Counseling process to their clients.

The presentation proved to be a great success and what we had predicted would happen to this law firm's clients was exactly what did happen. Their clients got excited, clear and focused. Estate planning became fun for everyone.

Again, as you can see, creative planning begins with creative thinking, and creative thinking begins with thinking beyond the nine dots with unhindered imagination and open-minded listening. With these two skills, the world will be yours.

In upcoming chapters, you will be asked to process other Critical Mental Angles. They are everywhere in our process. Depending on how you choose to process them, they can either be stumbling blocks or launching pads. They are stumbling blocks for those who will not believe they can be true, launching pads for those who see their potential and choose to seize the day.

CHAPTER 4

Understanding the Impact of the Three Phases of the Family Wealth Counseling Process

Our Family Wealth Counseling process includes three distinct but fully integrated phases—counseling, planning and implementation. Within these phases are five steps. When these five steps are followed in the proper order, with the necessary time and effort applied, our success rate with clients is exceptionally high. The following is a diagram of our Family Wealth Counseling process.

Counsel-ing Phase		Planning Phase		Implement-ation Phase
Information Gathering	Current Analysis	Plan Design	Plan Evaluation	Implement-ation

The five steps shown above are identical whether you are doing traditional estate planning, business-continuation planning or Family Wealth

Counseling. If you showed this diagram to your current advisors, they would most likely say, "That is what we do." They would be right. What Family Wealth Counselors do during these steps and the time we allocate to each step sets our approach apart, and we produce radically different results than traditional estate planning.

In the preceding diagram, each box is equal in size to represent an equal amount of time an advisor would devote to each step. In reality, depending on which advisor you work with, the amount of time devoted to each step varies. We have found that the most time is usually devoted to the areas in which the advisor feels most comfortable or knowledgeable.

The following is a typical time-and-energy allocation in the traditional advisor's estate planning process.

Information Gathering	Current Analysis	Plan Design	Plan Evaluation	Implementation

As you can see, the amount of time spent gathering information is quite compressed in the traditional planning scenario. Often this entire step is composed of gathering all the client's necessary legal and financial information and spending a couple of hours in general discussions about what the client might want to do. From there, the traditional advisor begins to analyze the current plan and design a new and improved plan.

This process does not allow enough time to explore and address adequately all the aspects of a family's wealth. Usually, the information the advisors gather is only financial. We have already stated that we believe the financial aspect of a family's wealth is the least important. The advisors are not certain what their clients want to accomplish. Once the plan is designed, an inordinate amount of time is spent in the evaluation process, because the clients are not absolutely certain this plan is what they want.

When clients become confused or scared, they end up doing nothing. Are they confused about what they want to do? Are they scared that they might be making a mistake, an irrevocable mistake? If either or both is true, clients will stop the process.

A recent survey found that the average wealthy family starts and stops the estate planning process five times. Five times. They know they need to do something, so they begin the process. Then, at some point along the way, they become confused or scared and stop. They often have all the legal documents drafted but never sign them. Fear and confusion are great debilitators.

Imagine that you decide to build that once-in-a-lifetime home. You hire an architect. At your first meeting, he asks, "How many bedrooms do you want?"

"Five."

"How many bathrooms do you want?"

"Four."

"How many cars do you want to put in your garage?"

"Four."

"How many square feet do you want?"

"About six thousand."

"Basement?"

"Yes."

"Pool?"

"Of course."

"How much do you want to spend?"

"No more than one million dollars."

He looks up, smiles, closes his notepad and says, "Okay, I think I have what I need. I will begin working up the blueprints over the next couple of weeks and will present them to you for approval. It is a pleasure doing business with you." The whole meeting has lasted about an hour.

Is all the information this architect has correct? Absolutely. But what do you think the odds are that he is going to come back with blueprints for your new house that will be exactly what you want? The chances are near zero. Why? He did not spend enough time in the information-gathering phase before he began drawing the plans.

As a result, you will be spending more time

evaluating the blueprints he brings you. You cannot be sure that what he has drawn is really what you want. You will need to scrutinize every detail and evaluate it. Dozens, if not hundreds, of changes will have to be made in the blueprints during the evaluation phase.

Contrast the traditional approach diagrammed earlier in this chapter with the time allocations in our Family Wealth Counseling approach depicted below.

Information Gathering	Current Analysis	Plan Design	Plan Evaluation	Implementation

You can see some striking differences between this diagram and the one preceding. In the traditional approach diagram, relatively little time is spent gathering information—requiring the evaluation period to be greatly expanded. A Family Wealth Counselor devotes a tremendous amount of time in the information-gathering or counseling phase. A longer Counseling Phase dramatically reduces the need for exhausting, frustrating and time-consuming evaluation of the designed plan.

Consider another scenario. You contact another architect about designing the same dream home. He says that, in order to do a proper job, he needs an entire day to discuss what you have in mind. He wants to discuss some of the hundreds of options. "Have you ever built a home like this before," he asks?

"Not really," you answer. "We have built before, but nothing of this magnitude. This is really big."

"All the more important for us to spend a day together talking."

The day arrives for your meeting. You sit down together in the comfort of your own home, and for the next several hours he asks you one question after another—dozens of them. You are not even sure that many of the questions have anything to do with building a house. When you voice this concern and ask why, he answers, "We have built hundreds of homes. These questions help you become clear on exactly how you want your house to look. We are designing more than just a building. We are designing your home!"

He asks you, "Will guests be visiting often? How about live-in servants? Will you be leaving this home for extended periods of time? Do you enjoy yard work? Will your grandchildren be coming to stay? Will you want to keep this home in the family for future generations?" The questions keep coming.

After hours of questions, he then pulls out book after book of floor plans and pictures of homes. He asks what you like or do not like about them. He helps you get a living picture of how your house might look. He asks you to imagine how each room in the house might appear. You even talk about how many electric outlets you want in each room and where the light switches should be located. He leaves no stone unturned. After hours of thinking, talking and dreaming, you are absolutely amazed at all the minute details that go into building a home. You are so impressed. He obviously knows exactly what needs to be done.

The day actually flies by. Twelve hours together. It seems like only a few minutes. It was fun. Challenging. Tiring. Above all, at the end of the day, you are clear as to the kind of home you want and what you want out of it.

Following that all-day meeting, he prepares a detailed letter that reflects what you decided during your day together. You receive the first draft, but there were a few important things that he missed. Also, after more time to think about it, you want to make some changes. No problem. The changes are made, and the process continues until the letter represents accurately everything you want. You sign it. He then goes to work drawing the blueprints for your dream house.

After a couple of weeks, your architect comes back with your blueprints. It is exactly as you had imagined. It looks fantastic.

How long will you spend evaluating those blueprints? How many changes do you think you will have to make to his drawings? The answers will likely be very little time and very few changes. The tremendous amount of up-front time you invested with your architect was rewarded by the reduced amount of time spent evaluating the blueprints and making significant changes.

Which of these architects would you prefer to hire? Which one has a more efficient process? What sets the second professional apart is not his ability to draw blueprints. The two may be equal in their architectural abilities. However, the first architect's process is going to be more than frustrating and quite confusing. It may even lead you to forget about the building project altogether. You do not want to invest an incredible amount of time and money building a home that is not exactly what you want.

In contrast, the latter process brings clarity of thought early in the process. The architect helps you become clear about what you want before he develops the drawings, not after. This removes stress, frustration and confusion as you move through this demanding process. If you have ever built a home, you can appreciate the accuracy of this illustration.

In addition to bringing greater clarity to the process, Family Wealth Counseling dramatically reduces the total time required. Compare the following two diagrams which reflect the time requirements of each approach.

The Traditional Estate Planning Approach

Information Gathering	Current Analysis	Plan Design	Plan Evaluation	Implementation

The Family Wealth Counseling Approach

Information Gathering	Current Analysis	Plan Design	Plan Evaluation	Implementation

For every hour we spend with our clients in our Counseling Phase, weeks or months are eliminated from the time it takes to finish the planning process. When both the client and the planning team are clear about what they want to accomplish, the analysis, planning, evaluation and implementation time are drastically reduced. Our extended counseling phase does not take time; it saves time.

What Happens in the Three Phases of the Family Wealth Counseling Process?

The following is a diagram outlining the entire Family Wealth Counseling process and its three phases. Under each phase are listed the three primary components and which advisor is expected to be the leader during that phase.

Phase 1: Counseling	Phase 2: Planning	Phase 3: Implementation
One Day Client Retreat	Analysis of Current Plan	Drafting/Execution Legal Documents
Life on Purpose Questionnaire	Design of Proposed Plan	Repositioning of Assets
Family Wealth Letter of Intent	Evaluation by Planning Team	Acquisition of Fin. Services/Products
Lead Advisor:	*Lead Advisor:*	*Lead Advisor:*
Family Wealth Counselor	*Entire Planning Team*	*Attorney*

The remainder of this book explains what we do during each phase and how we do it. The chapters in Section 2 are devoted to the Counseling Phase, the area of the Family Wealth Counseling process that is unique to us. The chapters in Section 3 explore critical subjects that must be addressed to develop an effective plan both for you and your future generations. In our technical supplement, we review the compelling results some of our clients achieved by completing the entire Family Wealth Counseling process.

SECTION II

THE UNIQUE COUNSELING PROCESS
OF FAMILY WEALTH COUNSELING

CHAPTER 5

The Client Retreat
The Most Important Day

Of all the pieces of the Family Wealth Counseling process, the Client Retreat is the most important. The Client Retreat sets the Family Wealth Counselor apart from all other advisors. To our knowledge, no other type of advisor is taking such an intense and comprehensive approach to helping wealthy families discover and fulfill missions for their lives and wealth. This, in our judgment, is the most critical component of the entire planning process, yet it is the one part that is most often minimized or ignored. We have found that many advisors have little, or no, training or experience in helping wealthy parents address life's "soft issues." Often, their primary specialties are the "hard issues"—tax and financial matters. A Family Wealth Counselor is very skilled at the hard issues but is also trained in the soft issues—relationships and feelings.

During our Client Retreats, we have discovered a common characteristic among older, wealthy couples. There seem to be two CEOs in each family: a Chief Executive Officer and a Chief Emotional Officer. It is fascinating—and sometimes a little frustrating—to put these two CEOs together, watch them share their different perspectives, listen to their dreams and fears for themselves and their families, and get them to dig deeply enough to address the critical areas of their lives. On more than one occasion, a couple will be sharing their feelings and one will say to the other, "Honey, I did not know that was how you felt."

Such a revelation would not be too much of a surprise if a couple had been married for five years, but many have been married close to fifty years. How is it that a person who has been married for fifty years could still be surprised to discover a long-standing attitude or feeling in a spouse? The answer is simple. This was the first time in their lives that they had ever talked in depth about these vital issues.

For this reason, we always insist that both spouses be present at and participate in the Client Retreat. It is not possible for the Chief Executive Officer to speak for both. Something would get lost in the translation.

"My wife does not want to be involved in any of this planning!"

Occasionally, in discussions about the planning process and Client Retreat, a husband will tell us, "My wife is not interested in any of this stuff. She even refuses to go to any of the planning meetings we have with our attorneys and account-ants." Or, "My wife has told me to go ahead and make whatever decisions about planning that are necessary. She does not want to be involved."

What these men have told us is absolutely true. Their wives do not want to be involved. But we need to explore the reasons for such a reaction. We have found that wives resist involvement for one or more of the following reasons.

(1) They have attended numerous estate-plan-ning meetings with their attorneys, accountants, trust officers, etc. and have found the meetings overly focused on the "hard financial issues." They are generally not interested in the technical terminology and are unable to connect emotionally with the process. Therefore, they feel they have little to contribute in these meetings and tell their husbands, "You go to the meet-ings; I am going over to see the grandkids."

(2) Another reason is that most Chief Execu-tive Officers have a very dominant person-ality. They sometimes overpower their wives with their thoughts, opinions and quick reactions. They sometimes fail to listen carefully, if at all, to their wives' views or perspectives. The wives know their input and opinions will not be heard or, if heard, categorically disregarded if different from their husbands' thoughts. So, after years of being ignored or overpowered, they deter-mine that contributing will be fruitless and of no consequence. Therefore, they tell their

husbands, "Count me out." The husbands may not even know this has happened. They think their wives are genuinely uninterested.

(3) Occasionally, there are husbands who are so used to controlling situations that they do not want their wives to be involved in any of these matters. They have effectively communicated this wish verbally and non-verbally over the years. They want to make all the decisions. They do not want to be distracted from their personal agendas by thoughts and comments from their wives. In this scenario, the husband does not want us to meet or even talk with his wife. This is the most troubling reason.

We have worked with couples where all three of these reasons were present. It only takes a few questions and one face-to-face meeting with the wife to find out what the problem is. The fact is, if we cannot resolve this problem and get both spouses involved in the Client Retreat, we know before we begin that the process will be doomed to failure. Nothing will happen. So, we know not to take the case.

Once, a man said his wife did not want to be involved and that she genuinely was not interested. We asked him two questions: "Do you mean to tell us that, if we can show your family how to give millions of dollars away to charity, your wife will have absolutely no interest in helping decide where any of that money will go?" Also, "Do you mean to tell us that your wife, the person who most likely knows your children even better than you do, does not want to have any meaningful input into what each child should get and how best to structure that inheritance?" The man changed his mind.

We requested he allow us to meet personally with his wife and him, so we could tell her our Family Wealth Counseling story. If after that meeting she still were not interested, we would consider going on without her. (We can say this because we have never told our Family Wealth Counseling story to a Chief Emotional Officer who did not "light up like a Roman candle" after hearing the presentation.) For her, this was the part of the planning process that had always been missing. This was the part of the process in which she truly could be a major contributor. Our story was something she was acutely interested in and excited about.

After another such meeting, the wife looked at us and said, "This is the first estate planning conversation I have ever had with an advisor that I both enjoyed and understood."

If the reason a Chief Emotional Officer has chosen not to be involved is because her part of the family's "business"—the heart part—has always been absent, she will find our approach much to her liking.

If the husband really does desire for his wife to be involved, but due to his overpowering personality routinely stifles her input, the way we conduct the Client Retreat eliminates that problem. The Family Wealth Counselor facilitates the discussion so that each spouse has the opportunity to respond to each question, to share their views and thoughts, and then discuss them in a respectful and productive way. This format is extremely productive.

Many years ago, before we fully understood the importance of both spouses being involved, we let a fiercely independent entrepreneur pressure us into taking him through our process without his spouse. We were going to do it his way, or we were not going to do it at all. We reluctantly acquiesced.

We went through the counseling process with him, analyzed his current situation, and designed an absolutely fantastic new plan for him. Once we completed our presentation, we asked, "Well, what do you think?"

"This is more than anything I ever expected!"

"Should we go ahead and begin the implementation process?" we asked.

"Well, I am not sure. I am going to need to talk to my wife first," he said hesitantly.

"Excuse me? You have to talk to your wife first?" we asked in amazement. "You told us that she was not going to be involved in any way."

"Yes," he said. "But I did not know it was going to be all this. I cannot make these types of major decisions and plans without her knowledge or input."

Rather than leaving him to try to present our plan to his wife, we volunteered to meet with her to go over our plan.

You can probably guess what happened. The wife had a host of concerns and wishes that the plan did not reflect. We ended up having another Client Retreat with both of them. As you can imagine, many of their goals and objectives changed with her insightful and sensitive input, requiring the plan to be redesigned completely. Ultimately, we ended up designing a second plan and adding three months to the process. We learned a very important lesson. If a couple's wealth was accumulated during their married lives together, and the heirs are their children, both spouses absolutely must be involved.

———

"Let's forget about all this 'touchy-feely' stuff and get on with the business of planning!"

Can you guess which one of the CEOs makes this kind of statement? This is a classic Chief Executive Officer comment, and we hear it quite often from them. They are not so concerned about the details of where they, their heirs or their wealth are going; they are just anxious to get there —to the bottom line.

We liken it to the army that was hacking and cutting its way through a jungle in Africa. The general sent a soldier to climb a tall tree to see if they could find out where they were. The general calls up, "Sergeant, where are we?"

The voice comes back, "General, I do not know where we are, but we sure are making great time."

Sounds like a typical Chief Executive Officer at work on his estate plan.

A similar analogy would be to call AAA and say, "My wife and I are wanting to take a vacation. Can you put together a Trip-Tik for us?"

"Well, where do you want to go?" the voice on the phone asks.

"East. Now will you put a Trip-Tik together and get it out to us right away," you say with some degree of irritation in your voice.

"But sir, where east do you want to go?"

"Stop focusing on details. I want to go east, and I want you to put a Trip-Tik together telling me how to get there," your voice increasing in volume and intensity. "Doesn't he understand?" you think. "I need and want a Trip-Tik, and I am not interested in planning out a detailed trip. Doesn't he know I am a very busy man? My time is precious. All he needs to know is that I want to go east. Isn't that enough?!"

Obviously, it is not. In fact, if you travel east long enough, you will end up right back where you started, having covered lots of ground, but not having made much progress—unless movement is your sole objective.

Likewise, having a few general ideas about what you want to do with your life and your wealth is inadequate to develop a comprehensive life-plan that will maximize your personal potential and financial leverage.

If you and your spouse wanted to go on a world

tour that would take you to twenty-four countries and last a year, how much time would you spend planning that trip? Probably weeks, if not months. Should it be any different to set aside a substantial block of time to determine what you want to do with your wealth—both for the rest of your life and when you are no longer here to use or control it?

The fact is that touchy-feely is a regular part of our lives, regardless of which CEO you are. Consider why you bought the car you did instead of the other cars in the same price range. You liked it. Touchy-feely. Why did you buy the suit you bought instead of all the other suits for sale at the same price? You liked it. Touchy-feely. And why did you buy the house you are living in instead of the other homes available at the same price? You liked it. Touchy-feely. Why do people choose the spouses they do? What drives their decision to marry a particular person, their minds or hearts?

You see, almost every decision we make is based to some degree upon feelings. Facts may or may not be included in the decision. "Where do you want to go to eat tonight, Honey?" you are asked. "Oh, I feel like Italian food tonight." The friends you choose, the advisors you retain, the clothes you buy—these and hundreds of other choices all have an emotional aspect.

Why should we suddenly now resist getting in touch with our feelings when it comes to making some of the most important choices of our lives? These choices will affect us as well as our families for generations to come.

"Just because we engage our hearts, does not mean we simultaneously disengage our brains."

However, since each of the family's CEOs are naturally inclined to be either more logical or more emotional, it is all the more important that they work together to bring both balance and perspective to the planning process.

Remember that people are most powerful when they are able to both think and feel at the same time—when their heads and their hearts are working as one. When you can get two people thinking and feeling as one, there is an exponential increase in the power and impact of the process—the whole is decidedly greater than the parts. That is why we insist both spouses be engaged fully, both mentally and emotionally, in this process. The combination produces phenomenal results!

How does the Client Retreat work?

A Client Retreat generally lasts one full day. We typically begin at 8:00 a.m. and finish about 8:00 p.m., depending on a number of factors. We prefer to hold a retreat in the couple's primary or vacation home, whichever they prefer. We never conduct a retreat at the client's office or ours. We want our clients to feel completely comfortable and safe as we talk about these very serious, personal and confidential matters. As Dorothy said in

The Wizard of Oz, "There's no place like home." Home is the best place in the world to relax and be you. Interruptions and distractions can and do disrupt the meeting, so we do everything possible to minimize them.

It is during the Client Retreat that we discuss each spouse's responses to the questions in our proprietary *Life on Purpose Questionnaire.*™ Chapter 6 is devoted entirely to addressing the importance of these questions, along with the vision and energy generated from the mutual conclusions that come from them.

We do not collect any financial or legal information prior to the Client Retreat because this retreat is not about assets or legal documents. We want to focus our time and energy helping the clients pinpoint problems to be solved and/or opportunities to be seized. In most cases, we uncover several of both during our day together, and these become the foundation for our future planning.

It is during the retreat and the weeks following that we help clients craft their own written family mission statement, the Family Wealth Letter of Intent (chap. 8). This is when it all begins to come together. As we labor over this document, a comprehensive, master life-plan develops that includes wealth but goes far beyond a typical tax plan.

A Collaborative Effort

Our work must be a collaborative effort. We do not have a magic wand (even though many of our clients think we do magic). We have already scoped out the terrain, and there are no shortcuts to getting there from here. We can only succeed in our work if everyone actively cooperates and fully participates. If we are going to accomplish from the Client Retreat what we want and need to accomplish, there must be a personal commitment from all parties.

The couple's commitment is to invest some of their time and some of their money (our counseling fee and expenses), and the Family Wealth Counselor's commitment is to invest his or her time and expertise to make this process work. The counseling process is very time consuming. There is no way to rush a masterpiece. It demands everyone's mental, emotional and spiritual energy to achieve the greatest result. However, as we pointed out in the preceding chapter, the time demanded by this phase proportionately reduces the time required to complete all other phases of the planning process.

If you have ever been involved in constructing a building, you know that getting started seems to consume a disproportionately long period of time. The construction crew must level the ground, dig and pour the footers, lay the foundation, and get all the building materials on site. Then, it seems that almost overnight the building goes from nothing to being framed and under-roof. That is the way it is with the Family Wealth Counseling process. It seems to start slowly, but it finishes fast.

Again, of all the days we devote to Family

Wealth Counseling, the single-most important day of the whole process is the day of the Client Retreat. No other day even comes close. It is a day well spent.

To follow is just one example of how powerful this day was for one of our clients.

Joe is the CEO of a rapidly growing company located in a large metropolitan area. Together, Joe and Jill have successfully nurtured their two children to adulthood. They are still in love with each other. Communication with the family is good, and they are proud of their children, even if they do not always agree about everything. Their net worth has ballooned to nearly twenty million dollars. Gifts of stock to the children were made when it was worth pennies per share. As a result, each of them has a trust worth about a million dollars now. Joe and Jill are in their fifties, in good health and vital. They have legal, tax, investment and insurance advice from the most qualified professionals, with up-to-date, sophisticated estate planning documentation.

Joe and Jill have already made a million-dollar gift to a trust for the benefit of charity, in addition to faithfully supporting their local church. Even with their affairs as well-ordered as this, they are still eager for the Client Retreat.

From the moment we begin on the day of the retreat, it is obvious that Joe and Jill have each done their homework. Independently, they have gone through the *Life on Purpose Questionnaire*,™ made notes of their thoughts and eagerly shared them with each other. The emphasis repeated is on each other. We are, at this point, simply privileged listeners. They are having a great time sharing who has been important in the formative years of their lives, why and how. How they met. What they share in common. How they are different and complement each other. Affirming each other. The relationships they have with their children. Hard times shared together. Fun times. Sad times. Challenges met and overcome. He is a hands-on type. She is a gifted and consistent letter writer. The positive energy they are sharing is powerful and tender. Occasionally, one responds to the other, "I did not know that!"

The most touching of these moments occurs with the sharing of their dreams of things they would like to accomplish. Both agree they want to share their wealth in significant ways but without fanfare.

Joe has observed two needs. "There are a lot of retired men in good health who need something to do to feel useful," he says. "I would like to establish a nonprofit company to do odd jobs around the house. We would recruit and train these men to do the work. Trucks would be equipped with tools. Once set up and organized, it could even be franchised. There are thousands of older women needing help to care for and maintain their homes. Our clients would have to meet certain qualifications. Like your mother, Jill. She needs help, and there is never anyone around to do it. We could call it Helping Hands, or The Widow's Might, or something like that."

Jill sits forward. She is listening with new

intensity, and with tears in her eyes she says, "I did not know you ever thought about this." Coming even more alive and energized they continue—*and we could do such and such and help so and so*—and on and on they brainstorm together.

Joe and Jill demonstrated why the retreat is the most important part of the process of Family Wealth Counseling. For this already healthy, emotionally fit, productive couple, it became the catalyst for them to take time and take stock of who they are—and why. They expressed appreciation for each other and what they have accomplished together, and they formulated how their lives will have significance beyond the pleasures provided by wealth.

CHAPTER 6

The Power Is in the Questions
Gaining Enhanced Clarity, Greater
Confidence and Increased Leverage

The idea that there is power in questions seems to be contrary to our American way of thinking. We have been taught to believe that power lies in the answers. "The one who has the answers, has the power!" Questions are merely a means to an end. Consequently, we have an abundance of professional advisors, but very few professional "askers."

We have observed that many professional advisors simply assume the desires of all clients are essentially the same—avoid taxes and pass the maximum possible inheritance to the heirs. Ok—next client. Because of this faulty assumption, the answers and solutions for all their clients will be essentially the same.

We have also observed an interesting phenomenon among estate planners. Professional advisors tend to design clients' plans after their own images. If advisors sell life insurance, their plan designs will always include life insurance. If they like Living Trusts, all plans will have a Living Trust. If they like Family Limited Partnerships, one or more will undoubtedly be part of every client recommendation. If they like Charitable Remainder Trusts, they will find some place to fit one in for all their clients.

We once heard an advisor say in his educational presentation, "We always use Generation Skipping Trusts in our planning with our clients."

Another speaker stated, "We always recommend a Qualified Personal Residence Trust for our clients." The operative word here is *always*. The advisors assume the questions are the same for all their clients. Therefore, the answers will be the same for all their clients. It is like the joke about the insurance agent who shakes your hand and says with great confidence, "Hi. I am Jim Smith. Life insurance is the answer. Now, what is your problem?" Unfortunately, this approach to planning is pervasive.

We were making a presentation to a planned-giving council in Michigan and mentioned an article that had appeared in *Trusts and Estates* magazine just the month before (June 1996). It reported the results of a survey of Michigan attorneys. Since we were in Michigan, it seemed appropriate to mention it. The overwhelming majority of estate planning attorncys surveyed did not ask questions regarding any philanthropic interests their clients might have. When asked why, they said they did not feel it was their place to probe into those personal areas of the clients' lives. Further, if clients brought the matter up, the advisors would only discuss philanthropy at the tax level. They were concerned that if they did ask about or probe in these areas they might upset and possibly lose the clients.

After the meeting was over, an attorney in the audience came up to us and said, "I just want you to know that I happen to be one attorney that asks the question." His nametag indicated his name as "Bill."

"Bill, that is fantastic. Exactly what question do you ask?"

"I ask every one of my clients if they have any charitable interests."

"Don't tell me, Bill. Almost every one of your clients responds by saying, 'No, not really.'"

With a surprised look on his face, he said, "Yes, they do. How did you know?"

"Bill, our experience has taught us that the type of question you ask often gets a negative response because clients are unaware of the exciting planning possibilities that we just spent the last hour and a half showing you. Charitable intent is often something that must be uncovered with specially designed questions."

We then suggested he ask a different question, "If you had to choose between giving one million dollars away to the IRS in estate taxes or giving that same million dollars away to your favorite charity, which would you prefer? Bill, do you think your clients would still have no interest in charity?"

He agreed, "Their answers would be completely different, and our plan designs for those clients would end up looking completely different as well."

Because of one simple question, the "destination" the client chooses will be completely different.

Yet the questions, the really important questions, are simply not being asked. Maybe, advisors feel uncomfortable discussing them. Maybe, they do not know the right questions to ask. Maybe, they really do not think it is any of their business. Maybe, they feel uncomfortable getting so personal. Who knows? But what we do know is that the power in planning is in the questions.

We believe this is another major, fundamental difference between the traditional estate-planning approach and our Family Wealth Counseling approach.

The *Life on Purpose Questionnaire™*

As a result of years of working with clients and learning what matters to them, we created our *Life on Purpose Questionnaire™*. It consists of sixty-four critical questions addressing virtually every area of a family's life. These questions:

- help us to get to know our clients

- help our clients get to know themselves and their spouses in many new and important ways

- help both spouses make sound decisions regarding the effective use of their remaining time, their unique talents and their accumulated treasures—producing the greatest possible benefits for them, their heirs and the world

The *Life on Purpose Questionnaire*™ has three sections: (1) Where Have You Come From? (2) Where Do You Want to Go? and (3) What Decisions Need to be Made?

Many of these questions are fun to answer. Some may be difficult. A few may even be painful. But each question helps clients uncover problems to be solved and opportunities to be seized in their lives.

Here is how the Client Retreat and the *Life on Purpose Questionnaire*™ combine to produce effective results.

Meet Rich and Cindy Bowling. The Bowlings are both sixty-five years old and have inherited a substantial amount of wealth. Their net worth is currently nine million dollars. Recently, they told the development director of a university they wanted to make a major planned gift. However, they had not yet "pulled the trigger" and made the gift. We were introduced to them through the director.

We were certain that, until the Bowlings gained enhanced clarity about why and how they might make this major gift and then got excited about doing it, the gift would not happen. The first step in helping them achieve this clarity was to take them on a Client Retreat using our *Life on Purpose Questionnaire*™. In our initial conversations with them about the purpose and value of our Client Retreat, Cindy made a most profound observation.

"We have six attorneys anxious to document what we want to do at four hundred dollars an hour," Cindy said, "But not one of them has ever offered to help us figure out *why* we want to do it." She said we were the first professionals who offered to help them decide why before we helped them decide how.

When we explained that a Client Retreat could give them greater confidence so they could take control of the planning process, both Rich and Cindy looked puzzled.

"How can this Client Retreat allow us to take control of a planning process when we know nothing about planning tools and techniques?" they asked.

We explained that the power is in the questions. Knowing the right questions to ask gave them control of the process. We were able to give them the questions.

Cindy responded, "In other words, having the right questions to ask ourselves and our advisors will allow us to tell our advisors what we want to do, instead of having to look to them to tell us what to do."

"Exactly."

Rich and Cindy immediately saw the value and the power of the Client Retreat and working through our *Life on Purpose Questionnaire*™ and agreed to set aside a day for the retreat.

The results were beyond anything they had imagined. It was indeed the life-changing experience they had been told it would be. They had gained enhanced clarity, greater confidence and saw numerous opportunities for dramatically increased leverage.

———

This is just one of numerous examples we could have chosen. Going through the Client Retreat and working through our *Life on Purpose Questionnaire*™ enables our clients to gain some perspective on their circumstances. With that perspective comes tremendous new energy for the planning process. The *Life on Purpose Questionnaire*™ helps wealthy families catch the vision.

The ability to effectively use your remaining *time*, your unique *talents* and your accumulated *treasures* in a clear, confident and highly leveraged way to do the most good for the most people and find the greatest fulfillment and significance is energizing beyond words.

We obviously do not intend to discuss or even list all sixty-four of our questions. Many questions are so important we have devoted entire chapters to addressing one issue raised by one question. But we will share a few others to give you an idea of just how different these questions are from the ones you are routinely asked in the traditional estate-planning process. We will then offer some thoughts as to why the questions are so powerful.

Question: *If you had just thirty days left to live, had perfect health and money was not an issue, what would you do with those last thirty days?*

This is a very sobering, if not frightening, question to be sure. You will likely never hear these words in your lifetime, but for the sake of participating in a very valuable mental exercise, let us imagine the following scene.

You are sitting in your local hospital's examination room, in a backless gown, after spending all day taking a battery of tests. You are waiting for the doctor to come and give you the results of the tests. He finally walks in. You can tell he is having difficulty looking you in the eyes. The news cannot be good.

He sits down next to you, finally looks you in the eyes and speaks, "The test results could not be worse. You have a very rare, incurable disease. It is already so advanced that what little treatment we do have would be useless, and there is no surgical procedure known for this illness."

He speaks your name and then slowly says those six dreaded words, "You have thirty days to live." The doctor then adds some extremely good news to his shocking pronouncement. He says that with the nature of this disease, you will have no negative physical manifestations until the very last day. Death will come at once. For the next thirty days, you will continue to feel and look as you do right now. You will notice no change in your energy level until the very last day. No one will even be able to tell you are sick.

"I have thirty days to live."

"Only thirty days!"

Your mind is whirling with the news that your days are numbered. Of course, your days have always been numbered, as is the case for all of us. But your actual number of days has just been revealed to you, and it is several thousand less than you had assumed.

Once the news sinks in, one penetrating question comes to your mind, "What will I do with my last thirty days on this earth?"

Will you take this month to finally read those books you have wanted to read? Will you spend these last precious few days with your children and grandchildren? Will you rush back to the office to finish that project that absolutely must be finished this month? Will you try to mend some fences with people whose relationships with you have been broken or destroyed? Will you finally take that once in a lifetime vacation you have always wanted? Will you see those people who have influenced and helped you most and tell them 'thank you?' Will you devote the rest of your time giving back something of all you have received? Will you prepare to meet your Maker?

At a time like this, the really important things in life become apparent, don't they? Under these circumstances, it is easy to distinguish between what is urgent and what is important, what is real and what is superficial, what is lasting and what is temporary.

The great tragedy for far too many of us is that life never becomes more precious than when it is almost over. Then, we hurry around and try to do what has been left undone, fix what has been broken, savor what has been overlooked and give what has been long overdue.

Few of us will ever know the exact number of days we have left, so we can get "our house in order" before we say good-by to this life. Can you imagine how our priorities might change if we lived our next thirty days as if they were truly our last? Can you imagine how much more at peace we would be if we actually did those final things now instead of waiting until our last thirty days of life really arrive?

At a national conference, a man shared a lesson he had learned from his grandfather. His grandfather told him, "Remember, Son, there will be a first time and a last time for everything."

He explained what he meant. If you kiss your mother good-by, there is a first time and there will be a last time. If you take a walk through the woods, there is a first time and there will be a last time. If you sit down to a meal with your entire family, there is a first time and there will be a last time. When you put on your shoes each morning, there was a first time, and there will be a last time. If you hold your child in your arms, there is a first time and there will be a last time. There will be a first time and a last time for everything in your life.

Living life with this truth in mind enhances our awareness of life and makes all the in-between times far more precious and meaningful. We would suggest that the things we would choose to fill our final thirty days with are our highest priorities.

If you had just thirty days to live, what would you do with them?

The greatest challenge is doing what needs to be done to make the person you are consistent with the person you really want to be.

Can you see how important it is that we be clear about our life-priorities? The tyranny of the urgent is never more clearly revealed than when we honestly ask this question. How we answer this very powerful question has everything to do with planning.

We could fill the rest of this book with powerful stories of how this simple question has impacted our clients' thinking and planning, as the answers became clear on what was really important.

———

Question: *What is the most meaningful charitable gift you have made?*

On more than one occasion, this simple question has brought about a flood of fond memories and even tears from our clients. Here are a few examples of our clients' stories.

During a Client Retreat with Kyle and Meredith Hall, a couple worth thirteen million dollars and earning more than one million dollars per year, we asked this question. As soon as we asked the question, they both looked at each other knowing exactly what the "correct" answer was for both of them.

"We have a home in Mexico where we go during the winter," the wife shared. "One winter when we were there, a friend took us to a local Salvation Army orphanage to visit. We were so impressed and moved by the love and care that we saw there, we have sent this orphanage five hundred dollars each year to help them with their work. That is, undoubtedly, our most meaningful gift we have ever given." A tear could be seen in the wife's eye as she shared this story.

"Five hundred dollars per year?"

"Yes."

"Really meaningful?"

"Incredibly meaningful!"

"Well, may we ask you a follow-up question?"

"Yes, please do."

"If giving five hundred dollars has been so meaningful to you, can you imagine how fulfilling it would be to give away one million dollars?"

Both of them looked at each other, looked at us, then looked back at each other and said, "We have never thought about doing anything like that before."

"Based upon what we know about your situation, it looks to us like you are going to have several million dollars to be giving away, since you have said you do not want to give that money to the IRS in estate taxes."

Talk about increased leverage! This was one example of how the right questions can lead to powerful results.

———————————

During a retreat with another couple, we asked the same question. They both immediately smiled at each other. They knew. It was the same for both of them.

"Each year our family sends $250 to support an orphan child in Africa. We do it as a whole family. We write letters to her, and she writes us back. It is the highlight of our year."

This family was worth more than $25 million and earned more than $2 million per year. A $250 gift. A mere 1/100th of one percent of their annual income had produced such joy and personal fulfillment.

Leaning towards them, we asked "If giving $250 a year to help someone in need has been this meaningful and fulfilling to your family, how do you think you would feel to give $2.5 million away to help others like this little orphan girl?" Silence. Stone silence. As if they just had been told they had won a fifty-million-dollar lottery, they were speechless.

We asked, "If you could give that much away, what do you think you might do with it?"

"Well," they looked at each other as the husband spoke, "I think we would have to give that some thought."

"Then you need to start thinking about it, because you are going to be giving away a whole lot more than $2.5 million."

During another retreat, we asked this question and as soon as we did, the wife burst into tears, weeping openly. We waited. Her heart was responding to the question.

Once she regained her composure, she said, "During the depression, I was a very young girl, about ten. Times were really hard for my family. We had so little. I remember one cold winter day my father came home and told us about the Browns down the road. They were in even worse shape than we were. In fact, their situation had almost become desperate.

"I remember my father asked me to get a burlap sack and come with him. We walked to the root cellar, and he carefully picked through the potatoes, selecting the best he could find. He then picked out a number of the best-looking apples and onions. He did the same for the carrots and the turnips until the bag was filled. I thought he was getting some food to bring into the house for us to eat. But as he closed the root cellar door, he took my hand, and we walked down the road to the Browns' house. He knocked, and when Mrs.

Brown came to the door, he had me hand the bag of produce to her. She looked into it and broke down in tears. She hugged me ever so tightly and thanked my father.

"I can see that picture in my mind like it was yesterday. My father taught me what it was to give and to give sacrificially."

It was a very moving and powerful moment. Then we asked if she had ever done anything like that since.

"No, never."

"Why not?"

She looked at us in near disbelief. The thought had never crossed her mind that she could or should do something like that again. She and her husband were not dirt poor, struggling to survive like her family was during the depression. They were worth millions, tens of millions. But there were families in their town who were still dirt poor. They could help them now! They could make a difference today!

To make a long story short, she chose to set up a family foundation in her father's honor. She used the income from a multimillion-dollar gift to the foundation to support the poor and needy in her community. It became this woman's life work.

Can you imagine what it did for her in the way of finding meaning, fulfillment and purpose in her life? One simple question changed her life.

Question: *Are the best years of your life ahead of you or behind you? Why?*

This simple question tells us volumes about our client's current perspective on life. How do you think the vast majority of older wealthy Americans, who can afford every luxury in life and do virtually whatever they please with their time, answer this question?

The answer may surprise you. The majority believe that the best years of their lives are behind them. This is one of America's great tragedies—an incredible loss of one of our most valuable resources. It is not a good thing to be old in America today.

When people believe the best of life is behind them, they are just biding their time. These great movers and shakers have come to believe life has passed them by. They are now "out to pasture," and while living in comfort, they are simply waiting to die.

Our goal is to help these wealthy Americans catch a new vision for their lives, find something new to move and shake. This will not come by trying to motivate them to add another zero to their net worth. That objective lost its motivation some time ago. Getting them excited about trying to spend even more on a consumptive lifestyle is not going to light their fires either.

We have found that unless we can help the wealthy find some reason to believe that the best years of their lives are ahead of them, they will not have enough energy and motivation to complete the planning process. They need to find something that gives them a new reason to live—to move and shake again.

We have also discovered that simply avoiding taxes is not enough. Avoiding taxes may be a good initial motivator, but it seldom provides adequate spiritual/emotional energy to carry wealthy families to an enthusiastic implementation of a comprehensive life-plan.

When clients believe that the best years are behind them, we must ask, "What motivates you to continue to live, to get up in the morning or to do something big?" For most of our clients, this question uncovers a faulty life perspective they had unconsciously embraced. However, now that it has been recognized, they choose to reject it completely.

Our joint challenge, then, is to counsel our clients and help them find some work, some cause, some challenge in life that changes their answer to this question. Now, they firmly believe that the best years, even if they are in their eighties, are still waiting to be lived. Often, hours of discussion result from this one simple question. Sometimes, these discussions continue for weeks, even months.

This is such an extremely important area that we are going to spend all of chapter 7 outlining how people can discover their real life-purpose and "fire within."

You can see why we believe the power is in the questions. Armed with the right questions, wealthy families can make effective, meaningful and life-changing choices that would have never been considered had these important questions not been asked.

By working through our *Life on Purpose Questionnaire,*™ our clients gain **enhanced clarity** as to what they want to do with their lives and their wealth. They gain **greater confidence** that they can indeed articulate to their advisors what they want to do and can effectively evaluate their advisors' plan designs and determine if the plans will get them where they want to go (i.e., maintain control). The motivation that drives this planning process, that gives the couple the emotional energy to travel this new and unfamiliar territory, comes from recognizing the dramatically **increased leverage** they have at their disposal and the desire to again begin moving and shaking.

As you can tell from the powerful stories we have shared, the *Life on Purpose Questionnaire*™ leads to much more than simply *minimizing the damage.* It enables our clients *to maximize their potential.*

The power is in the questions.

CHAPTER 7

Discovering Your Life Purpose and Stirring Your "Fire Within"

In this chapter, we first want to define the general concept of life-purpose. After working with hundreds of people all over the United States, it has become obvious that few people have a clear understanding of what life-purpose is. Fewer still have mastered their own definition of life-purpose.

In our *Life on Purpose Questionnaire*,™ we ask our clients to briefly describe their current understanding of their life-purposes—what are they here to do? The majority of our clients have difficulty articulating a response. Few have answers. Those who attempt to respond generally offer a superficial answer. They have never given this idea serious thought.

An equally powerful question asks our clients to determine the purpose for their wealth. The idea that people and things could, or should, have a purpose seems to have been lost in our modern, materialistic American culture.

Does every human being have a life-purpose? Are we on this earth simply due to some biological function of life? Are we just waiting for some future failure of other biological functions to end our lives? Is there more? Is there a purpose for our lives?

Modern thought pushes the idea that we are nothing more than a massive compilation of protoplasm. No matter how impossible the odds, the fact that we are here proves that accidents can happen. We are simply several billion "accidents" now living on this planet.

The modern mantra is "Let us eat, drink and be merry for tomorrow we shall die." Or, as we see on bumper stickers, "He who dies with the most toys wins." Or, as reflected in an old beer commercial, "You only go around once in life, so grab for all the gusto you can."

Is this all there is? Is this our life-purpose? In today's culture, the answer seems to be yes. And, if so, we should make all we can, take all we can, consume all we can and enjoy all we can because after this there is no more. When it's over, it's over.

However, we would challenge this philosophy. We believe there is another explanation.

Have you ever wondered why you—an individual of stature in your community with substantial means and education—have never been awarded the Nobel Peace Prize? Likewise, have you ever wondered why a poor elderly woman—an individual who lived in the slums of a Third World city with little education, no material wealth, no station in life; an individual who served a handful of starving, dying, orphaned children—did receive that most prestigious award?

The answer is obvious. Intellectually, we have embraced the notion that we are here as a result of an accident. However, in our hearts, we have a higher understanding of purpose and of dignity that elevates the value of human life.

The world recognized purpose and dignity in the exemplary life and sacrificial service of Mother Teresa. We honored this woman for fulfilling her humble, yet noble, life-purpose.

So, we come back to our original question. What is life-purpose? If we accept that there is only the physical world, we cannot realize a complete and satisfactory answer. Acknowledging only a part of our being—our physical side—leads to only part of the right answer. What is the rest of the answer?

In reality, we are truly physical beings, but we are also social beings, emotional beings and spiritual beings.

The general definition of the life-purpose concept is to discover the purpose for the whole of who we are physically, socially, emotionally and spiritually.

Each year, our firm organizes and underwrites a mission trip to Mexico to build homes for homeless families. It is a life-changing experience for all who go. Overlooking that poverty-stricken community prompted us to ponder a number of sobering questions. Why are we living in the most prosperous country in the history of the world? Why were we born in America and not in some ghetto in Rwanda, Haiti or Mexico? Why do we have healthy bodies while malnutrition, TB or other diseases plague others? Why do we have such abundant wealth? Is it just good luck? Hardly. We believe there is a plan for us—a life-purpose.

Our goal in life should be to discover and carry out our own life-purpose. How do we deploy our accumulated wealth to do the most good for the most people during our short time on earth? We start with understanding our fundamental human desires.

Four Fundamental Human Desires

Human beings have four fundamental desires that must be fulfilled to find meaning and purpose in life. When these fundamental desires are equally met, a person will be healthy, focused, balanced, happy and fulfilled. When not met, any number of problems will occur. We will illustrate some examples later in this chapter, but we begin with identifying and defining the desires.

1. The Desire to Gain Independence

Deep within us, we *desire to gain independence*. To be free. We do not want to be obligated to anyone. But, even in a free country such as America, financial freedom is not granted automatically by law. For many of us, we must earn our financial freedom. The desire to gain financial independence is why many of us sought higher education or started businesses.

If you have ever started a business, recall your initial reasoning. You probably wanted to improve your life, to get ahead and to be your own boss. When the opportunity arose, you seized it—and all the inherent risks that went with it—in an attempt to build a secure, financial future for yourself and your family. The wealthiest business owners have obviously succeeded—often far beyond anything they ever imagined when they first started.

Those who have financial independence treasure it. Those who do not, long for it. Night schools are filled with adults still trying to get ahead. Lotteries are a multibillion-dollar business fueled by people longing to hit it big, so they can be financially independent. No one can deny the presence and strength of this internal desire.

2. The Desire to Help Others

The second fundamental desire is to *help others*. The motivation to help someone who needs what we can provide dwells within all of us. Whether it is your spouse, children, grandchildren, neighbors, friends, other community members or your employees, the desire to help resides within each of us. A mother's relationship with her child is a most vivid example of this desire to give —to sacrifice for the good of another.

This desire can make a man instinctively risk his life to save a young boy who has wandered into the street in front of an oncoming car. It can motivate a woman to walk away from a profitable career as a doctor and move to the jungles of Africa to run a primitive medical clinic. It tugs at our hearts when we see the pictures of starving children on television. This desire causes you, in the wee hours of the night, to stay up and lovingly hold your crying child who is afraid of the dark. This inner impulse to give of ourselves and our belongings to others we deeply care about is real and powerful.

3. The Desire to Feel Significant

The third fundamental desire is to *feel significant*. Psychologists' offices are filled with people whose lives are falling apart because of a poor self-image. These individuals do not feel loved. They do not feel appreciated. They feel like failures. In the United States, this problem is almost epidemic.

But many of us are on the healthier side of this coin. There are people whose work makes a difference in the world some way. Examples: the Red Cross worker, the teacher, the social worker and the missionary. Despite the fact that the work does not translate into a great deal of accumulated wealth, these careers produce strong feelings of significance for the workers. For many wealthy people, feelings of significance come in a different form. Even though other areas of their lives may be in shambles, many creators of wealth have been able to gain an immense feeling of significance from successful material accumulation. In contrast, inherited wealth does not produce the same feeling of significance. In fact, heirs often have feelings of inadequacy and insignificance. It is important that wealthy parents understand this fact.

4. The Desire to Find Immortality

The final desire is to *find immortality*. No one wants to die. Given the choice, we would prefer to live forever. The medical industry has become a multibillion-dollar industry for one reason— people do not want to die. Standing at the bedside of someone in intensive care is both a chilling and an impressive scene. Equipment surrounds the patient—machines monitoring vital signs, machines dispensing drugs, respirators and other machines doing who knows what. The room is full of technology. Why? The person does not want to die.

But check the mortality tables. Mortality is one hundred percent. One day, the old ticker is going to stop. And then what? Is it over, or will you continue to somehow live even after your physical body ceases to function?

It is this desire for immortality that causes us to want to be remembered by someone for something meaningful. How do we continue to live even after we are dead? We offer some profound options for your consideration in coming chapters.

These four fundamental desires have everything to do with how we discover our life-purposes. But how we integrate these desires leads us to vastly different results. The most common approach is what we call the *Compartmentalized Approach* to finding your life-purpose.

The Compartmentalized Approach to Finding Your Life-Purpose

Typically, we see the four fundamental desires as separate and distinct aspects of our lives. Consequently, we relate to them independently, as the following illustration depicts. Our goal is to spend an equal amount of time in each of these areas of our life. The greatest frustration people discover is that giving equal time to all areas is impossible. No matter what area of life we seek to address, we feel guilty because we are neglecting the other important areas.

While you are at work, you feel guilty because you feel you should be home with your family. After all, Dad, "You promised."

When you are home with your family, you feel pressured because you have so much work to do. In an attempt to compensate for the neglect of the family, you skip the charity board meeting Tuesday night, which adds even more guilt and frustration to your life. The more you try to balance your time and pursuits, the more stressed, frustrated and guilty you feel.

Figure 1 depicts this compartmentalized approach to life—trying to touch all the bases with equal amounts of time and interest. This is the way most people try first. However, we must tell you that it simply does not work. You cannot find your life-purpose utilizing this approach. Here is the theoretical ideal:

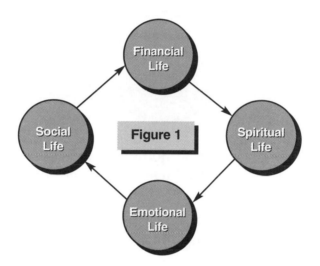

The Imbalances that Develop Following the Compartmentalized Approach

After years of observing this futile approach to finding purpose in life, we have seen that imbalances often develop accidentally. The following are four figures that depict common imbalances we have found.

Figure 2 represents people who have a poor self-image and have been so consumed by trying to feel important and find a sense of significance

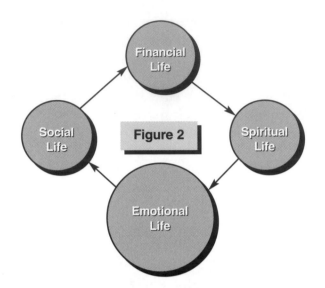

that the other areas of their lives have been under-developed. Their lives have become completely out of balance.

Figure 3 illustrates people who have become so consumed with being "heavenly" minded they are

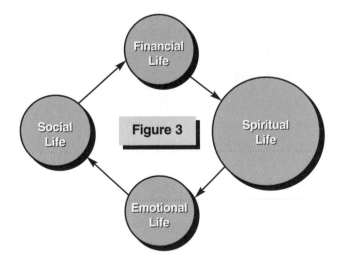

no earthly good to anyone. They are so philosoph-
ical about life that their lives become somewhat
hollow. Their lives are out of balance in these four
areas, and we find their true life-purposes are left
undiscovered.

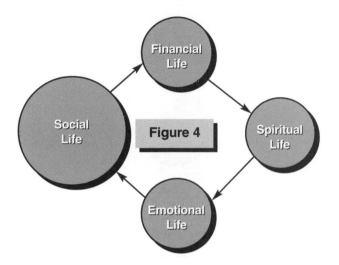

Figure 4 is an example of people who have so
devoted themselves to helping others that they
neglect the other fundamental areas of life. Even
though this overemphasis on serving and helping
others seems noble at first blush, these people
often neglect themselves. Many times, they are not
socially, emotionally, financially or spiritually
healthy.

Lastly, Figure 5 is the common imbalance we
see among "fiercely independent entrepreneurs."
They started their businesses to build a secure
financial future for themselves and their families.
They became so engrossed in the process that,
instead of running their businesses, they found

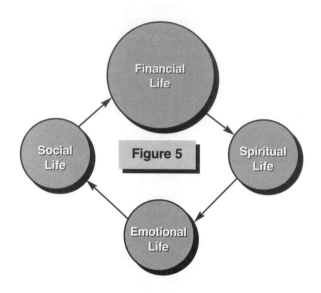

their businesses running them. They have gotten on the success treadmill—and they are running fast. They became incredibly successful monetarily, but the other critical areas, as a result of this over-demand in the financial area of their lives, were neglected.

The last thing in the world that any of us desire is to spend our entire business careers climbing the ladder of success only to discover, once we have reached the top, that the ladder is leaning against the wrong wall. We have seen this happen all too often. Entrepreneurs may be very successful in business, but often this success has been at the expense of their health, their marriage and their children. The good news is that, as long as you are still on this side of the grass, it is not too late to climb back down the ladder, move it to the right wall and then climb back up to the top.

The Synergistic Approach
to Finding Your Life-Purpose

We would suggest an alternative, and we believe a superior, way to finding the purpose for life. We call it the *Synergistic Approach*. We believe that, instead of treating each of the four fundamental desires of life as separate and distinct areas, we should merge them into concentric circles as follows.

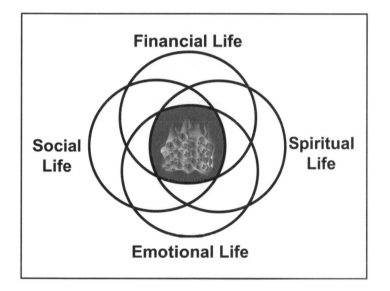

The goal in life is to find those activities, causes, relationships and opportunities that are common to all four fundamental desires. When you are devoting your time and energy to those specific tasks, you are fulfilling all of your desires and meeting all of the needs in your life at the same time. Once you are able to identify those things that fall into that core area and you begin devoting yourself to those things, you will find a fire beginning to burn within you like you may have never experienced in your life.

When you feel that fire within, you will discover the purpose for your life and the purpose for your accumulated wealth. This Synergistic Approach is like taking the rays of the sun and focusing them through a magnifying glass onto a piece of paper. It only takes a few seconds before the paper catches fire. Likewise, when you can narrow your focus from the thousands of possibilities of life and concentrate your energies on those few activities that can simultaneously meet your financial desires, your social desires, your emotional desires and your spiritual desires, your life will light up like the Fourth of July.

Someone once said, "The two most important days in a person's life are the day they are born and the day they discover *why* they were born."

George Bernard Shaw made a very revealing statement that relates perfectly. He said:

This is the true joy in life . . . being used for a purpose recognized by yourself as a mighty one . . . I am of the opinion that my life belongs to the whole community and as long as I live it is my privilege to do for it whatever I can. I want to be thoroughly used up when I die. For the harder I work the more I live. I rejoice in life for its own sake. Life is no brief candle to me, it is a sort of splendid torch which I've got to hold up for the moment and I want to make it burn as brightly as possible before handing it on to future generations.

Do you think that George Bernard Shaw had found his fire within? Did you notice the fourth sentence in his quote? "For the harder I work the more I live." That is a sure sign you have found your life-purpose. You are energized when you work. You are never bored or burned out.

When we can help a couple or better yet an entire family find their life-purposes and the purpose for their family's wealth, there is almost an explosion of excitement, motivation and passion that drives the balance of the planning process. Once they know what they are here to do, they cannot wait to begin doing it.

It is this experience, this discovery of purpose, which changes their attitude from the best years of their lives being behind them to being the years yet to come.

CHAPTER 8

The Family Wealth Letter of Intent
The Most Important Document

The Family Wealth Letter of Intent is the written essence of the decisions that come out of the day-long discussions at the Client Retreat. It will become the family mission statement—a written declaration of who they are and what they wish to do with the rest of their lives, how they wish to employ their talents, and how they plan to distribute their accumulated wealth.

We find it fascinating that almost all the wealthy business owners we have worked with have some form of a written mission statement for their businesses, but the thought of doing the same thing personally has escaped their consideration. We find it to be an oversight that is more accidental than intentional.

The Family Wealth Letter of Intent is, without a doubt, the single most important document that will be drafted during the entire planning process. This document will set the target that we will be aiming for in all the planning that follows. If we hit that predetermined bull's-eye, we will achieve exactly what the clients want.

A primary reason why traditional estate plans are not implemented is a lack of clarity. The Family Wealth Letter of Intent gives crystal clarity to the family and to all the advisors on the team. One of the most frequent complaints we hear from other traditional estate planning professionals is that their clients are not sure exactly what they want to do. In this state, it is almost impossible for advisors to recommend or design any kind of a plan, traditional or otherwise.

We have also found that even when a couple is clear about their goals the planning process may cause them to become confused and/or forget what it was that they wanted to do so many months earlier. The Family Wealth Letter of Intent becomes something akin to our nation's constitution, a document that has been referred to thousands of times over the past two-hundred-plus years to verify the original intent of the founders of this country. Similarly, as your planning team considers the different alternatives, the Family Wealth Letter of Intent serves as the constitution. We check all the planning alternatives and results against your written constitution.

Two years ago, we met with the Robinsons and all their advisors to do a final review of the case design. The planning team had met by phone and in person several times previously and had agreed the plan design was sound. The Robinsons were fully supportive of the plan. As far as we knew, everyone was on the same page and in complete agreement. Minutes into the meeting, we learned otherwise.

The two attorneys and the accountant began the meeting by suggesting planning alternatives they preferred. They discussed the alternatives for almost three hours in front of the Robinsons. They suggested that an outright gift of the stock to the children using the lifetime exclusion would be a superior alternative to the strategy we had already agreed upon. The Robinsons sat quietly for the entire three hours. We did the same. We just let the other advisors talk.

Finally, Mr. Robinson looked at us and said, "I can tell you have something you want to say."

We hesitated for a moment. Then, one of us replied, "We have been here for three hours talking about this other option, and we have not spent one minute talking about the Robinsons' philanthropic objectives that they have put in writing for us to follow. These new alternatives will have a negative impact on their ability to give to the charity they have stated they wish to support. Tom, you and Gladys need to say something."

After we threw the ball back into his court, he paused for several seconds, took a deep breath and said, "Yes, I do want to say something. In fact, I want to say two things. I do not want to pay any estate taxes, and I want to give three million dollars to the Holocaust Museum."

The advisors looked at the Robinsons and said, "If that is what you really want to do, the original plan is the best way to do it."

In fifteen minutes, the implementation assignments were passed out, and the meeting was over. The plan was being implemented based upon the written constitution that had been drafted months before. The Family Wealth Letter of Intent essentially saved the day. It kept the Robinsons focused on what mattered most to them—where they wanted to go.

In another case, the Family Wealth Letter of Intent was drafted in collaboration with an elderly widow's one son, Bruce, who was managing their substantial family wealth. Based upon the guidelines laid out in their Letter of Intent, we went to work designing a plan. It was a very complex plan, primarily because of their very significant amount of wealth, but with hours and hours of planning we had created a plan design that did everything they wanted done.

We went back to present the preliminary plan design to Bruce and two advisors for their critique and input before taking it to his mother for review. After hours of careful and meticulous review of every detail in the plan, Bruce expressed great satisfaction with the design. One advisor, however, expressed some concern about one aspect of the plan.

He said, "Gentleman, this is truly a brilliant plan design. I have never seen anything quite so comprehensive or well integrated. But, I do have a problem with this six-million-dollar testamentary strategy. It seems too complicated for the results it accomplishes. I would suggest that we just eliminate it from the plan altogether. We can have the family just pay the three million dollars in estate taxes when Bruce's mother dies, and then they grow the asset back up to the six million dollars in eleven years. Your proposal shows that they will have to wait for eleven years to get the six million dollars, and all the income from that trust during that time will go to their family foundation."

Bruce, an astute businessman who was extremely clear in what should be accomplished, looked at the advisor in surprise and said, "Why would we want to do that? With this design, we get six million dollars in eleven years, our foundation will have six million dollars in eleven years and the IRS gets nothing. With your proposal, the IRS will get three million dollars, now. We will still end up with six million dollars eleven years from now, but our family foundation will get nothing. Why would we want to do that?"

The attorney was completely stunned. He had never had a client who was so clear in what he or she wanted and so able to sort out the planning issues. The attorney actually apologized to the other members of the planning team for calling into question the plan design. He was both shocked and impressed. The testamentary strategy remained as a part of the implemented plan.

This is why the Family Wealth Letter of Intent is the most important document you will draft in the entire planning process. It sets the bull's-eye at a fixed location, so everyone involved in the planning process is in full agreement on exactly what the goals are. It ends ninety percent of the disagreements and confusion that interrupt, frustrate and stall the planning process.

How the Family Wealth Letter of Intent Is Constructed

During the Client Retreat, we take notes on what we discuss, what problems we identify, and what opportunities are before us to seize. With these notes and a copy of each couple's *Life on Purpose Questionnaire*™, we reduce to writing the essence of the decisions made at the Client Retreat and the reasoning behind them. We craft the first draft of the Family Wealth Letter of Intent using our clients' words and thoughts. This is to be the clients' letter to their children and advisors. It is not our letter to them.

It generally takes several days for us to put together a first draft of a Letter of Intent. Once we have the first draft, we send it to the client for careful and thoughtful review. There is only one rule for taking receipt of the first draft. The clients cannot simply say, "It looks good to us; let's do it."

The client must make changes. Our experience has shown that reducing to writing the essence of who others are and what they want to do is close to impossible on the first attempt. We cannot have said everything exactly right, included all that is needed, and expressed it the same way the clients would say it to their family and advisors. It is our goal that when the clients' children read this letter, they will say, "This letter sounds just like Mom and Dad."

Usually, there is a period of four to six weeks of refining, modifying and editing the Family Wealth Letter of Intent before it reads exactly the way the clients want it to read. The second reason we do not hurry through this phase of the process is because we have learned that clients continue to reflect upon the day we spent with them and the questions we asked. More often than not, they change their minds about what they want to do, what they want to say or how they want to say it.

The clients need time to process mentally what is being expressed in this letter. The rest of their lives and all their planning will be built upon it. We must be sure the letter accurately represents who the clients are and what it is they want to accomplish. This part of the process cannot and must not be hurried over.

We learned this truth very early. We had hurried through this part of the process once. We quickly drafted a Family Wealth Letter of Intent for a family. The clients saw it, said it was fine, and off we went to begin the planning. Everything seemed to be rolling along, until we were in a meeting with the client's accountant to review the case. (Then, we did the review with the clients and all the advisors at the same time, a practice we no longer do.)

During the meeting, the accountant told the client, "I have been running some of my own numbers, and I think we can increase the amount going to your kids from twenty-three million dollars to $23.5 million. Of course, this will reduce your charitable giving from seventeen million dollars to nine million dollars. Instead of paying nothing in estate taxes, you will have to pay seven million dollars. But," he proudly emphasized, "your children will get an extra half-million dollars."

We countered, "But Sam, you told us that you only wanted to give your children twenty-three million dollars and not a penny more. You also told us in your Family Wealth Letter of Intent that you were excited about giving as much to charity as you could, and avoiding all possible estate taxes was something you wanted to do. This plan will do everything you stated you wanted to do in your Letter of Intent."

What he said next we have never forgotten. It was a painful reminder of the dangers of rushing forward. Sam looked at us and said, "That was not really *my* Letter of Intent. It was *your* Letter of Intent for me."

At that moment, we knew the case was closed. Our process, and we, had lost credibility in the eyes of the client. As you might expect, nothing was ever implemented. Not our plan. Not the accountant's plan. Nothing. Sam still was not clear in what he wanted. When a client gets scared or confused, they will do *nothing*.

Reviewing the Family Wealth Letter
of Intent with Your Family

Once the clients have approved every paragraph, every line and every word, of their Family Wealth Letter of Intent, they sign the letter. When this is done, we are ready to move to the final step of the counseling phase, presenting their Family Wealth Letter of Intent to their family and advisors. This is an important final step before we move forward into the planning process.

We prefer to have the children see what their parents have in mind. One of the greatest mistakes some parents make is doing this kind of planning in a vacuum. We will discuss this issue extensively in chapter 13. But, for now, we feel very strongly that getting input from the children can be as important as getting input from the parents. The children should not feel as if this is their parents' plan for the next generation. They should feel that this is their family's plan for the family wealth. The difference between these two mindsets must not be minimized.

The children must agree that this is a good plan for them as much as it is a good plan for their parents. At one of our National Association of Family Wealth Counselors' semiannual training conferences, an heiress spoke for our opening banquet. She shared that her first experience with her own wealth was when, at eighteen years of age, she was taken to an attorney's office. There, she was told how much money she was worth— five million dollars. Hearing this number for the first time was very disorienting and troubling for her. She shared that she did not like all of the emotional ramifications of being wealthy.

The input from the children on what their parents are going to do for them, and to them, is critical. Adult children's insights and perspectives can be most helpful. If they object to any portion of the Family Wealth Letter of Intent or have other suggestions, getting those issues out on the table —so such issues can be resolved—must be done prior to beginning the planning process.

The value of allowing your children to discuss the Letter of Intent prior to planning and implementation cannot be understated. Grant and Dawn are the two children of our clients, Bob and Betty Harbert. Grant and Dawn were given the opportunity to review their parents' Letter of Intent. They saw that their parents intended to leave each of them several millions of dollars. In the meeting, they told their parents that they already had more than enough wealth and did not need or want anymore. They lovingly told their parents that, if philanthropy was so important to them, they would prefer Bob and Betty receive the joy of giving their inheritances away to the charities they cared about rather than to them. Betty and Bob were absolutely shocked.

This opened up new conversations with their children that they had never had before. They chose to set up a public family foundation and all four of them work together to give the inheritance away to worthy charitable organizations. Can you imagine how different and far less satisfying the results would have been if the children had not been included in the process? Can you imagine the frustration of discovering all this after you have just spent a great deal of time and money designing and implementing a new plan? Our counsel is to bring the heirs into the discussion as soon as you are clear about what you want and then be ready to listen to what they have to say.

Reviewing the Family Wealth Letter of Intent with Your Team of Advisors

This is the final critical step in the counseling process. Once the parents and the family are all completely "on board," it is time to review the Family Wealth Letter of Intent with the team of advisors. It is critical that all the advisors clearly understand the target at which their planning is aimed. During the review, members of the team may call into question the clients' motives and challenge the appropriateness of the listed objectives. This is not because they are trying to be difficult. It is typically because they are struggling to understand what is going on. Many times, advisors have never seen or heard of doing estate planning this way. They often find themselves out of their comfort zones and, therefore, out of control of the process. We will discuss how to build a successful planning team and have everyone pulling together in chapter 15.

The client's advisors, like their children, must have time to process the content of the Family Wealth Letter of Intent. They must be comfortable with its contents. The client should be looking for answers to three important questions from their advisors. First, do they see any legal or ethical obstacles to achieving the goals and objectives as stated in the Family Wealth Letter of Intent? Second, do they know anything about the client's current plan that would prevent them from carrying out the Letter of Intent? Finally, can a plan be designed that can accomplish everything stated in the Letter of Intent?

Completing the Counseling Process

Once we have completed all the steps in this counseling phase, we are about sixty percent finished with the entire planning project. This is their formal approval of the letter and their authorization to begin the planning process using this letter as our planning "constitution."

Sample
Family Wealth Letter of Intent

We close this chapter by including the following sample Family Wealth Letter of Intent with a great degree of trepidation. We have found that, as soon as we show a sample of anything we do, many conclude that this must be the "package" Family Wealth Counselors are "peddling" to everyone. Nothing could be further from the truth.

Showing you just one of hundreds of Family Wealth Letters of Intent is like trying to impress you with the magnitude of the Smithsonian Museum of Art in Washington, D.C. by showing you one painting. At best you can see what a rare masterpiece looks like, but it would not be wise to judge the entire museum by viewing only one painting. For this family, this was their personal masterpiece. Your masterpiece would, and should, be different.

We do tend to follow the same basic organizational outline for most of our Letters of Intent and to that extent you will find this sample useful. You can see that the Letter of Intent is not a mere listing of financial and estate distribution goals and objectives offered in a sterile vacuum. The financial information is integrated into the broader life aspects of the parents. The couple's goals and objectives are in a context of life, not just in a context of money and taxes. This couple's life-purpose is clearly articulated throughout the letter.

As you read this Letter of Intent, you are looking into the heart, the mind and the soul of this couple. Take some time to ponder what it is that they have said and the impact it will have on this family's future generations.

The John and Amanda Couch Family Wealth Letter of Intent

Purpose

This letter has been prepared to communicate to our children, family and professional advisors what is important to us as we seek to be good stewards of the wealth that has been and is being accumulated. We desire that they more fully understand our values and beliefs regarding the accumulation, preservation, use and distribution of our wealth. It is our intent to plan our personal and financial affairs in the context of our core values and beliefs in order to prepare our children for the responsibilities of wealth, and to provide a model for transferring our virtues, values and influence to them and to generations yet unborn.

How We Obtained Our Wealth

We recognize that true wealth is made up of more than money. In addition to money, wealth includes those virtues, values, and purposes that form the foundation of one's character.

Although both of us came from homes that in some respects were less than ideal, we nevertheless learned valuable lessons that marked us and contributed significantly to who we are and what we have become today. From our parents, we learned the importance of honesty, hard work, personal integrity, and faith. For Amanda, her primary care giver was her grandmother who loved her and nurtured her in addition to modeling for her a strong personal faith in Christ. We also learned from our family experience that the highest calling in life is to value our marriage and to raise our children successfully.

It is these primary virtues of honesty, hard work, personal integrity and being well prepared that have been the foundation of the success of Couch and Company. While these primary virtues and core values are the cornerstones on which the company has been built, the company is also a product of John carefully preparing himself, setting goals that he wanted to accomplish and seizing the opportunity when it presented itself. He has built his company on the personal belief that he must first earn the trust of his customers and then keep it. It is important for him and the company to not even walk close to the line of unethical conduct but to do business the right way every time.

In our first jobs as children, we understood the importance of accepting the responsibilities that we had been given as well as the need to document and organize activities in order to successfully accomplish the tasks.

Our Beliefs Concerning Finding Meaning

We share an abiding conviction that neither social position nor status provides anything inherently satisfying. Rather, it is understanding and responding to the God-given purpose in each of us that provides both fulfillment and contentment.

We believe that our highest calling in life is to raise good, responsible, and contributing children who pattern their lives after the example of our Lord. Therefore, it is our desire that our children discover the unique gifts and purposes for which they are being prepared and called, and that they would identify and follow the most satisfying uses of their time, their talents and their treasures. This will allow them to discover the place in life that utilizes their exceptional abilities and provides them their best roles. Through Couch and Company, John desires to build a company of significant financial value that will provide the children an opportunity to work within the company should they desire to do so.

We believe that accomplishment contributes more significantly to self-esteem, confidence and the development of strong virtues than does a lavish bestowal of inherited wealth. It is our strong conviction that good character based on the virtues of honesty, truthfulness and faith is the only assurance of true survival in life. It is our desire that our family be good citizens who contribute to others in our community. Further, money is high on the list of life's illusions of what constitutes true security, and if used incorrectly could even damage our family.

At the same time, we recognize that we live in a world full of financial uncertainties. Wealth does often provide a certain degree of protection and assurance during turbulent times. We would like to have at our family's disposal adequate financial resources if and when needed.

Our Responsibilities to Ourselves

We feel our first responsibility is to each other, to our financial security and to our personal life style. To this end, we intend to participate more fully in the financial-management process to personally gain the most from this process and to coordinate the efforts of our advisors.

We feel to be financially independent we need $480,000 annual after-tax income. This number includes some gifts to children. Further, we believe that liquid assets of $250,000 should be sufficient as an emergency reserve. We would also like to purchase a vacation home at some point in the near future.

Our Responsibilities to Our Heirs

We honor our responsibility to our children. We recognize the value of education for Patrick, Michael and Joseph. It is our objective to bequeath to our children sufficient resources for them to pursue their own goals and objectives and to equip them better for the responsibility of handling family wealth in a manner that enables them both to enjoy their inheritance and to manage it properly. It is our desire to bestow on them enough wealth that they will feel they can do anything, but not so much that they might choose to do nothing.

We also understand that money can distort perspective and become more of a burden than a blessing. According to Matthew Henry:

> Riches are a reward, if with them come wisdom and knowledge and joy to enjoy them cheerfully and to communicate them charitably to others. Riches are a punishment if one is denied a heart to take comfort in them, for they do nothing but tantalize and tyrannize over one.

Therefore, we exhort our children to hold riches with open hands, seeing neither material possessions, power nor social position as a measure of success and realizing that virtue is the true indicator of a life well lived. We would like our children ultimately to inherit our net worth—not all at one time, but over a period of time. Because we are young, we want to maintain the flexibility to change the terms of our distribution to our children as we follow their personal growth. We want to maintain the freedom at any time to provide current and future gifts to our children.

We very deeply want our children to be good citizens who contribute joyfully and generously to those causes with which they most identify and those causes that embrace and promote their primary virtues and core values. We want concern for others to be a prominent characteristic of their lives.

Our Responsibility to Others

It is our objective to reduce taxes in favor of charitable gifts wherever possible, as long as these gifts do not interfere with our ability to meet our personal lifestyle needs and the needs of our children. To the extent financial resources are sufficient, we would like to begin the process of philanthropy during our lifetime. We very much want to actively support local charities and ministries that assist the elderly and children. We would also like to support those organizations that are doing good work dealing with environmental concerns and scientific research.

In addition to the allocation of financial resources, we would like to be more personally involved with these charities when practical for us to do so.

We would like to design a philanthropic program that involves our children as much as possible. It is our hope that the process of shared philanthropy will allow our family to maintain a sense of unity as each child follows his own path in life.

Our ultimate objective is to equip and encourage our children to continue under their management, guidance and control the philanthropic legacy that we are beginning for our family with this Family Wealth Counseling process.

Sincerely,

John E. Couch   Amanda S. Couch

SECTION III

THE UNIQUE FAMILY PLANNING
ISSUES ADDRESSED IN FAMILY
WEALTH COUNSELING

CHAPTER 9

Understanding the
Psychological Pyramid of Priorities

One of the most powerful and important planning concepts is the Psychological Pyramid of Priorities. It identifies how people prioritize things. It is basic and instinctive. It is part of our human nature. Yet, it is very common to see this pyramid routinely ignored or violated in the planning process—to everyone's frustration and dismay.

Once the pyramid is understood, it simplifies and clarifies the proper steps to fully implement plans. The concept is incredibly simple, yet it is often the simple things in life that confound the wise. Knowing the pyramid does not make it powerful. Applying this concept to the planning process does.

The Psychological Pyramid of Priorities has three levels, or tiers. The first priority is the foundation of the pyramid. The second priority, obviously, is built upon the first, and the third level is built upon the other two below it. Except in the rarest of cases, it will not be otherwise. Adhering to this pyramid allows an advisor to create a plan clients will feel comfortable enough with to implement.

Here is how we illustrate the Psychological Pyramid of Priorities to our clients and their advisors.

The Base Level of the Psychological Pyramid of Priorities— Taking Care of Ourselves

One of the most basic and fundamental human instincts common to us all, rich or poor, is self-survival. Volumes have been written on this instinct and how it impacts human behavior.

To minimize this instinctive human drive, even among the wealthy, is foolhardy. Although people may be worth millions or even tens or hundreds of millions, most recognize how quickly things can change. Most wealthy people today did not inherit their wealth. They created it themselves out of years of sweat, sacrifice and risk.

Now they are comfortable and want to stay that way. They do not want to go back to struggling to pay the bills and make ends meet. They had enough of that lifestyle in decades past.

Contrary to popular opinion, most wealthy people live well below their means. This may sound absurd. It may be hard to imagine how people can live in a two-million-dollar house, have a Mercedes and two BMWs, take three months a year to live in a one-million-dollar winter home in Naples, Florida, have a million dollars in the bank, and still be living below their means.

The wealthy could spend more than they do. But they do not. They usually have substantial discretionary income beyond what they consume. They often have accumulated assets they could not possibly consume in their lifetimes even if they went on a spending spree every day for the rest of their lives.

Somewhere along the way to where they are today, they chose to cap their lifestyles. It may have been a conscious decision. It may have happened as a result of finally having everything they wanted in life. It may have been that they never increased their lifestyles from years past even though their net worth and income have multiplied many times over. No matter what the reason, they are living well below their means.

How much is enough for us?

Regardless of this tendency, there seems to be one question that wealthy people rarely contemplate, seriously or otherwise. That question is, How much is enough for us?

How much income do we feel we need to maintain our current lifestyle? It should surprise no one that wealthy people are not living on a budget. Often they have only a vague idea of how much they spend each year on their lifestyles. They have enough on hand to buy whatever they want, so no one tracks spending. Consequently, the question of how much is enough is not answered easily.

Notice that we do not ask, "How much do you actually need to maintain your current lifestyle?" We ask how much you *feel* you need to maintain your current lifestyle. Over the years, we have learned that no matter how logical, rational, or analytical people are they still will not make a decision unless they *feel* comfortable with it.

We often get responses like this, "Well, probably $250,000 annual spendable income would allow us to maintain our current lifestyle, but we would feel a lot more comfortable with $350,000."

The number we work with in planning this case is $350,000, not $250,000. We have seen that feelings often override facts when they are in conflict with one another. This couple is telling us they really want $350,000 of annual spendable income.

The next question we ask is, "How much do you need in emergency reserve to avoid possible future financial disaster?" It seems that a simple mathematical equation could give us the answer, but it does not work that way.

Memories of economic collapse and financial ruin—something younger Americans have yet to experience—have indelibly marked many older Americans who either lived through the Great Depression or were raised in homes where the depression had a major impact.

The instinctive and understandable reaction of those who have experienced true financial hardship is often "We can never have enough in reserve because we can never know just how long or how deep the next 'Great Depression' will be."

The answer to this concern is not a simple mathematical calculation. It requires in-depth conversations to help distinguish facts from feelings as we seek to answer this critically important question.

These are emotional discussions that go to the root of the instinctive human drive to survive—to take care of ourselves. These are not financial issues. Advisors who do not understand the pyramid are not sensitive to these perceptions and, consequently, move their clients into plans that are out of their clients' comfort zones.

Until a person *feels* comfortable that he or she has set aside enough to stem the worst financial disaster the person believes could happen, that individual will never release anything to children, charity or anyone else.

That is why we produce detailed, integrated

cash-flow scenarios for our clients. They must see that the sum of money they feel they need adequately provides them with the security they want. Unless they feel financially secure, they will not be emotionally ready to move to the second level of the Psychological Pyramid of Priorities.

The Second Level of the Psychological Pyramid of Priorities— Taking Care of Our Heirs

In addressing the second priority, wealthy parents must ask themselves, "How much is enough for our heirs?" This question is just as complex and emotional as the first. However, now the emotion is not one created out of deep fear and anxiety, but out of deep love. In most cases we are going to the opposite extreme of the emotional pendulum.

Warren Buffett made a profound comment on the topic of inheritance. He said, "I want to give my children enough of an inheritance that they will feel like they can do anything, but not so much of an inheritance that they might choose to do nothing."

When we discuss this quote with wealthy parents, the overwhelming majority readily concur. Yet almost none have tried to identify the minimum and maximum levels of wealth that would be best to pass on to their heirs.

The goal of passing as much of the family's wealth to the heirs as possible is one of traditional estate planning's primary assumptions. Planning strategies are designed to maximize the heir's inheritance. In fact, this is often the only planning goal. The chant rings out, "Max to the kids. Max to the kids."

Estate planners have told us that the only thing that really matters—the goal of the estate planning "game"—is to see how much wealth clients can transfer to their heirs. Whether the rest of the money goes to charity or the IRS is apparently irrelevant.

We feel that where the other half of the family's wealth goes should be just as important. When we ask our new clients how much wealth they want to pass to their heirs, they often look at us in disbelief and say, "Well, everything, of course!" They believe there is no other answer loving parents could give.

When they answer this way, we ask them another clarifying question, "When you say 'everything,' do you mean everything before tax or everything after tax? Because if you mean everything that is left after taxes, you only mean fifty percent of everything."

We must assure them that loving parents can have another answer. Few other advisors have raised this question, much less provided any method by which to determine what an appropriate inheritance might be.

That is why the statement from Warren Buffett is so valuable. There are minimum and maximum boundaries for an appropriate inheritance. We seldom are faced with parents who ask, "How little is too little?" They most often are struggling to answer, "How much is too much?"

When our clients are struggling to find an appropriate inheritance for the children, we take them through the "itemizing-their-inheritance" drill. We have them make a column for each child and then list exactly what they want each child to inherit. The exercise will go something like this.

"Well, we want them to each have their own home."

"How much will that cost?"

"Two hundred fifty thousand each."

"Okay, what else?"

"We want them to be able to keep our vacation home in West Palm Beach, Florida."

"How much is that worth?"

"One million dollars."

"What else?"

"Our kids all love to sail, so we would like for them to be able to own their own sailboat and have the money for the marina and boat maintenance."

"Fine, how much will they need for that?"

"Two hundred thousand dollars."

"Good, what else?"

"We want to be sure that our kids can provide our grandchildren the best education possible."

"And how much do you want to make available for that?"

"Thirty thousand dollars a year for each grandchild."

"Fine, anything else?"

"Yes, we want them to each have one million in the bank for emergencies."

"No problem. Anything else?"

This exercise continues until the parents cannot think of anything else that they would want their children and grandchildren to inherit. We once had a man say after going through this exercise, "If they get anything else, they will have more than I do!"

"So," we ask, "if your heirs get all this, you would consider it to be an appropriate inheritance?"

"Yes."

To their surprise, when we add up all the numbers and explain the time value of money, the children's inheritance is almost always dramatically less than the amount they had in their mind before the drill.

It is interesting that the total inheritance, once it is tallied, often does not go much beyond fifty percent of the family's current net worth.

The one exception is when a family business is involved, it makes up the majority of the family's wealth, and they want the business to go to the children. Then, these results will not apply. In those cases, the entire value of the family's wealth may indeed end up being passed on to the heirs. The important thing in any case is that the parents know how they have arrived at the inheritance figure, instead of simply pulling some arbitrary number out of thin air or resorting to the default answer, "Everything."

On as many occasions as not, the heirs actually end up with a larger inheritance with our new plan than they would have received under the existing plan. With many current plans, the children would receive even less than fifty percent of the family's total wealth.

Whatever amount of wealth ends up being "enough of an inheritance that they will feel like they can do anything, but not so much of an inheritance that they will do nothing," the next question that parents must ask is, "What will we do with the rest of our wealth?"

Assume that a couple determines, after our itemize-their-inheritance drill, that fifty percent of their wealth is an appropriate amount for their heirs. In this case, we tell them, "If you want to pass fifty percent of your wealth on to your heirs, and you do not mind the other half going to the IRS in estate taxes, you will not need us to go further and do any planning for you. Your current 'default' planning option is adequate. But, if you would prefer to self-direct that Social Capital to the charities and causes you care about, you will need us to do a good bit more planning."

This discussion leads us to explore the final tier of the Psychological Pyramid of Priorities.

The Third Level of the Psychological Pyramid of Priorities— Taking Care of Others

This is where the fun begins. The parents feel completely secure that they are going to be able to maintain their lifestyle and ride out any kind of emergency for the rest of their lives. They are providing their heirs with an appropriate inheritance. Now comes the big question, "What do we do with what is left?"

Obviously, charitable giving is a wonderful answer, but one that is rarely used. Why? In our experience, it is because most charities approach wealthy donors with an inverted pyramid. Charities approach donors to explain their needs— asking that the charity's needs be met. There is nothing wrong with asking that your needs be met. However, based on the Psychological Pyramid of Priorities, donors will not meet the charity's needs until they are certain that their needs will continue to be met and their heirs' needs will be met. If they do not know how much they need to accomplish these higher priorities, they will be reluctant at best, and completely unwilling at worst, to bestow a major gift on a charity.

The charities may ask, "Well, then, why are we able to acquire multimillion-dollar planned gifts from our donors if what you are saying is true?"

The issue is not whether they have acquired major gifts, but rather—are those gifts as major as they could have been? What about all those donors from whom the charity solicited a major gift but never received one? Was there any wealth left on the table that could have gone to the charity but went to the IRS instead? The answer, we believe, is usually in the affirmative.

We suggest this is the case because the Psychological Pyramid of Priorities was inverted and violated. It is not what they did give to charity that is the issue. It is what they did not give, but could have given, that is the issue. Until the family determines how much they need and how much their heirs need, they will always give less than they can or maybe even should.

Some years ago, we were referred to Dr. and Mrs. Jim Hohlt. They were one of the few clients we have had that already had a charitable trust established before we met them. He was on the board of trustees of a regional university. A couple of years prior to Dr. Hohlt meeting us, he was approached by the director of development about making a planned gift to the school. After some reflection, Jim and his wife, Liz, decided to fund a charitable trust with one hundred thousand dollars of highly appreciated securities.

Do you think the director of development was pleased to accept this planned gift? Of course! However, two years later, Jim and Liz met with us. We took them through the entire Family Wealth Counseling process. When we were done, we set up and funded a second charitable trust with $1.7 million more of appreciated assets—seventeen times more than he gave two years earlier. What was the difference?

It is simple. We followed the Psychological

Pyramid of Priorities and helped them answer the two questions that had never been asked by any of their advisors, "How much is enough for us, and how much is enough for our heirs?"

Once they had satisfactorily answered these two questions, Jim and Liz discovered they had extra wealth left over—$1.7 million to be exact. Now, the couple was emotionally willing to make a second planned gift because they saw that this part of their wealth was truly surplus.

———○◦○———

If wealthy people have not adequately answered the questions of how much is enough for them, their children and others, they give substantially less than they could. They do not want to over-give and create possible lifestyle maintenance problems for themselves or reduced inheritance issues for their family.

Each wealthy family must answer fully these three essential questions. Without doing so, the likelihood of getting a creative master life-plan implemented falls to nearly zero. A planner must have fixed benchmarks upon which to base his or her plans. With no clear answer as to how much is enough for clients to feel comfortable, to maintain their current lifestyle, no plan for wealth transfer to the family can be developed effectively. Likewise, with no specific set figure for the appropriate amount of wealth to be passed on to the family, there is no way to determine if there is any surplus. This thought process and the answers that come from it are absolutely critical to doing effective and strategic planning.

This Psychological Pyramid of Priorities expresses our most basic human instincts of: (1) taking care of ourselves, (2) taking care of our own, and (3) taking care of others. Moving through these planning-priorities in the proper order not only simplifies the entire planning process, it also makes it more rewarding. It is worth the effort.

CHAPTER 10

Planning with Your Heart
as Well as Your Head

One of the most difficult tasks in estate planning is including the human side of the equation. The planning process itself is heavy on the technical side. There are legal documents, Estate Tax tables, Gift Tax tables, Annual Gift Exclusions, Applicable Lifetime Exclusions, Generation Skipping Tax exemptions, gift and estate tax deductions, unlimited marital deductions, valuation adjustments, revocable and irrevocable trusts, inter vivos and testamentary trusts, GRATs, CRUTs, FLPs and CLATs.

Then there are the integrated cash-flow ledgers, multiple insurance illustrations, net-present-value calculations, time-value-of-money projections, interest and growth-rate assumptions, and mortality tables.

If that is not enough, all the meetings are held

in an advisor's formal conference room with everyone dressed in business attire. The room is full of professionals who make their living by analyzing and writing words and running numbers. They are masters of the details. They are brilliant technicians. The brainpower in the room is staggering.

Assets you have traded much of your life to accumulate—businesses, homes, and real estate—are reduced to nothing more than commodities to be repositioned and revalued to improve "the bottom line."

Worst of all, our children and grandchildren can and often are reduced to nothing more than a small but useful group of tax shelters to be taken advantage of in the planning process.

Is it any surprise that planning often lacks any human element? Parents and their advisors end up letting the head issues overrule the heart issues of life during the planning process.

Viewing Your Family Members as "Tax Shelters"

Consider this. A man and his wife both are giving their children and grandchildren twenty thousand dollars each year, their joint annual exclusion amount. Has anyone asked them why they are doing that? Perhaps more importantly, why is the amount twenty thousand dollars? Why not twelve thousand dollars? Or fifty thousand dollars?

The answer usually has less to do with whether making these gifts is good for the heirs as flesh-and-blood offspring and more to do with maximizing the advantage of using heirs as tax shelters. Think about it. These gifts are made primarily to enhance the parents' tax planning, not to enhance the welfare of their children and grandchildren. If you question the truth of this observation, simply ask yourself who prompts parents to make such gifts and further recommends the size of the gifts? The answer is usually the tax advisors.

You see, like it or not, family members can and are being used as tax shelters. Have you considered how the heirs feel knowing that the primary if not the sole reason they are getting these annual gifts from their parents or grandparents is because there is a tax incentive? Do these gifts have anything to do with their parents' love for them? Or are they making these gifts with ulterior motives and strings attached?

Ask yourself, when those children or grandchildren get their annual gifts, do they come with cards or personal letters expressing love and affection, explaining why the beneficiaries are receiving this inheritance and expressing the hope that they will use the gifts wisely?

What beneficiaries usually receive with their gifts are letters that must be signed and returned to the trustees in thirty days. They must waive the right to withdraw their gifts. This does not necessarily communicate a great amount of feeling and affection.

Generation Skipping Trusts
"You Own It, but You Don't"

Have you ever considered the emotional impact on heirs of Generation Skipping Trusts? Enough time has passed since these trusts became law that research on this type of trust is available. Generation Skipping Trusts, sometimes referred to as GSTs, are having a negative impact, mostly emotional, on the beneficiaries.

The *Inheritance Project* has done extensive research into how the beneficiaries of wealth handle these trusts. This research is turning up some very interesting and troubling discoveries. A GST may be the hardest trust of all to deal with emotionally because "you own it—but you don't." Are GSTs set up because they are really best for the family members who were going to have to live with them for the next one hundred years or more, or because they are good tax-planning tools?

The heirs' perceptions are very interesting. They sense that trusts in general have nothing to do with trust at all. These trusts have everything to do with *dis*trust.

Whether that was really the parents' motivation is irrelevant. For the heirs, perception is reality. Unless they are told otherwise, the message is loud and clear, "My parents did not trust me with my inheritance." How does it make heirs feel knowing that a trust was set up that they could not control? That they were not deemed responsible or trustworthy enough to be fully and totally able to handle their wealth—ever?

Family Limited Partnerships
"Irrelevant Ownership"

The use of Family Limited Partnerships, referred to as FLPs, in planning is another example of potential planning without a heart. The typical scenario of an FLP is that the parents retain control of the entire partnership by keeping the general partnership units while gifting the limited partnership units either directly to family members or into a trust that will ultimately end up benefiting family members.

Of course, the limited partners, the offspring, have absolutely no control over these assets. They are at the mercy of their parents as to whether there will be any income coming from it or how the assets will be invested. They learn nothing and possibly even gain nothing from their inheritance.

What these parents have communicated to their family's future generations is, "We do not trust you to make good decisions or to be wise in handling this wealth you are receiving. Just hold onto these units and be quiet. We will take care of everything."

What message is being communicated to the children or grandchildren through this tax-planning and wealth-control strategy? It is safe to say this strategy does not lead to a flood of warm, fuzzy feelings toward the parents. Often, heirs even feel used and manipulated.

"Dad is just doing business again. We are his little pawns in his game to beat the IRS."

It May Not be Wrong,
but It May Not be Wise

Do not misunderstand the point. We are not saying any of these tools and techniques are, in and of themselves, wrong or bad. We use these tools and dozens like them all the time.

What we are saying is that decisions to use these tools and techniques must be evaluated with the heart as well as the head. We must explore the "soft" side of an option as well as the "hard" side. Tragically, this is rarely done in traditional estate planning.

One of our cardinal rules in the Family Wealth Counseling Process is to always ask, "How will the client feel about this particular strategy?"

It does not matter how good the technique is or how well it works in their particular situation, if the clients do not feel good about it, it is not going to happen. The couple will not do it. We must find an alternative strategy that makes both "head" sense and "heart" sense.

Unfortunately, the other family members—the beneficiaries of this accumulated wealth—are seldom given that same opportunity to have input before a plan or strategy is implemented. In fact, the overwhelming majority of estate planning is done behind the closed doors of an advisor's conference room with just the parents and their advisors considering options, making decisions, and implementing plans.

We find this practice fascinating. An owner of a business usually does not decide to set up an elaborate new employee-benefit plan without consulting at least a few key employees to see if it is something they want or need. Are they in favor of it? Will they participate? Will it be a valuable perk? Yet, just the opposite seems to happen when putting together the "benefits package" for their own flesh and blood.

Often, the children know nothing of their parents' plans until they are sitting in the attorney's office listening to the last surviving parent's will.

Look at Your Plan's Impact through the Eyes of Your Family Members

There is a natural tendency for fiercely independent entrepreneurs to do their planning the way they run their financial empires, "This is *my* wealth, and I will do with it what *I* please." This attitude may work extremely well in managing your assets, but it is not effective when transferring that wealth to future generations so that it will be a blessing to them and not a curse.

Parents must make a conscious effort to move around to the other side of the table. In other words, they must look at the plan's impact through their children's eyes. They must consider their children's feelings and emotions. We ask our clients to put themselves in their children's shoes and imagine living out the rest of their lives after receiving their inheritance. Do they like the outcome they have imagined?

We always insist that parents go through this mental exercise. They need to ask themselves the same kinds of questions we ask ourselves when designing their plan. How will the children and grandchildren *feel* about this plan? Are we doing something *for* the family or are we doing something *to* the family? Of course, the simplest way to find the answer to this question is to ask the children directly.

The idea of including all the family in the planning process creates an entirely new set of emotional and practical issues that parents may not be willing to address. Often, they do not feel comfortable fully disclosing all their financial details to their children. However, we strongly believe that full disclosure is the best rule in these matters; although, we acknowledge there are exceptions to every rule. Just the fact that the parents trust their children enough to "tell all" goes a long way toward improving the plan's impact on the children.

In-laws versus Outlaws

When possible, we encourage the direct involvement and input of the children, adult grandchildren and even the in-laws in the decision-making process.

Have you considered the impact a multimillion-dollar trust in your daughter's name *only* might have on her marriage? She will be receiving two hundred thousand dollars a year from her trust while her husband makes only fifty thousand dollars annually and works all year long to earn it. What will this do to his feeling of equality within the marriage? Although this inheritance will no doubt make them "financially happier," will it make them personally happier and help them maintain a strong, vibrant marriage in the years to come? Or will the gift inadvertently sow seeds of envy, division and possibly even divorce? The newspapers are full of tragic stories of wealthy heirs. This is not a far-fetched theory that could not possibly happen to your heirs. It is the way real life works, and wealth provides no insulation from real life.

Such parents do their wealth-transfer planning with an eye to producing maximum tax benefits. They fail to consider carefully and adequately the human ramifications of those tax-planning strategies and inadvertently sow seeds of destruction in the lives of their children.

Blessing or Cursing Your Grandchildren

As another example—what about the grandchildren's trust that was set up using the GST exemption? They were each to receive one million when they reach twenty-five years old. It may be a great tax-planning strategy, but what will it ultimately do for or perhaps to these twenty-five-year-olds? Worse yet, what might it do to them even before they turn twenty-five, knowing that they will receive cash and assets of one million dollars each? What might it do to their work ethic, motivation to get a good education, and career goals when they know that after their twenty-fifth birthday, they will be receiving at least eighty thousand dollars a year even if they do nothing?

Think about how that trust will take power and authority out of the hands of their parents and how it might paralyze the parents' influence and control? When the mother and father insist that their son graduate from high school, he may simply refuse and move out, knowing that in seven more years, he will be "rich." Did the grandparents intend for this to happen? Definitely not. They were just trying to take full advantage of the tax incentives available to them.

If you think the solution to this potential problem is not letting the grandchildren know anything about the trust until they are twenty-five, you simply exchange one emotional danger for several others.

When planning is done without the heart, without feelings, without considering the human side of the equation, and is only done to reduce taxes, the results can and often are disastrous to the lives of the recipients of that so-called efficient tax plan.

Wealth Does Not Build Character; It Only Reveals It

Parents must remember, *wealth does not build character; it only reveals it.* We have seen parents who believe that although their children are currently lazy, undisciplined and selfish their inheritance will somehow magically transform them into hard-working, disciplined and generous people. If you put millions of dollars in "bad" children's hands, all you have given them is the opportunity to be worse. If you put millions of dollars in "good" children's hands, it will allow them to be and do even more good. Wealth simply magnifies the underlying nature of those holding it; it does not change it.

It seems obvious that a parent's greatest challenge in planning is building solid virtues and noble character into the children and grandchildren, so they will have the underlying fiber to use the wealth in a way that will be a blessing to them, their family and to others. Chapter 14 addresses this issue in greater detail.

Feeling What Inheritors Feel

The *Inheritance Project's* materials are extremely helpful to parents who wish to explore fully the heart side of planning. There are five major emotional conflicts inheritors face. All five can be overcome. However, with careful advance planning they can simply be avoided. That is why we encourage parents to engage their heirs in the process while they are still around to be both role models and mentors to this new generation of wealth holders.

To the extent that parents recognize the emotions and problems that come with the wealth they are passing on, they can effectively address them. They can devise ways to minimize or avoid them altogether in the planning process, just as they are trying to do with taxes.

Inheritors' Fears

It is interesting that the greater the level of financial security provided by an inheritance, the more emotional insecurity there is. Even though these heirs are financially secure, they struggle internally with debilitating concerns about self-image, responsibility and even survival.

Deep, nagging questions eat away at their psyche. *With all my wealth, how can I prove myself in any endeavor I might undertake? Am I a valuable person without my wealth? Without this wealth and the advantages it provides, could I even make it on my own? If I did not have all this wealth, would my friends still be my friends?* These are just a few of the haunting questions that loom in the minds of the inheritors of wealth. Lavishly bestowed wealth often increases heirs' insecurities rather than decreasing them.

Inheritors' Isolation

The possession of wealth leads heirs to conclude, sooner or later, that they are different from most people. Of course, when it comes to the amount of wealth they have, it is true. But this difference may be transferred incorrectly to other areas of life.

They feel separated, insulated, alienated and disconnected from the rest of the world. This is a lonely and painful feeling. This sense has been conveyed to them in many ways as they grew up living in country estates with walls surrounding the enclosed lawns and city apartments with guards protecting the buildings.

They cannot have normal relationships with many people because their wealth can be intimidating to others. Instead of being a means of having deeper, fulfilling relationships, their wealth isolates them. This forces them to be lonely or to hide their wealth, so they can have a "normal" life.

The movies *Aladdin* and *Roman Holiday* are perfect examples. In *Aladdin*, Jasmine chooses to flee the castle to get a taste of real life. In *Roman Holiday*, Princess Anne sneaks out of the royal compound one night to experience how the rest of the world lives. In both cases, it took little time for them to realize how ill-equipped they were to live normal lives.

Both these heirs longed for what they had been cut off from, what they could see, but not experience. Such isolation is anything but a blessing.

Inheritors' Delayed Maturity

The protected and sheltered lives heirs enjoy as children may keep them from growing up. Things are simply given to them. They are not required to think, plan, budget or set boundaries. They have unlimited resources, so the goal often is to eat, drink and be merry. If they waste ten thousand dollars, no problem, there is always more. Heirs often fail to learn how to even balance a checkbook, much less learn how to responsibly spend what is in it.

Wealthy heirs can also become snobs. They may think of themselves more highly than they ought and fail to learn social skills, humility, grace and compassion. They become the infamous spoiled, rich kids.

Children must learn to become emotionally autonomous from their parents. They can do this when parents equip them with the virtues, values and skills needed to make a success of life with or without wealth. This is the most important inheritance parents can give to their children.

Inheritors' Lack of Direction

Abundant wealth often leaves heirs in a fog. They have no clear plan or purpose in life. Their wealth has given them the opportunity to do anything, yet they find themselves doing nothing of value for themselves or anyone else, except enjoying the abundant life their wealth allows.

If inheritors have no specific goals or objectives in their lives, they can have their engines running at full throttle, yet with no rudder in the water, they will drift from one hobby to the next, from one degree program to the next, from one career to the next. They are going nowhere in high fashion. They simply have no plans for their lives.

When people know they have so much money that they never need to work, they find it extremely hard to commit to anything, especially something that will require sacrifice or possibly even pain. Yet, without commitment, relationships and accomplishments will never be successful, and life will be hollow.

Inheritors' Guilt and Shame

Heirs very commonly feel both ashamed and guilty about their unearned fortunes. They have what hardly anyone else has and what so many people in our country and around the world need, and they have done nothing special to deserve it except come from the right womb.

It is this unmerited wealth that is so emotionally debilitating. Since wealth was never discussed at home while they were growing up, they assume that wealth must be a bad thing, something people should not talk about. They may further internalize this to believe that since they have money, they must be bad, too. Often, this mindset is ingrained in them very early.

Another reason for guilt and shame might be how the family fortune was earned. If it was through exploitation, manipulation or less than virtuous means, the wealth can be tainted in the heir's mind, which can create other emotional conflicts.

In attempting to overcome this guilt, inheritors will either try to work exceptionally hard to deserve their wealth, work hard to hide it, continually apologize for even having it or sometimes all three. These attempts to overcome guilt inhibits them from feeling free to be themselves instead of always feeling the need to prove themselves worthy of their good fortune.

Planning with Your Heart as Well as Your Head

The majority of wealthy people we work with are first-generation wealth creators. They started with nothing. They exercised their undying work ethic. They labored endless hours to become successful. They lived modestly for much of their early lives while building their financial empires.

These fiercely independent entrepreneurs have absolutely no personal experience with the emotional and psychological issues that accompany inheriting substantial wealth. For the most part, their advisors are not wealthy and have no personal experience in these emotional issues of wealth transfer either—unless vicariously through some of their clients' inheritors.

Because of this lack of knowledge and experience in this area, it is critical that parents get information to help them plan with their hearts as well as their heads. There is no shortage of professionals who can help with the head part. But there is a dramatic shortage of those who address the softer issues within the context of the factual issues of transferring wealth to heirs.

As we have shown, there is more that comes with an inheritance than just the wealth. A Family Wealth Counselor has been trained in both the heart and the head issues and feels comfortable talking about both. It is the integration of these two disciplines that makes our approach to planning unique and should make such an advisor an essential member of any wealthy family's planning team. Half of the battle is recognizing the emotional planning pitfalls. The other half is making sure you have a planning team that knows these pitfalls and how to address them within the context of tax planning.

CHAPTER 11

Resolving Family Conflicts and Repairing Broken Relationships

No one is surprised that family conflicts and broken relationships are not the exclusive domain of the wealthy. These tragic situations are found in all economic strata. However, the amount of wealth a family possesses does seem to greatly magnify both the quantity and the extent of these problems.

This chapter will not be an easy chapter for many people to read. Some may even choose to skip it because the hurt from family conflicts and broken relationships in their lives is too painful, or they have come to believe that certain relationships are beyond repair.

This chapter, however, has been written to offer you hope. There is no pain so deep that it cannot be removed, or no relationship so completely destroyed that it cannot be successfully repaired—if at least one person is willing to try.

In those situations where reconciliation of these family conflicts and broken relationships is not possible, there are some very practical steps to gaining permanent peace and freedom. Regardless of whether reconciliation is accomplished, we all need to find personal peace and learn how to let go emotionally and get on with our lives.

No matter what the outcome, we can all have victory.

Causes of Conflict in Wealthy Families

Before we can begin a discussion on how to resolve family conflicts, we must first understand the root causes of family conflicts that ultimately lead to broken relationships. Not all of a family's conflicts manifest themselves in intense and on-going arguments. In many cases, conflicts and wounds are held within and never verbalized. Freedom to discuss the conflicts and express the pain is often repressed. In many situations, these topics may even become taboo and are to never be mentioned. Often, one party in the conflict may not be aware that a conflict exists. Resolving these conflicts is sometimes difficult because the parties have never even discussed the conflicts with one another.

Over the years as we have worked with many wealthy families, we have found that virtually every family conflict and subsequent broken relationship seems to fall into one of six basic categories.

1. General Neglect

Years ago, we heard this statement within the context of asset management, "Any asset left unmanaged becomes a liability." The point was that you should not invest in something and then ignore your investment.

For example, imagine buying a home and then ignoring its maintenance for the next twenty years. What will happen to the home? What will happen to its value? What if you bought a car and drove it for fifty-thousand miles without having it serviced? What would happen to that car?

The same is true of relationships. Any relationship left unmanaged becomes a liability. There are no truer examples of this than relationships with children. There is a big difference between children growing up and children being raised. As long as you feed and shelter children, they will grow up. There is nothing magical about that. *Raising* children is another story.

A very common internal family conflict that wealthy families have is the absence of one or both parents when the children were young. In many cases, family employees (i.e., nannies and housekeepers) have partially or completely raised the children. The negative ramifications of this practice go beyond the scope of this chapter, but suffice it to say, this scenario creates serious problems.

Neglecting relationships with family members does not lead to a lack of relationships. Rather, it leads to bitter relationships. Children, even into adulthood, feel unloved, abandoned and cheated.

The fruit is almost always bitter. Often the bitterness affects their own self-worth, their marriages and even how they raise their own children.

Consider the Cohens. They live in the Southwest. An existing client in the East had referred them to us. Herb was interested in reviewing his family's estate plan. When we introduced Family Wealth Counseling to him, he was so impressed with the concept of retaining control of his Social Capital that he asked us to present it to a nonprofit he was a board member of and also to the Jewish Federation in his state. We told him we would schedule a Client Retreat to discuss these ideas. Barb, his wife, was reluctant to go on the retreat, but she finally agreed.

We arrived at their home and began their retreat. Barb was having a difficult time answering the questions. Herb was extremely talkative and very open. One of the questions we asked was, "What kind of relationship did you have with your parents, and how are you most like your father and mother?"

Herb described a horrible relationship with his father. In fact, he described how he stood over his father's coffin and poured his heart out to his deceased father. He asked, "Why didn't you ever come to my basketball games when I was in junior high, high school and college? Why didn't we ever really talk? I really loved you and wanted to spend more time with you."

He related that, while he was having this meaningful conversation with his father, a sobering reality hit him: he had just had the best conversation of his life with his father, and his father was dead.

The next question we asked was, "Are there any other damaged relationships with family members that need to be resolved?"

Herb looked at me with a pained look on his face. He said, "Well, I was married before. I have three children from my first marriage whom I have not seen in twenty years."

We were surprised and asked, "You are kidding? You have not seen your children in twenty years?"

He said, "No, nor have I spoken with them."

We responded, "It sounds as if your kids are going to have the same experience at your funeral that you had at your father's funeral."

He looked up at us and said, "That is, if they even come."

Then he stood up, went to his china closet, and pulled out a Kiddush cup. In the Jewish faith, this cup is used when you say blessings on the Sabbath and religious holidays. He brought it over to me and asked me to stand by the window so I could really see it. It was silver and very old. He showed me the names of his ancestors dating all the way back to the early 1800s. It had been passed down father to son for more than 175 years. He showed me where his grandfather's, then his father's names were inscribed on it.

He turned and looked at me and said sadly, "Who can I leave this to? Am I going to leave it to my wife's daughter? She is not even Jewish."

We said we felt his son should have it. We advised him to reach out to his children, that perhaps a messy divorce had led his children to believe he was a monster.

He looked at us and said, "I kind of deserved some of that."

We encouraged him, saying, "But the truth is that you are a wonderful person now. You need to let your children at least know what kind of person you turned out to be. Do you have the courage to contact them?"

Herb asked, "What do you mean?"

We said, "Think of the rejection you might get. It is going to take some courage to make those calls. Can you do it?"

As the retreat progressed, he became more and more excited about the idea of reaching out to his own children. Several hours had passed. We apologized that we had a plane to catch, but we obviously were not finished.

Herb told Barb, "You need to ride with us to the airport, so we can keep this going." There we were bouncing around in the back of the Jeep and asking them these very powerful questions.

Suddenly, Herb said, "I just thought of something. During the war, I could not get a basketball because all of the rubber was used for the war effort. They were not making basketballs, and I loved to play the game. My friend and I crumpled tinfoil to shoot baskets. When I was about eleven, my father found a basketball for me. I have no idea where he got it, but I was the only one in the area who had one."

With tears in his eyes, Herb sighed, "You know, I forgot about that."

"It sounds like your father really did love you," we offered.

He responded, "I guess he did in his own way."

It took this man fifty-five years to realize that his father really did love him. It may have been the most significant revelation of his life.

We pulled up to the airport. We were running late. The last call for our flight was being announced, and we knew we would never make it.

Herb said confidently, "No problem. I will run with you." He asked his wife to stay with the car, and he ran with us through the airport to be sure that we caught our plane. We did not have time to say good-by, but we could see in his eyes both peace and hope.

Any asset left unmanaged becomes a liability. It is just as true of human assets as it is of financial assets. We will tell you the rest of the story later in this chapter.

2. Rejected Family Values

Many times, we have seen the children of wealthy parents reject their family's primary virtues and core values. They choose a course for their lives that is the antithesis of everything the family stands for. Children may become involved in drugs, marry outside their family's faith or live a promiscuous and immoral lifestyle. Often, this is their way of responding to the general neglect they experienced at home. A child may turn out to be lazy and unmotivated. To the fiercely independent entrepreneurial father, this is like scratching your fingernails on a chalkboard. Nothing creates more of an excruciating discomfort for a hardworking father than having a lazy son.

The tragic conflicts and broken relationships that have resulted from children's rejection of their parents' underlying virtues and core values could fill several volumes. The daily newspapers all too often feature true stories of wayward children of wealthy families.

3. Failed Expectations

"Dad, I have never been able to live up to your expectations. No matter how hard I try, you are never satisfied."

How many times have we heard this sad cry from the children of wealthy parents?

Wealthy parents often unconsciously think that because their children have had the best of everything—the best schools, the best clothes, the best tutors and coaches—they should be the best at whatever they do. It can be hard for extraordinary parents to accept that they have ordinary children.

More times than not, these kids will never be the brightest, the most athletic or the shrewdest business minds in their class. Yet living in the shadow of an extraordinary parent forces them to strive for levels of achievement that they simply cannot attain. As a result, their lives are filled with the frustration and pain of knowing that they are disappointing the very people they love the most and want to please. Generally, they will eventually give up trying.

Another way in which failed expectations create family conflicts is when a child's career has been predetermined by an edict of the parents—like the young prince who is destined to become king regardless of whether he wants to or not. His future has been predetermined.

We have seen many fathers who have, as part of their business plan, designated a son to take over the family business. It has just been assumed that the son would be the heir apparent to the business "throne."

The only problem is that the son's skills, temperament or career goals may not line up with becoming the CEO of the family business. He wants to please his father, but he does not have the talent or the interest to go into the family business.

The Bennett family had to deal with such an issue. The matter had become such a sticking point between Henry, the father, and his son, Tim, that they had all but stopped speaking to each other. This fractured relationship was revealed during our Client Retreat.

Henry wanted Tim to go to Stanford and get a degree in business and then get his MBA from Harvard. Tim was bright enough. He was a straight-A student. He was a good child, clean cut, moral and well mannered. Everything a mother and father could want in a son. Except, Tim was not interested in the family business. He was interested in music. He wanted to go to the Julliard School of Music, one of the finest in the country.

Henry told Tim that if he went to Stanford and majored in business, he would pay for his entire college education. If Tim insisted on going into music, he would have to pay for his college education himself. Henry would not help him at all.

The stress on the young man was incredible. He longed to please and be accepted by his father, but he also had an intense desire to play the cello with a symphony. Tim chose to pursue his own passion instead of his father's, and the relationship between this father and son was all but severed. We will continue this story later in this chapter.

Failed expectations have created a huge number of conflicts in the wealthy families we have worked with.

4. Self-Gratification

One of the great advantages of wealth is that there is plenty. One of the great disadvantages of wealth is that there is plenty. Children who have the opportunity to get everything they want will usually end up wanting everything. This disease, we call "affluenza," is usually transmitted from the parents to the children by common association.

Children who grow up with access to "easy" money, lots of free time and little responsibility become consumed with getting and doing what pleases them. They often become so self-focused that they only live for themselves.

If their parents ask them to contribute something to the family, to make some sacrifices for the good of the whole or to assume some responsibility, they will make life miserable for everyone else until they get their way.

This can make for a very unhappy home life for everyone. Even after the children move out, they often keep "coming back to the well," so they can continue the opulent lifestyle they had grown accustomed to while living at home.

How does a young man or woman, after living a life of luxury, move away from home and start with nothing? The culture shock is extreme. What often happens is the children go out and try to recreate the lifestyle they were used to at home. They run themselves into major trouble financially, because they cannot afford to live the way their parents do.

Parents may continue to underwrite their children's lifestyles, but the children never become responsible or self-sufficient. They remain permanent dependents.

This self-gratification problem can persist indefinitely and can create major disagreements and conflicts between family members.

5. Lack of Honesty

You might think this refers to lying to your children and spouse, and you would be right. But there is so much more than simply being truthful in what you say. All of us have lied on purpose, probably more than once. There may be no more devastating violation of a human relationship than to deceive someone you love intentionally. Small infractions can be overcome when discovered. Major ones, on the other hand, can end relationships. These are the kind that end marriages and business partnerships.

There is another kind of dishonesty that is incredibly pervasive among the wealthy. More often than not, we hear about this type of dishonesty from the children when they discuss their relationships with their fathers.

We were talking with the daughter of Jerry Watkins, a very wealthy business owner. When we spoke about him, Beth said very coldly, "I do not trust my father. He is not honest."

We were almost numb with shock. Jerry was one of the most honorable men we had ever known. He had told us that he had walked away from several major business opportunities because for the deals to work some numbers were going to have to be "fudged." He wanted no part of those kinds of deals.

He was the kind of businessman who would refund a dollar to a customer whom his clerk inadvertently overcharged. He was like a modern-day Honest Abe Lincoln. We could not understand why Beth would not trust this man, her own father. But what she told us was truly heart-wrenching.

She reflected on her childhood and said, "When I was eleven years old, I had a school recital. I was the featured pianist for the evening program. I was dressed in a formal gown, and the auditorium was full of proud parents, family and friends anxious to hear the evening's performance. I had reserved seats for my parents at the end of the front row. The day of the recital, my dad told me that he was going to have to be at a business meeting that afternoon and would come directly to my recital. I stood backstage waiting for Dad to arrive. The seat next to my mom remained empty. The recital started—still no Dad. I was next. I looked again to see if he was there. The seat was still empty. When I walked out on stage to perform, I glanced over to see if my dad had arrived. The seat was still empty. I cannot describe the intense disappointment and pain I felt that night. We had been home for about an hour when my dad finally arrived. He was very sorry he had missed my recital. The business meeting ran over. I wanted to forgive him, but I was so hurt. He had promised me he would be there. But he lied."

She went on, "When I was fifteen, there was a father/daughter banquet at our church. It was a very big event and everyone was wearing dresses and suits. All my friends were going. The dinner was on a Friday night, and Dad called to say that he was running a few minutes late and asked if Mom could run me to the church; then he could just meet me there. The dinner started and ended. I sat alone for the entire dinner and program. Just as it ended, my father arrived. He said he was very sorry and that things at the office had gotten out-of-hand. He promised me he would take me out to dinner some evening, just the two of us, to make up for it. He never did.

"Then there was my high-school graduation. I was class salutatorian. He arrived late. He missed my speech. He was very sorry, but things just came up at work."

By this time she was crying openly as she relived these painful memories. "Can you see why I do not trust my father? Can you see why I do not think he is an honest man?"

Jerry never overtly lied to his daughter whom he loved deeply. But he might as well have. He promised to be there for her, but instead let the tyranny of the urgent get in the way of the priority of the important. Lack of honesty takes more than one form and can create conflicts in relationships that can and do last for decades.

We will finish this story later too.

6. Parental Favoritism

This area of conflict also has many facets. There are the cultural prejudices that make a father believe that his daughter should not become the CEO of the family business because she is a woman, even though by both temperament and training she may be the most qualified. "My son will run this company, or I will sell it," one bullheaded business owner said when we suggested that his daughter might be better suited to run the company.

This same mindset causes parents to also believe that their daughters' inheritances should be smaller than their sons' inheritances. Of course, it is the parents' wealth, and they can do with it as they please. But this predisposition to favor male children over female children creates more than its share of conflicts among children and their parents.

We have seen parental favoritism demonstrated in favor of the oldest son over a younger son, based purely on the fact that he is the oldest. Sibling conflicts over this very act of discrimination go back millennia in time.

Another insidious demonstration of parental favoritism is treating the children differently than their spouses.

"In-laws have only secondary standing in our family," many parents subconsciously think. "We claim the grandchildren as all ours, but the in-laws who helped my children produce them are not 'real' members of our family."

This attitude creates conflicts between the sons- or daughters-in-law and their fathers- and mothers-in-law. It also creates conflicts between the children and their spouses. Many times, their spouses are excluded from family meetings, from being beneficiaries of trusts and from any knowledge of the families' financial affairs. In fact, many legal documents are intentionally drafted to keep in-laws out.

Taking Care of Unfinished Business

When we use this phrase, people immediately know what we mean. Taking care of unfinished business means proactively resolving any family conflicts and rebuilding broken relationships. In almost every family, there is some unfinished business that needs attention.

Some years ago, we were invited to speak on Family Wealth Counseling at an international medical conference. The topics were wide-ranging and, for the most part, of little practical value to anyone who was not a medical doctor. However, there was a session led by a psychiatrist that was truly profound.

The psychiatrist had been in clinical counseling for more than twenty-five years. He opened his presentation with a very provocative statement. He said, "The need for ninety percent of all psychological counseling would disappear overnight if people would learn to do one simple thing."

He had the audience in the palm of his hand. All the complexities of life and its inherent conflicts were going to be reduced to one simple thing. He paused to prepare the audience for this profound insight.

He repeated, "The need for ninety percent of all psychological counseling would disappear overnight if people would learn to—forgive!"

He went on to say that we need to forgive three things. (1) We need to forgive God for making us in a way we do not like, or allowing people or circumstances in our lives to cause us pain or sorrow. (2) We need to forgive ourselves for the ways in which we have failed those we love and ourselves. (3) We need to forgive others who have hurt or disappointed us.

Think about it. Ninety percent of all psychological problems will go away if you will simply choose to do one thing—forgive.

We know the normal reactions. We have heard them all many times. "I cannot forgive that person for what they did to me." "That person is not even sorry for what she did. I am not going to forgive her." "He is dead now. There is no way to forgive him. It is too late."

Do you want to resolve those family conflicts? Do you want to reconcile the broken relationships in your life? Are you willing to say what needs to be said? Do you want your family to be whole, healthy, happy and have fellowship during the final days of your life? Are you willing to set aside the urgent and concentrate on the important?

Seeking Forgiveness

Often, when we encounter these unresolved conflicts among family members, we will ask the parties, "If it were possible to heal this relationship and resolve this conflict, do you want a loving, intimate and meaningful relationship with the other person?"

Almost without exception, the answer is yes.

So essentially what we have are two people, each of whom wants to have a healthy, happy and fulfilling relationship with the other, who do not know how to get rid of all the garbage that stands between them. The answer is simple. The action may be difficult, but the answer is simple. Forgive one another.

The Rest of the Stories

Two days after our Client Retreat with the Cohens, we got a one-line fax from Herb. It only read, "I made the calls."

We picked up the phone, called him and asked, "What do you mean, you made the calls?"

He replied, "I called my ex-wife. I have not talked to her in ten years. In fact, the last time I had talked with her it was not too pleasant because we were back in court. She was extremely gracious with me, much to my surprise. She was very forthright and told me all about our kids."

He paused, then said, "I am a grandfather. I have a three-year-old grandson. My son and his wife had a baby and live in Houston. My middle daughter also lives in Houston. She is married, but does not have any kids. My oldest daughter lives in Chicago."

He had called them all. His son was thrilled to hear from him. He and his son were coming in to see his mother over the Christmas holidays. The three were going to have breakfast together the day after Christmas. Herb was going to meet his grandson. He was very excited.

When he called his younger daughter, she burst into tears and sobbed for ten or fifteen minutes. Herb had to hold back the tears himself. It was a very difficult call. He said he could not make up for the last twenty years, but would be glad to answer any questions about what happened. He said he would like to have a relationship with her going forward. He reassured her that he did not have a terminal illness, he just wanted to have a relationship with her, if she would be interested. She also was coming to visit her mother during the holidays, and she took his phone number.

He then spoke to his oldest daughter in Chicago. Her response was cold as ice. She did take his phone number, but he did not hold out much hope that she would call him.

We asked if we might call him over the holidays to see how the visit with his son went.

He replied, "Please do. I want you to know how much I appreciate your encouragement to call my kids. I would have never done it without you. And, by the way, it looks as if I will have someone to give my Kiddush cup to after all."

For the first time since his son was a young boy, Herb saw his son. He is six feet and two inches tall, very good-looking, and Herb's grandson is an absolute doll. Herb's son is an excellent father and married a wonderful woman. They invited him to come to their home for a visit in the near future. He had taken the first steps toward healing the broken family relationships of more than twenty years. The joy Herb has found in the healing process has been inexpressible.

Remember the Bennetts and their son, Tim, who wanted to pursue music instead of business? After reflecting on the magnitude of the loss of his relationship with his only son, Henry decided the loss of his relationship with his son was worse than the loss of his company's future CEO. He recognized that the problem was really his and not Tim's. His ultimate goal for his son was for him to be happy and productive and to follow his calling in the same way Henry had followed his.

Unannounced, Henry went east to see his son. He called him up, told him he was in town and would like to talk with him. Tim was surprised by all this and did not quite know what to make of it. Henry picked up Tim at the dorm. They went to a quiet little park and sat down on a bench under a large oak tree.

"Son," Henry began, "I would like to begin by asking you to forgive me for the way I have acted about your career. I was wrong. You must follow your dreams the same way that I followed mine. You must do what you are on this earth to do. If you have found your calling in music, I am thrilled. So few people ever find what they are really meant to do with their lives."

Henry began to choke up, "Son, I want you to know I am proud of you. I am proud of the kind of young man you have become. You carry our family name well. If you want to spend your life playing the cello, then I want to help you enjoy it and develop your skills to their highest level. I will pay for your education, and I will be sitting in the front row when you play your first concert."

They both cried and hugged for the first time in over a year. They sat on the bench for what seemed like the longest time holding onto one another, rocking and crying. The healing was complete. The restoration was total. The family was once again united. A father and a son were once again friends. Forgiveness was sought, and forgiveness was extended.

Only six years later, this young man was playing the cello in a major symphony. Tim's proud father was there for his first performance, watching his successful son exercise his gift and follow his call.

In regard to Jerry Watkins' daughter, who had been repeatedly disappointed by her father, we suggested that she tell him how she felt about his actions. She said she could not, but we told her if she wanted to get beyond the past and into the present she needed to speak to him. That way, he could seek her forgiveness, and she could give it.

The day came. The two were in the same room. They sat face-to-face. We had prepared Jerry, saying that we had discovered why his relationship with his daughter had been so distant for all these years and that he needed to be ready to seek forgiveness for things he had done in the past. We did not tell him what they were. That was his daughter's place.

Beth began sharing the stories that she had told us earlier. She could hardly keep her composure as she recalled those painful memories.

As Jerry heard the first story, his chin began to quiver and tears filled his eyes. He had not thought about that recital since it happened. To him, it was such a little thing. But it was obvious that the memories flooded back for him just as they had for his daughter. Before Beth could even finish the story, he jumped up from chair, hugged her and asked her to forgive him for being so insensitive. They cried and hugged. She still needed to share the other times. With each story it was obvious his pain and shame was intense. They hugged and cried some more. The healing was complete. The reconciliation was total. Forgiveness was sought, and forgiveness was given. Beth had her father back, and Jerry had his daughter back.

Do you know what they did that night? Jerry took his daughter out to the dinner he promised her years ago.

We are amazed at the healing and freedom that comes with forgiveness. More times than not, it comes as easy as asking for it.

Extending Forgiveness

When two people really love each other deeply and they both want to resolve a conflict, healing and reconciliation can begin. But what about those cases when the other person does not even know that they have hurt or offended someone else? Or what if the person knows he or she has offended another person but refuses to seek reconciliation? Or, worse yet, what if the offender is already dead? Then what can a person do to gain freedom from the burden of holding on to that pain and resentment for life?

One thing we know for certain is true, holding on to resentment will hurt a person much more than the offender. We have seen people who are eaten up with bitterness and anger, and the other person does not even know they have caused the offense. One thing is for sure; the other person is not being hurt at all. But the people holding on to resentment must keep it alive by rolling it over in their minds, replaying the offenses again and again. They find themselves carrying on imaginary arguments with the other people, telling them off in royal fashion.

It is evident when someone is carrying a grudge and refusing to forgive. When people talk about the events or the offenses, the person will get involved emotionally, reliving the offense. The person may get angry, pound fists, yell or cry.

All the while, the resentment eats away at the holder's heart and soul. Resentment slowly kills, just as certainly as if that person were to continually inhale small quantities of carbon monoxide.

These are the situations where the exercise of forgiveness is most critical and also most difficult. But do not lose heart. There is a way to extend forgiveness to others even when they do not know they need it, they do not want it or they are not here to receive it. There is a way to peace and reconciliation. There are five powerful steps to extending forgiveness without the offender's involvement.

STEP 1: Make a written list of all those people who have hurt or offended you at any point in your life and reconciliation has not occurred. Do not worry about how long the list becomes, and do not hurry through making the list. It may take a week or two to be sure you have every one of your offenders on your list.

STEP 2: By each name, write the offenses for which you are holding these people guilty. Be specific. They abandoned you. They stole from you. They slandered you. They physically abused you. Whatever it is, put the whole ugly mess on the list.

STEP 3: Go away to some lonely, secluded place and talk to your Creator. Give your list to Him. Verbalize that you are voluntarily extending forgiveness to each person on your list. You are setting them free of their "crimes" against you. You are dropping all charges against them. You are officially declaring them not guilty, forgiven.

STEP 4: Feel free to express your hurt and resentment. Also be willing to admit that your bitterness and hateful attitudes about them have been just as wrong as what they have done to you. Let go of both the person and the offense. Acknowledge that you will not try to change or correct that person in any way. You are turning the people over to a higher authority.

The key is to release them. Once you break the chains of resentment that bind you to them, you truly will be free of that person. You set yourself free from the resentment.

STEP 5: Once you complete Steps 1-4, destroy your list and do not tell any of the people what you have done. The last thing in the world you want to do is go to one of them and say, "Oh, by the way, I decided to forgive you for being such a jerk." As soon as you say that, that person will be right back on your list. This is a private decision between you and your Maker. No one needs to know that this has happened. Once it is done, let it go!

One lady chose to destroy her list by tying it to a large rock and then throwing it into her lake, symbolically separating herself from all the pain and hurt that those people and events had caused her. After completing this process, she was finally free emotionally from her father who died more than thirty years earlier.

Another man chose to burn his list in his fireplace, symbolically sending all those past offenses and hurts up in smoke. Finally, he was emotionally free to go on with his life, leaving all that baggage behind.

Conclusion

There is nothing mystical about resolving family conflicts and repairing broken relationships. There are only two ingredients needed: one, the desire to resolve and repair, and two, a willingness to forgive and seek forgiveness. While there are situations where the problems will be so severe that professional counseling may be advisable, the vast majority require only desire and forgiveness, commodities that all of us can access.

Once the family's unfinished business is completed, the planning process can move forward with unity, energy and strength. Trust can be re-established, communication lines can be re-opened, and the family is positioned to work together.

Traditional planning seeks to isolate the family problems and then plan and draft documents around the problems so as to contain them and not let them become any worse.

Family Wealth Counseling seeks to heal the wounds, not simply bandage them while they fester. We want healthy, happy and functioning families. With reasonably functional families, the wounds and injuries can be healed, never to be worried about again.

CHAPTER 12

Preparing Your Heirs for Their Inheritance

When the founders of the family fortune consider transferring the family's wealth to upcoming generations, they usually do so exclusively within the context of the transfer itself. They spend large amounts of time determining how to avoid the taxes and create airtight legal documents to preserve the wealth from claims of creditors and irresponsible heirs.

These well-drafted plans may be the state-of-the-art in tax planning, incorporating precision language in each document. Yet, what determines whether an estate plan is successful cannot be merely whether it has escaped taxation and litigation. The determining question is, Has the family been able to successfully retain the family wealth and use it in ways that are truly beneficial both personally and globally? But the single most important question that should be asked by these founders of wealth is, Have we been truly successful in our wealth transfer plans if our heirs are not able to retain their inheritance and have their lives enhanced emotionally and financially by receiving it?

Jessie O'Neill, the founder of the *Affluenza Project* and the heir of a wealthy family, lists the following outcomes when a financial inheritance is passed on without an emotional inheritance.

- Inability to delay gratification
- Inability to tolerate frustration
- Low future motivation
- Low self-esteem
- Low self-worth
- Lack of confidence
- Lack of personal identity
- Social and emotional isolation
- Feelings of failure, depression, anxiety
- Unrealistic expectations and lack of accountability
- False sense of entitlement
- Inability to form intimate relationships

If parents were to pass on their entire financial empires successfully to their heirs, but these negative emotional dysfunctions were also passed along with it, would anyone consider the family estate plan successful?

Numerous studies in recent years have revealed some very sobering statistics concerning the success of traditional estate planning in pre-serving the family's wealth, let alone the heirs' emotional health.

- Sixty-five percent of wealthy families have lost the family wealth by the end of the second generation.

- Ninety percent of wealthy families will have lost the family wealth by the end of the third generation.

It is a classic example of *shirt sleeves to shirt sleeves in three generations* or *rags to riches to rags in three generations.* In Holland, the saying is, *clogs to clogs in three generations.*

Traditional estate planners have suggested that the primary culprit behind the disappearance of family wealth is the crippling estate taxes that are levied on wealthy American families.

However, in Australia these statistics are almost identical to the United States'. Yet, Australia has one major difference: it has no estate tax! Wealthy Australian families are losing their wealth at virtually the same rate as wealthy American families. The United Kingdom has almost identical statistics as well.

Obviously, avoiding estate taxes does not ensure the successful retention of the wealth by the children or the grandchildren. So what is the reason for these pathetic results? The answer has nothing to do with how effectively a family eliminates taxes or has great legal documents drafted. The answer is in how well heirs have been prepared to receive wealth.

How do the parents and founders of the family fortune prepare their heirs for their inheritance? It begins with building trust and communication.

Building Trust and Communication

Roy Williams, author of *For Love and Money*, points out that these two elements are critical to the successful transfer of family wealth from one generation to the next. Trust and communication between parents and their heirs in these areas are not optional: they are essential. Consider the following illustrations.

Jared Mills had never turned over the responsibility of managing the family's multimillion-dollar investment portfolio to his sons.

"They could never manage money as successfully as I do," Jared said.

He is correct. He is correct now, and he will be correct after he is dead. The sons will never learn to manage money because Jared never trusted them enough to give them the chance to even try. He never communicated to them how to select or be an effective money manager. Consequently, the first time the boys will get their hands on the money, Jared, who could have been their best teacher and coach, will be dead, leaving them adrift at sea with millions of dollars, no idea how to manage it, and no one to advise them. No trust. No communication. Unfortunately, this is not an isolated example. It is almost routine among wealthy families.

Another example is the father who never tells

his children how much wealth the family has because he does not trust them with that kind of sensitive information. They finally learn about the amount of wealth their parents had in the lawyer's office after the last parent dies. They are completely ill-prepared to manage the family's wealth. No trust—no communication.

It is quite common among wealthy families for their children to be resentful of that wealth. They often see their father as being filled with greed, consumed with power and living an opulent lifestyle, while the rest of the world struggles to even survive. They often view the family wealth as something evil. They take the side of those who are down and out, the weak and the poor. They may even see their parents as "the enemy." These children intentionally go to the other extreme in their lifestyles, rejecting this cursed disease of "affluenza." They drive old cars and shop at thrift stores.

What they may have never seen or understood is that their parents have perhaps anonymously given millions of dollars away to help the poor in their city—a gift only made possible because of their parents' brilliant business prowess. The children also do not know that their parents pay their employees very well and provide generous benefits, giving the employees' families a better life. They do not see any of this. They simply do not know. Why? They do not see it because there is no trust and no communication. Some wealthy parents do not choose to include their children in their charitable giving. The children do not understand how their family's wealth can be used to help others, to help those who are down and out—the poor, homeless, sick, and hurting—the very people they so wish to help.

If wealthy families are going to keep their wealth in the family for future generations to enjoy and use for good, they must do more than simply implement effective financial techniques and strategies. This traditional approach to planning guarantees nothing except a high failure rate.

Parents need to draw back the curtain covering the family's wealth and reveal to the children what is behind it. It can be done slowly and over time, but the sooner the better. Children need to see what will someday be theirs. Talk with them about the purpose of wealth and how it can and should be used. Talk with them about the responsibilities that accompany the control of wealth.

Think of this process in the same way you would if you were bringing in a top executive to eventually run your company. He would go through years of mentoring and training to become competent, comfortable and ready to step into the shoes of a CEO. The same is true with the transfer of family wealth. A plan without communication is no plan, or it is nothing more than a plan to fail.

We were in a Client Retreat with Bill and Mary whose net worth is over one hundred million dollars. Bill shared that they did not have any estate taxes to pay. Each child was already worth ten million dollars, so they were going to give all their wealth to their private family foundation.

He was correct. He already had a "zero estate tax plan" in place. We then asked Bill, who was a venture capitalist, how much money he and Mary had given to charity last year.

"Four hundred thousand dollars," he answered.

"Was it easy to give that much away?"

"Easy?" he chuckled. "I worked all year long evaluating charities, charitable projects and various grant proposals to determine which we felt were worthy of our support."

"So, giving four hundred thousand dollars away last year was really a challenge?"

"Oh, yes."

"Do you realize, Bill," we said, "that when you die, your family foundation will have over one hundred million dollars in it? The law requires that five percent of the trust assets and income must be distributed annually to charity. That is five million dollars each year. How prepared are your children to distribute effectively five million dollars to charity each year?"

The blood drained from his face, and with a look of horror, he gasped, "Oh, no!" It had hit him for the first time that, even though he had a zero estate tax plan in place, he had failed to consider how totally ill-prepared his two children were to continue the philanthropic heritage he had begun, much less increase the giving by a multiple of twelve.

Worst of all, the children did not even know

that there was one hundred million dollars going into a foundation that they would be required to manage. A disaster waiting to happen.

But communication is not enough. There must also be trust. The progress of a young man who is an aspiring pilot is a good example. He begins his training in class, learning about the aerodynamics and operation of a plane. Then he goes out with an instructor in a small single-engine plane for lessons. The instructor begins trusting him by letting him take the controls yet is always right there in case he makes a mistake. Once he has demonstrated measurable standards of progress, the instructor will trust him with his first opportunity to solo. His solo flight consists of simply taking off, circling the field and landing again. He is completely on his own, an exhilarating and frightening experience for both the new pilot and the instructor. Once he has passed that milestone, he is now back with the instructor learning all of the other aspects of flying. Dozens of additional flying hours are logged.

Then comes the day when he must pass his Visual Flight Rules tests allowing him to fly completely on his own anywhere he wants, except in the clouds or fog. He must go through extensive additional training to earn his Instrument Flight Rules certification. Finally, he may fly a single-enginc plane anywhere he wants at any time he wants.

If, however, he wants to fly in a twin-engine plane, there is more training that he must go through to be checked out on flying a twin. Once he has demonstrated his competence, he can fly wherever he wants in a single or a twin. But let us say our young pilot aspires to become a commercial pilot. To do so, he must take even more extensive training and get his commercial pilot's license. Further, he does not want to simply fly "puddle jumpers" on commuter flights. He wants to fly 747s. More training, more flight hours, more check flights. Then finally, after years of additional training and flying, he is given the opportunity to sit in the left seat of the cockpit of a 747—the big one. He is trained and experienced. He knows what to do, and he does it well.

Passing on family wealth is much the same thing. In a figurative sense—if you are going to leave your children a fleet of airplanes for their inheritance, it makes sense while you are both alive and well to teach them how to fly. If not, you may end up having to lock the planes up in a hangar and give the keys to a trustee who is then required to baby-sit their inheritance, because the heirs are not trained or trustworthy enough to fly without supervision.

You must turn over some part of the family wealth after you train them and then trust them to fly. They will probably make some mistakes, some errors in judgment. But better to make a mistake in a single-engine plane circling the airstrip at five hundred feet than to make the same mistake flying a 747 at thirty-five thousand feet with a plane full of passengers. If they succeed in the first test, you can trust them with more.

The first two keys to successful wealth transfer

are *trust* and *communication*. Trust and communication are not achieved through creative tax planning strategies or airtight trust documents. They are achieved through an investment of time and money in relationships—family relationships.

An ancient proverb says, "Wisdom along with an inheritance is good." This is exactly what we are espousing here. Leave your children the wisdom to know what to do with their inheritance, so it will bless them and others and not be a destructive curse.

Again, successful transfer of wealth cannot be judged solely by how little taxes the estate paid or how sheltered the assets are from waste and lawsuits. It must also be judged by how mentally and emotionally prepared the heirs are to receive and be proper stewards of their inheritances.

The Perfect Training Ground for Preparing Heirs

This nagging concern over whether heirs will be mentally and emotionally prepared to receive the family inheritance has troubled the wealthy for thousands of years. King Solomon (circa 700 BC), the Jewish king whose wealth and wisdom was legendary, struggled with this very same issue. He expressed his concern over this frustrating dilemma when he confessed:

Thus, I hated all the fruit of my labor for which I had labored under the sun, for I must leave it to the man who will come after me. And who knows whether he will be a wise man or a fool? Yet, he will have control over all the fruit of my

194

labor for which I have labored by acting wisely under the sun.

Is there a way to affect whether our children will be wise or fools with their inheritance? The answer is definitely, yes!

Overcoming Emotional Dysfunctions

Consider the exposure unplanned wealth can create for your heirs. Suddenly, your heirs are wealthy. How can they know whether people are genuinely interested in them or merely interested in enjoying the benefits of their wealth? Your heirs may eventually begin to question whether their friends love them or their money. This uncertainty can be very destructive to heirs' self-esteem.

Also, they risk becoming obsessed with consumption. Their whole world can begin to revolve around their individual wants and desires. The younger heirs are when they receive their inheritances, the greater the chance of this outcome.

Further, they risk losing the important connection between work and reward. They have been rewarded for doing nothing except being born and surviving the older generations.

So, how can you pass this wealth on to your heirs without making them insecure, lazy and/or spoiled? You can teach them about philanthropy!

Immediately establish a family foundation and fund it with an appropriate amount of money. Charge these future heirs of your family's wealth with the task of distributing these funds to worthy charitable causes. (For example, if you focus your philanthropic efforts in Third World countries, it is incredible how much can be done with very little money.)

You might ask what this would teach them. In reality, what they can learn from this experience, especially if repeated frequently during your remaining lifetime, is very significant. Can you imagine what it would feel like for your heirs to know that they have, for example, built an orphanage in Guatemala that will continuously feed and house twenty orphan children? (Five thousand dollars to build it and ten thousand dollars to feed them for the next five years should cover it.)

Knowing that they have made a difference in the lives of twenty desperately needy children should be profoundly fulfilling for your heirs. Even though they did not use any of their own money, they still gain all the emotional and psychological benefits of this philanthropic project just as if they had put the money up themselves. The heirs say, "Look what *we* did!" Not, "Look what Mom and Dad or Grandma and Grandpa did!"

You have helped improve their self-image. You have directed their focus away from selfishness. You have enabled them to do a meaningful work. What a powerful combination of benefits for such a small investment.

If you live long enough and repeat this often enough for this kind of philanthropic activity to become a way of life for your heirs, it is unlikely they will fall into the common problems created by inherited wealth.

This philanthropic context can be a perfect training ground for teaching heirs about investing and managing money, setting up budgets and the cost of operating a "business" as well as all the emotional and psychological benefits already mentioned. Philanthropy provides the best of all worlds and is the perfect platform for preparing your heirs to be ready, financially and emotionally, for their inheritance.

Receiving Back More Than You Give

How can giving so little be so meaningful? It is a simple fact that what comes back to you in charitable giving is always disproportionate to the size of the gift you make, regardless of whether you are giving away $250 or $2.5 million. If this is true for wealthy parents, it is also true for the children and grandchildren of wealthy parents.

Philanthropy builds character, develops a positive self-image and provides a real sense of accomplishment in those who participate in it. Beginning a significant philanthropic program now and including all your heirs can be the best training ground of all. It can be a fantastic growing experience for both you and your heirs. It can also become a wonderful activity that will draw your family closer together in a way that no other family activity can.

Even for families who have experienced broken relationships among family members, focusing family activities on helping others instead of on the family itself allows even strained relationships to be rebuilt again as family members are working together, doing good and helping others.

You have nothing to lose with this Family Wealth Counseling strategy except your concern over how successfully your heirs will handle their inheritance when it comes.

Examples of Families that Succeeded in Preparing Their Heirs

Example #1

Recently, the father of one of our clients passed away. Ben, our client, became reflective on how his father and mother helped prepare him and his siblings for their substantial financial inheritance.

As Ben shared the vivid pictures of his memories, it was obvious his father, Craig, was a man of great principle who had started his business in the midst of the Great Depression. One of the primary virtues Craig developed within his children was responsibility. Responsibility was taught incrementally. By around age twelve, each of the children started working on the family farm and eventually began participating in the family business to teach them how to be self-supporting and responsible. Craig then further prepared Ben by placing him in the role of president of the family business. Craig had the opportunity to mentor Ben in this role for several years prior to his passing.

Ben told us that Craig lived by this edict of wisdom, "Whoever can be trusted with little can also be trusted with much, and whoever is dishonest with little will also be dishonest with much." When the children proved that they were capable of accepting additional responsibility, Craig would give them more. Often, he would come alongside his children and help them make an investment decision and mentor them in their efforts. As the children increased in wisdom and expanded their application of the training Craig had imparted, he would lessen his role as mentor.

Ben spoke of how money concepts were taught to the children both at home and in the business. The family lived modestly, and Craig instructed the children to run the business by the same conservative principles. When money had to be spent for personal and business needs, Craig made sure it was absolutely needed and that the expenditure was the right thing to do. Craig had a discerning attitude toward the use of money.

As Craig was teaching the children these wise, conservative business and financial principles, the mother was teaching and modeling a complementary virtue of giving. The children were able to see and experience how the act of giving brings great joy and satisfaction to those involved. Through both parents, the children developed a very balanced perspective on the purpose of money. They have learned to be frugal in their personal and business lives. More importantly, they have learned to become charitable givers in and outside their community. The parents' discernment and wisdom have been successfully transferred to the children. The parents were able to leave a legacy as a result of their commitment to training their children and not just financially endowing them.

Example #2

Commitment to the mentoring and training of your children is a lifetime endeavor. As parents of three adult daughters, Nancy and Jim are for the first time enjoying life as empty nesters. Yet, these parents firmly believe that they need to be involved in the training and mentoring process a second time. They had the privilege of training their daughters in the values and spiritual beliefs they held. All of the daughters, now married, are normal, down-to-earth people. They just happen to be heirs to millions of dollars. Eventually, these millions will be distributed to charitable foundations and managed by the daughters. Jim chose to actively groom his sons-in-law to become involved in the management of these funds. The only way to ensure the inheritance is managed as the parents wish is to mentor each of the husbands in the areas of life, family, business, leadership and service. In this way, the parents will be able to pass down their family legacy to their daughters' families.

Jim had created a limited partnership, so each daughter and husband could jointly participate. He funded it with stock, real estate and other business holdings. Since its inception, every week, Jim and his sons-in-law have come together to discuss family business and the principles of stewardship, giving and serving others. Jim is building a stronger family relationship with the sons-in-law and training each of them to become good managers of what eventually will be entrusted to them through his daughters.

The value of these mentoring relationships is that Jim can now observe both the strengths and weaknesses of each son-in-law and take appropriate measures to help them develop into mature, wise and discerning men. They will then be better equipped in serving not only their wives and families, but also the wealth inherited from Jim and Nancy.

We asked Jim, "Is it hard work?" He smiled and said he receives great joy seeing his sons-in-law become mature and productive leaders. We posed a second question to Jim, "When will you finish your mentoring process?" He answered, "Never. You can never prepare them enough, because we do not live in a static environment."

Example #3

This third family operates a mid-size general construction company. Bill Willis had found himself with an estate and business planning challenge. He expressed his concern about how he would transfer his business assets upon retirement. Bill has one son-in-law, Andrew, participating in the business and three daughters with no interest in the business.

He had three primary financial objectives: first, to provide an equal inheritance for each of his daughters; second, to provide a strategy to remove the business assets from his estate; and, third, to alleviate the family business successor from being dependent on the parents' net worth as collateral for construction opportunities. Bill created a second construction company with a similar business name. Andrew has now operated that company for ten years. Over that period, Bill directed business into Andrew's construction company. As Andrew's construction company became profitable, the profits were placed back into the business to establish Andrew's own net worth and bonding capabilities.

The mentoring relationship Bill established with his son-in-law helped meet Bill's objective. It allowed Andrew to build a successful construction business through Bill's leadership and resources, and it prepared Andrew to receive the family business.

In the examples above, we can see how the parents have been able to mentor their heirs through modeling their principles and beliefs. The children have benefited through the nurturing relationship of their parents during their adult lives.

Example #4

Too many parents have lamented after their children are grown, "If we knew we were going to have this much, we would have done things differently with our children."

Within five years of his marriage to Janice, David Wallace's business endeavors were proving successful. He and Janice saw their net worth reach in excess of five million dollars. As the Wallaces' business holdings expanded, so did their young family. David and Janice's three boys are very productive in their business activities and have been very interested in philanthropic opportunities.

In talking with David about how he and Janice had prepared their heirs for inheritance, we discovered some very interesting attitudes and truths about the subject. In fact, both terms *heir* and *inheritance* were conspicuously absent from our discussions. Rather, terms such as *family wealth* and *stewardship* were prevalent.

David and Janice believe their family's success is directly linked to the concept of Stewardship vs. Ownership. David put it this way:

> A steward does not look at an asset as his to begin with. Too many of my wealthy friends have this incorrect attitude and perspective of ownership; therefore, the wrong treatment of assets results. Some parents say, "These are my assets. I paid the price to get here, and my kids are going to have to do the same! Until then, I will make all the decisions!" What these parents fail to recognize is their stewardship over both the assets and their kids. How can that attitude lead to anything but resentment? The fact is neither the assets nor the kids really belong to them. They have simply been entrusted with the children and the assets as parents and stewards.

When David and Janice realized that the family asset base was expanding beyond their own needs, they established trusts for the young boys. David and Janice talked openly to the boys about the family assets. They placed an emphasis on preparing the boys to be stewards of the Wallace family wealth. There have never been any family conversations about an inheritance. Rather, the focus has been on a planned transfer of the responsibilities and privileges of stewardship. David believes that this cannot begin at death via inheritance. It must happen during his lifetime.

As an example of trust and communication building, one of their son's summer projects during college was to develop a Family Asset Review. The project involved identifying each family asset along with the asset's value, income, indebtedness and any other pertinent information. David and Janice made this information readily available. The project not only heightened their son's awareness about the details of the family wealth but also served as an excellent resource for the entire family.

David and Janice also reinforced their values through action. David told us:

> As stewards, it is an honor to work. It is also an honor to serve others through our work, with our time and other resources. As soon as they could drive, the boys have had jobs. My kids have seen that hard work can be one of life's greatest joys. Sure, I told them that, but they had to learn it for themselves. Even when they were younger, I refused to shield them from hard work. They worked on the construction sites, seeing and learning about every aspect of construction. At an early age, they learned about the true economic value of their labor and their decisions. As time passed, they learned that wealth and its privileges are earned with honest, hard work. It is not ill-gotten. Today, they are very comfortable with the family wealth.

Children are more comfortable with the notion of inherited wealth when they are connected to a purpose for its existence that extends beyond their own personal interests. The vision becomes bigger than the family itself. A shared virtues/values approach connects the family members to the community in a way that makes sense of the family's wealth. Philanthropy builds character and gives meaning to our existence.

David further provided this insight and encouragement:

Generosity and the attitudes of stewardship go hand in hand. Throughout the years, Janice and I have shared the enjoyment and deep satisfaction that is associated with serious-minded philanthropy. Now the boys' generosity exceeds our own. I am delighted. They have become very creative and ingenious in their philanthropy. They are getting some important things done.

For David and Janice, sharing their faith, building trust and maintaining communication have always been important aspects of their relationship with the boys. David said, "I never want to cut off communication with my kids. Communication is absolutely necessary for building trust. Trust is absolutely necessary for a successful relationship in a family or in a business."

The importance of trust and open communication, coupled with the understanding that they are unconditionally loved, became readily apparent when the boys approached the decision of being directly involved in the family business. The question was not so much "Should I come into the family business?" The question was "What do I want to do with my life?"

Conclusion

If a family concentrates an equal amount of time and effort in financially and emotionally mentoring their heirs to prepare them fully for their inheritance, the likelihood of successfully transferring wealth that will be retained by subsequent generations and be a blessing to them is exponentially increased. This is why we believe that the Family Wealth Counseling approach more adequately addresses all of these issues within the context of life planning as opposed to merely tax and trust planning.

Heirs need to feel trusted and know that the lines of communication between their parents and them are open. They need to be mentored in how to handle effectively the privileges and the responsibilities that will someday be theirs.

These issues are best discussed with your children, not in the lawyers' conference room, but in your own living room. This part of the planning process is about loving people and using things, not about loving things and using people. Your children need to hear that from you.

CHAPTER 13

Building a Strong Family Tree
A Lasting Legacy for Future Generations

We often ask our wealthy clients what they want most for their children and grandchildren. The answer is always the same: We want our children and grandchildren to be happy.

Nothing is more gratifying than watching your own children grow up to be happy, useful and productive members of society. Likewise, nothing is more heartbreaking than to see them grow up to be miserable, useless and unproductive. These extreme outcomes are not a matter of the luck of the draw or the result of some good-seed/bad-seed explanation. They are often the direct result of the condition of the family tree.

On the next page is a picture of an apple tree, an illustration we use to depict a family tree.

Life-Purpose
(What You're Here To Do)

Core Values
(What's Important To You)

Primary Virtues
(Who You Are)

There are three parts to our "family tree": (1.) the root system, (2.) the tree itself, and (3.) the fruit on the tree. The root system represents the Primary Virtues upon which the family tree is built and upon which the tree draws its life. The tree itself represents the Core Values that are a natural outgrowth of the root system. Core Values are those activities and priorities in life that we choose to pursue. The fruit on the tree represents our Life-Purpose, what we are here on this earth to do.

We have already addressed Life-Purpose in chapter 7, so we will focus our attention on Primary Virtues and Core Values. These two aspects are absolutely essential to have a healthy family tree.

The Difference Between a
Primary Virtue and a Core Value

When we ask our clients to define *values* and *virtues*, they often struggle to distinguish the two clearly.

We define *value* as "what we believe to be important or has worth for us, something that has utility." It is something we prize; it is valuable to us. Money, for example, can be said to have value because of what it can do for us. Cars, homes, jewelry and real estate are all valuable. Recreational activities as a means of entertainment may be valuable to us.

We define *virtue* as "what we believe to be right, good and proper." There is a critical component of "rightness" or "goodness" that is missing in the definition of a value.

Money, real estate, homes and cars are not thought of as right or good. They are thought of as valuable, useful or important. Virtues, on the other hand, address character, integrity and goodness—being and doing what is right.

Often these definitions alone do not adequately provide clarity between the two terms. The following comparison chart helps to further define and differentiate *values* and *virtues*.

Virtues	**Values**
External	**Internal**
(created outside of us)	*(created by our own design)*
Objective	**Subjective**
(a matter of fact)	*(a matter of opinion)*

Universal	Local
(commonly accepted)	*(widely divergent)*
Moral	**Amoral**
(perception of right/wrong)	(no perception of right/wrong)
Immutable	**Variable**
(unchangeable)	*(ever-changing)*
Eternal	**Temporal**
(transcends time)	*(ends with us)*
Divine	**Human**
(extends from nature of God)	*(extends from mind of man)*

External vs. Internal

Virtues are external. We did not conceive them in a moment of brilliance or invent them in one of our more creative moments. They were bestowed upon us. For example, consider the virtue of telling the truth. Was that your idea? Or did someone teach you that telling the truth was the right thing to do?

Values, on the other hand, are created by our own design. What is important to us is just that— important to us. We decide what is important, what we like and what we want to pursue.

Objective vs. Subjective

Virtues are always objective in that people will recognize a virtue as a matter of fact. Again, using truth as an example, we may not be able to determine what the truth is in a certain situation, but we all agree that the truth is what we want.

A value, though, is a matter of opinion. If one person was a baseball fan and another was a football fan, which would be "right?" Neither. It is a matter of opinion, a value.

Universal vs. Local

A virtue is accepted universally. You can go to virtually any corner of the earth, any culture, any religion and you will find consensus among all as to the "rightness" of a particular virtue.

Values are widely divergent. If you go to Chicago, you will find people there tend to be Bulls' fans. In Indianapolis, just 150 miles south, people tend to be Pacers' fans. Values change from geographic location to geographic location, from culture to culture and from religion to religion. They all hold different things to be important and valuable.

Moral vs. Amoral

Virtues carry the perceptions of right versus wrong. Parents tell their children and grandchildren, "It is right to tell the truth. To tell a lie is wrong."

A value carries with it no such moral underpinning. If you like Harvard University and someone else likes Ohio State or if you like opera and someone else likes drama, there is nothing in these preferences that makes them right or wrong. There is nothing moral at stake here.

Immutable vs. Variable

Virtues do not change from generation to generation, from nation to nation, or from culture to culture. They remain the same.

Values change. Do you remember what was important to you when you were eighteen years old? Are those same things still important to you? Values change, even within one's own lifetime.

Now we must ask why anyone would attempt to build a comprehensive, intergenerational, wealth transfer plan based upon values knowing that they are, and will continue to be, in a constant state of change.

Eternal vs. Temporal

Virtues have existed from the beginning of recorded time. You can go back into our most ancient manuscripts and you will find that the same virtues we embrace today were embraced thousands of years ago as well. This is why virtues-based planning is so powerful. Time has tested and proven these virtues survive and thrive throughout time.

Values come and go. They are here today and gone tomorrow. Are there things you value that your children have no interest in whatsoever? The answer is probably, yes, maybe even several things. That is why it is so frustrating trying to pass on our Core Values. If they are not rooted in the Primary Virtues, they can die with you.

Divine vs. Human

We believe the reason why virtues are external, objective, universal, moral, immutable and eternal is that they are the extensions of the nature of the Divine.

Values are mankind's best attempt at coming

up with virtues. That is why values are internal, subjective, local, amoral, variable, temporal and human. Every human being has his or her own unique combination of Core Values. It is rare to find two people who value all the same things.

Distinguishing Between the Two

Scan down the following list and determine whether each item is a value or a virtue. Remember that a virtue always contains an element of universal rightness; whereas, a value is a matter of subjective opinion.

Virtue or Value?

____Sports

____Music

____Making Money/Getting Rich

____Business Success

____Giving to Others/Philanthropy

____Social Status

____Honesty

____Material Possessions

____College Education

____Temperance

____Financial Freedom

____Personal Responsibility

Of the twelve items listed above, only four are virtues: (1) Giving to Others/Philanthropy, (2)

Honesty, (3) Temperance, and (4) Personal Responsibility. The rest are all values.

After years of study, we have compiled a list of what we call the Primary Virtues. They are primary because you can go to any race, culture or religious group at any period of time in history and find these Primary Virtues regarded by the group as necessary for strong families and a healthy society.

Honesty
Always telling the truth

Humility
Thinking of others as more important than yourself

Sacrifice
Giving of yourself with open hands and a loving heart

Industry
Working hard and taking pride in your work

Responsibility
Being answerable for yourself and your actions

Temperance
Knowing when enough is enough

We have not met any parents who did not want these virtues to be present in their heirs' lives. Would you not love to have someone describe your child to you as being as honest as the day is long or to hear someone say that your son would give a person the shirt off his back? How about having your daughter's employer tell you, "She is the hardest worker we have, and when I give her a job to do, it is always done well"? It would make you proud, wouldn't it?

What if you confronted your child about a mistake he or she made and your child responded with, "Yes, Mom and Dad, I messed up. I will personally see to it that I fix it"? You would be impressed no doubt with your child's sense of personal responsibility.

What a joy it would be to hear your child say, "I already have enough. I do not need or want any more."

These utterances would make any parent proud. Their children would be demonstrating high levels of virtue, character and integrity.

If an overriding goal of wealthy parents is for their children to be happy, there is no better way to achieve that goal than to inculcate these Primary Virtues in them and into your planning. The sooner they learn these virtues, the better. But it is never too late, no matter how old your children are, to go to work on this task. We will give you many insights, perspectives and strategies for influencing your adult children toward these Primary Virtues in the next chapter.

Often, however, these virtues are missing in heirs' lives. In the absence of these Primary Virtues, something else moves in to fill the void—vices. Consider what can happen when an heir rejects one or more of these Primary Virtues.

An absence of **Honesty** breeds
Corruption, Mistrust, Manipulation, Duplicity, Cheating

An absence of **Humility** breeds
*Self-centeredness, Conceit, Discrimination,
Pride, Bigotry, Disrespect*

An absence of **Sacrifice** breeds
Greed, Selfishness, Unforgiveness, Lack of Concern,
Lack of Love, Envy

An absence of **Industry** breeds
Low Motivation, Shallow Commitments,
Lack of Direction, Laziness

An absence of **Responsibility** breeds
Irresponsibility, Poor Accountability,
Unreliability, Blaming

An absence of **Temperance** breeds
Excessiveness, Overindulgence,
Extravagance, Addiction

These vices are not limited to the wealthy. Vices are common among all people, regardless of their net worth. But what we have observed is that wealth increases the ability to indulge in many vices. As we pointed out in the preceding chapter, wealth does not build character; it only reveals it.

An ancient Jewish proverb says it well, "Luxury is not fitting for a fool." If a child is going to pursue vices instead of virtues, is an inheritance of any kind appropriate? This question is not asked often enough.

Judging a Child Based upon Virtues and Not Values

One of the greatest areas of conflicts occurs between parents and children when values and virtues are blurred. An example of this was the very successful businessman Henry Bennett, whom we wrote about in chapter 11. Henry had a strained relationship with his oldest son, Tim, because he wanted Tim to take over the family business, but Tim wanted to go into music. Henry thought his son should get a "real" job and make more of himself. They were barely civil to one another.

What had happened here was the father had failed to distinguish between his personal Core Values and the family's Primary Virtues. He was trying to force his own Core Values on his son, but his son had developed another set of Core Values. But they both were living out in their lives in exemplary fashion the same Primary Virtues— Henry in his business and Tim in his music.

Once Henry Bennett realized the difference between virtues and values, the frustration and disappointment disappeared almost immediately. It is true that Henry would have liked for Tim to have taken over the business. But he now recognized that for Tim to be truly happy in life he needed two things: (1) to fully embrace the Primary Virtues, and (2) to use his own personal Core Values to discover and live out his life-purpose. This was a very liberating revelation for this father.

Children will never be happy and will never maintain their parent's Core Values by force or decree. Unless children voluntarily maintain the same values, as soon as the parents are gone, so are their Core Values. Frankly, in light of this understanding of the difference between Core Values and Primary Virtues, does it matter if the parents' Core Values die with them? Is that such a bad thing?

As one father said (using our family tree metaphor), "I do not care what my children's tree grows to look like or even what kind of fruit it produces—as long as it is growing from the same 'root system' as mine."

Attempting to build a family heritage using values as a foundation is like building a home on shifting sand. To build a legacy with virtues is like building a home on bedrock. Initially, the buildings may look quite similar. However, the former will most assuredly collapse, likely sooner than later, while the latter will certainly endure for many generations to come. For families that want to establish a lasting family heritage, there seems little doubt upon which foundation they should elect to build.

In our opinion, these discussions are absolutely essential to develop successfully a comprehensive, multigenerational wealth transfer plan that will work effectively to benefit the heirs and enable them to grow as human beings and pursue their highest and best purposes in life. We have not worked with a wealthy couple yet that, when confronted with an enhanced clarity between values and virtues, the planning decisions were not significantly affected as a result.

If you want to build a strong family tree that will sustain the harsh realities of time, you must cultivate a strong root system of Primary Virtues. Then, let your "saplings" grow as they will, become all they can and achieve what they are called to do. Just sit back and enjoy their adventures.

With this added emphasis in planning, you

have greatly increased the chances of long-term success in transferring your family's wealth to future generations. This may be both the most important investment of your life and the one that will produce the greatest number of dividends.

The Stories of Two Different Families

Brenda and Jack Colvin were second-generation wealth. The Colvins had been married fifty years and had three children, two sons and a daughter. They also had eight grandchildren. When Jack was thirty-five years old, his father had died leaving him the sole heir to a very successful family business. Like many entrepreneurs, Jack devoted most of his time to the business. He worked day and night and weekends. The result was the value of the family business increased ten-fold.

Jack and Brenda's children grew up never lacking for anything. As teenagers, they spent their summers at camp or traveled with their friends' families. Upon reaching the age of sixteen, each child was given their car of choice. Brenda Colvin was a very public person. She was away from home almost as much as Jack. This left the children to be raised primarily by nannies. The children were sent to the finest private schools money could buy. Even though their grades were poor, all three attended the best colleges, thanks to their parents' generous contributions.

When the Colvins' sons graduated from college, they went immediately into the family business. They were given generous salaries and perks.

Their daughter married just prior to graduating from college. Her husband was a starving actor, so the Colvins supported their daughter to make sure she maintained her lifestyle. Soon, grandchildren arrived. The Colvins now began to meet all the wants of their grandchildren.

The company continued to grow until Jack Colvin retired and gave the management of the business over entirely to his sons. They promptly raised their salaries and increased their perks. The three key people who were not family members but who had worked for the company their entire lives eventually retired. Once in total control, the sons began expanding the business, rapidly taking on debt their father had refused to pursue. Instead of spending time at the office, they spent time at the golf course or vacationing. They remembered how their father never spent time away from the company. Their attitudes were to enjoy life. If you got into difficulty, use money to buy your way out of trouble.

As for the Colvins' daughter, shortly after the birth of their third child her husband decided that he no longer wanted to be married. She had never worked. Accordingly, she looked to her parents to support her lifestyle, and they did.

The business had always supported everyone in the family. There was no reason to think a day might come when there was no business to meet the needs of the family.

It was not too long after this when we met the Colvins. We had only known them through acquaintances and what could be read in the local paper. Now, standing before us were two people emotionally and financially devastated, because the entire financial empire they had built over their lifetimes for themselves, their children and grandchildren was gone. They were in their mid-seventies and had just learned that their family business was bankrupt because of their sons' excessiveness and lack of work ethic. The only assets they had left were the family home and Jack's IRA. In order to maintain even a modest lifestyle for the rest of their years, they were going to have to sell their home.

As for their sons, they were now faced with tremendous debt and the realization that they needed, for the first times in their lives, to get real jobs. Sadly, they were in their mid-fifties and had little knowledge or skill to offer any company. They had no idea how to run a company or even work for someone else. The daughter was also in trouble because she could no longer look to her parents as her sole source of support. The entire family was devastated. Never did they imagine that one day the wealth their family had accumulated would be gone. The beginning of the end was the parents' failure to practice and transfer the primary virtues that form the foundation for successfully passing on family wealth.

The Colvins had never seriously considered the long-term ramifications of excessive wealth in the hands of unprepared children. Like a garden left untended, over time only weeds will thrive. Wealth without honesty, humility, sacrifice, industry, responsibility and temperance will sooner or later become a wasted asset.

Fortunately, we also meet and counsel with many families who have happier stories to tell. One such family is Jan and Carol Bard.

When we first met, the Bards were living in a lovely retirement community. They had two married sons and three grandchildren. Their wealth had come from the sale of a family business, disciplined saving over the years and a long-term view of investing.

The family held very strong beliefs about their responsibility to be good stewards of the wealth that had been entrusted to them. As such, one of the first things taught to all family members was the need to give back to the community. Everyone was expected to tithe ten percent of his or her income. This included money earned from cutting grass and paper-route deliveries by younger family members.

Neither the Bards nor their children had any debt. Their homes were paid for as well as all of the family automobiles. When the Bards' grandchildren graduated from college, their parents gave them a car. It was the responsibility of the child to make regular payments into a savings account so that when the time came to replace the car the money to purchase another one outright was available.

One of the outcomes of our working together was the establishment of a family foundation. With the foundation, they were able to create a lasting legacy that cxcmplificd their primary family virtues and their core values. Their family foundation represented the family's strong work ethic, discipline, and their desire to serve the needs of others. It gave the family a way to look beyond themselves and serve the community that gave them their wealth in the first place.

The Bards lived their daily lives trying to practice the virtues we discussed earlier in this chapter. By embracing these virtues, the family realized the responsibility the wealth created. With the formation of their family foundation, the family found a unified purpose. Jan and Carol have new meaning and purpose in their final years. For their children and their grandchildren, their family foundation will forever stand as a testament of those primary virtues held so dear by Jan and Carol. The family wealth their inheritors will ultimately be called to steward will provide rich and powerful opportunities to discover their various life-purposes and to find joy, meaning and fulfillment in carrying them out. In this way, the Bards have indeed built a strong family tree that will most certainly survive for generations to come.

CHAPTER 14

Influencing Your Adult Children
It Is Never Too Late

During our retreats with clients, we often talk at length with them about the role they have played and are currently playing in the lives of their adult children. Far too often, we hear these parents say it is too late to influence their children because the children are grown.

This is often a very painful situation for them. They realize that perhaps they did not do all they could have parenting and mentoring their children while they were growing up. They know that their children are adults and believe the opportunities to influence their children have passed. Many times, these same parents do not have a close, intimate relationship with their children.

Harry Chapin's hit song of the '70s, *The Cat's in the Cradle*, was wildly successful, possibly because it reflected so accurately the consequences of yielding our lives to the tyranny of the urgent. The song struck a common chord with parents and children alike. The story told is all too common among those who have spent much of their lives in a headlong pursuit of the "American dream." Here is the sad tale:

A child arrived just the other day,
Came to the world in the usual way,
But there were planes to catch and bills to pay,
He learned to walk while I was away.
He was talking before I knew it, and as he grew
He said, "I'm going to be like you, Dad,
You know I'm going to be like you."

And the cat's in the cradle and the silver spoon,
Little Boy Blue and the Man in the Moon,
"When can we play, Dad?" "I don't know when,
We'll get together then.
You know we'll have a good time then."

My son turned ten just the other day,
Said, "Thanks for the ball, now c'mon let's play.
Will you teach me to throw?" I said, "Not today,
I've got a lot to do." He said, "That's OK."
And he walked away and he smiled and he said
"You know I'm going to be like you, Dad,
You know I'm going to be like you."

. . . .

He came from college just the other day,
So much like a man, I just had to say,
"I'm proud of you, won't you sit for a while?"
He shook his head and said with a smile,
"What I'm feeling like, Dad, is to borrow the car keys
See you later, can I have them please?"

And the cat's in the cradle and the silver spoon,
Little Boy Blue and the Man in the Moon,
"When you coming home, Son?" "I don't know when,
But we'll get together then.
You know we'll have a good time then."

I've long since retired and my son's moved away,
I called him up just the other day.
"I'd like to see you, if you don't mind."
He said, "I'd love to, Dad, if I could find the time.

You see, my new job's a hassle and the kids have the flu,
But it's sure nice talking you, Dad.
It's been real nice talking to you."
And as I hung up the phone it occurred to me,
He'd grown up just like me.
My boy was just like me.

When our clients say it is too late to influence their kids, we challenge that conclusion.

We ask them, "Are you different people now than you were twenty years ago?"

"Oh, yes," they say.

"Do you think you will continue to change over the next twenty years."

"Yes, most likely we will," they answer.

"Well, then, if you are still in a state of constant change at your age, why would you assume that your children's lives are fixed in stone?" It seems to us that the real question is not whether it is too late to positively influence their children or not. The real question is whether parents want to be down on the sidelines intimately involved in their children's lives as they are playing the game of life or whether parents prefer to be sitting in the bleachers and passively watching their children's lives played out. The children are going to change. The parents must decide whether they want to be actively involved in influencing those changes or not.

Our clients begin to see that maybe it is not too

late to make a positive impact on the direction of their children's lives. Even if the relationship is fractured, there is hope for repair and reconciliation as we outlined in chapter 11.

As long as parents are alive, they impact their children in one way or another. Even if parents have no contact with their children, the absence impacts who the children are and what they will ultimately become. Parents will impact their children, either negatively or positively, until the day they die and often even after that. Parents' prints are all over their children—either in positive ways or negative ways.

It is important to know that the concrete in life never completely dries. We are all constantly being shaped by old and new relationships, current and past circumstances. We are all a work in process.

This should give parents reason for renewed hope. It is not too late. Parents can still have a positive influence in their children's lives. Parents can still make up for lost time.

The purpose of this chapter is to give parents some very specific examples of how other wealthy parents have reentered their children's lives actively and effectively. Often this requires some coaching for the parents, so they do not repeat past mistakes or re-open old wounds. Fortunately, love covers a multitude of sins. What people lack in ability, they certainly can make up for with desire.

The most important question that parents must answer is whether they want to be involved in their children's lives in a positive way. If your answer is no, you should go on to the next chapter. If your answer is yes, you will be pleased to learn that it is not nearly as difficult as you might think. If you care for your children and want to have a happy and loving relationship with them, a positive influence on them will be the natural by-product of your relationship.

Understanding the Difference between Power and Influence

If you are going to impact your adult children's lives, it is critically important that you understand the difference between power and influence. If you do not know the difference, you are probably an accident waiting to happen in your children's lives. Let's look at the difference between these two ways of relating to people.

Power is exerted through control. People with power make things happen. They make people do things. They have the power to exert their will upon others. For example, the President has the power to veto legislation. A general can order his troops into a battle to their deaths. An employer can fire an employee and change that life forever in a moment.

Having power over young children is critical. Parents need to be able to have their young children go to bed, take a bath, clean their rooms and keep their hands away from a hot stove. It is necessary and appropriate. But, inevitably, children become adults and establish their own standards to live by, their own personal faith, their own pursuits of life's opportunities and their own boundaries for the amount of risk they want to assume in their lives.

Once children reach this natural point of human development, they will begin to resist others' exertion of power over them. This is natural and positive. They are becoming their own people, the "captains of their own ships." This is not the time to nag, complain, or threaten your children. If your children have not embraced your standards by adulthood, trying to force them on the children using your power and control usually only leads to further rebellion against you. In addition, they may reject not only your standards, but also you. This is when relationships and families fall apart.

The first reality you must accept is that you do not have control over your adult children, and you cannot tell them what to do. Both parents and children will live longer and have happier lives if parents understand this.

You can no longer tell them what to do or where to go. You must not try to "bribe" them with promises of material things or threaten them by withholding such things. If you try this with adult children, you may win that one battle, but you will ultimately lose the larger war.

Once your children chronologically become adults, you need to treat them as adults, peers and friends. Power and control are gone.

This is where influence enters. Influence is the ability to impact people's lives by giving them new insights, new perspectives, more accurate information, new visions, new opportunities and new experiences. Influence comes from recognition of a person's authority. The best modern example of a person who had no power and control, but possessed incredible authority, was Mother Teresa, a woman who had no material possessions to her name. She spent her life helping starving orphaned children in a destitute Third World country. She held no political office. Nonetheless, she earned the Nobel Peace Prize and international recognition for her example and work.

To borrow an old phrase, "When Mother Teresa spoke, the world listened." She influenced politics, religion, international policy and countless individual lives.

Influence earns; power demands. Parents must begin playing a new role in the lives of their adult children. This role may be both unfamiliar and uncomfortable, but it is one that is both appropriate and effective.

As parents share wisdom, insights and visions with their adult children, the children are free to consider and act upon these new paradigms. Their movement or change in direction will be initiated by them, not by you. In this situation, you serve simply as a coach, a mentor, a visionary, a technical resource, an advisor and a friend. You offer, and they accept or reject your input. Whatever they choose to do, you should rejoice in the relationship and remain a friend and mentor. Often, adult children will test you the first few times by doing the opposite of what you suggest. They want to see how you will react when they exercise their autonomy. If you blow up in anger, your relationship moves backwards. If you shrug your shoulders and say, "It is your life; I have given you my best input," your relationship moves forward.

Do you see the difference between power and influence? Attempting to influence your adult children works. Exerting power over them does not. Once you understand this, you are ready to begin making some real advances in your relationships with your adult children.

Perhaps, the best way to show you how you can successfully influence your adult children is to give you some examples from the lives of other wealthy parents.

Examples of What Parents Have Done to Influence Their Adult Children

Bob and Mary White

After spending the day in a Client Retreat, Bob and Mary decided they needed to include their children and their spouses in developing their Family Wealth Letter of Intent and called a family meeting. It was important to inform the children about the purpose and value of this meeting, what they could expect and what was expected from them. Bob and Mary wanted it to be a time to evaluate their lives, while redefining the meaning of the extended family. It would be a time to explore the family's strengths, temperaments and perceptions of each other, as well as to clarify the family's purpose.

They met in a beautiful rustic cabin over-looking a forest with a river not thirty yards from the cabin. The cabin was built on pillars so that it sat ten feet above the ground. In the quiet setting, the view was awesome as well as private.

As the meeting started, it was clear that the children and their spouses were very apprehensive. They did not know what to expect.

Bob told the family that he and Mary wanted to include them in the process of developing their Family Wealth Letter of Intent. The parents wanted to have the family's input as the master plan was developed to carry out the Letter of Intent. He wanted to start a process with them that they could continue with their children. They hoped to create a positive family tradition that would allow them as a family to maximize their time, talents and treasures.

The family's apprehension shifted to gratitude. This was especially true with the children's spouses. Several of them expressed that to be involved in a process that included such private matters as the family's finances was a vote of confidence. The trust and communication level of this family rose dramatically.

During several additional meetings, the family came together to share their thoughts, to listen and embrace each other as we helped them through the development of their Family Wealth Letter of Intent. The finished product clearly reflected the family's primary virtues, personal strengths and core values. In fact, out of this process the family developed a unique family crest.

Bob and Mary had brought the family to a new level of communication and influence that will continue for generations.

Charlie and Kathryn Wilson

Charlie was born in rural Nebraska, the son of a meat cutter in a packing plant. There were three children and a very special mother. Life was tough in the 1930s and became even worse when Charlie's father was killed by a drunk driver on the way home from work. It was extremely difficult for a boy of ten to pick up food stamps from the relief office and take them to the grocer for beans, bread and milk. He knew then that he never wanted to be poor again. In middle America during the 1930s, adversity built strong character. Charlie worked hard and learned that honesty and hard work are virtues that are to be appreciated. He also learned that studying and being smart also helped.

After returning from World War II, he met Kathryn, a fine woman, and they married. She had been raised in a family that believed material things are not nearly as important as being good people. This belief became their family foundation during all those years when they were not well-off financially.

Life had treated them well, and the family business that Charlie started in 1950 was now worth over five million dollars. One son expanded the business in a new direction that added millions more to the bottom line. Several of the children and some grandchildren were in the business and their efforts added to its growth as well. But, like most families, they had grown apart.

A couple of years ago we took Charlie and Kathryn through a Client Retreat. As part of the retreat, they completed our *Life on Purpose Questionnaire*™. The retreat was a life-changing experience. They discovered that there were so many things they wanted to do for others. They found they could accomplish these objectives by using their Social Capital for purposes consistent with their beliefs, rather than paying estate taxes, capital gains taxes and some income taxes.

When the planning was completed, their anticipated retirement income had increased, and they had benefited from substantial income tax deductions from gifts they would not make until their deaths. They used this "new" money to make gifts to the children and gifts to charities.

They created a public family foundation and called it the White-Stein Family Foundation, which included the name of Kathryn's beloved mother. It took about a year for the children to understand how the foundation worked and how and why they could be a part of it. But Charlie and Kathryn used the foundation as a way to get the family re-engaged in one another's lives. Now the highlights of their years are the family's quarterly foundation meetings.

Since its beginning, all of the children have personally contributed to the foundation. Their family is now providing scholarships to a community college. They have helped to build a town square and have been instrumental in starting a housing program for people who wish to move to their community. Other people have joined in their efforts to make the community a better place to live. Their foundation is still small compared to what it will become when Charlie and Kathryn die. The children are currently meeting regularly with advisors who are teaching them about the management of the investments in the foundation.

The children feel that by the time Charlie and Kathryn die they will have the knowledge and experience to manage effectively both the personal wealth they will inherit as well as the foundation's Social Capital.

They are learning about what good things wealth can do and the many lives it can affect. As a family, they have a common cause that has brought them closer than they have ever been before. Charlie and Kathryn's foundation allows all family members to participate, learn and work together.

They have found that their family actually becomes a source of strength to one another as they reach out to help others. They have found a purpose for both their lives and their wealth.

Charlie and Kathryn have opened up a whole new world to their children. Because they decided to get involved again in their children's lives, they will influence their progeny for generations.

Wayne and Alma Bandy

Two of the three Bandy children were what most people would term "normal." They were hardworking professionals, had nice families and led responsible lives. Wayne and Alma had no problem communicating with their two "good" children. The "good" children knew and understood the majority of their parents' finances and would have no problem in future years continuing to lead responsible lives after gaining additional wealth.

The "black sheep" in the family, Tom, had led an erratic and financially unstable existence and had routinely needed help. According to Wayne, he was a mess.

We helped Wayne see the need to begin building a stronger relationship with his wayward son. Wayne started meeting regularly with Tom and began working extensively with him to teach his child (now in his late 30s) his perception of being financially responsible. Wayne took him to meet with his stockbroker, his accountant, even the local bank manager with whom the father had a good relationship. Tom began to respond favorably to his father's personal interest in him and his coaching and counseling.

In the past, when Tom had an extra dollar it was always gone. Now, Wayne was very pleased to find that Tom had started a systematic program of investing for his future. He no longer spent every dollar that he had, and he actually became very proud of his newfound financial discipline.

Wayne has dramatically influenced Tom because he chose to get back involved in his son's life and coach and mentor him. Not only did Tom learn a lot from his father, the two actually ended up becoming the best of friends—even after all those years of conflict, frustration and no genuinely meaningful relationship.

Arnold and Theresa Roe

Arnold and Theresa were the ultimate consumers. They had big cars, big houses and were big spenders. Their children were learning a superficial lifestyle. During the initial counseling phase of our work with the Roes, we were able to open their eyes to the virtues of philanthropy.

Just as this family's members had previously immersed themselves in superficial activities, Arnold and Theresa now became more and more excited about new philanthropic activities. Living in their winter resort home, they quickly made a mark on the local community through philanthropy.

Arnold and Theresa decided to get their children involved. They wanted to help bring a balance to their children's perception of money and purpose. Just as they had learned from their parents to partake of a superficial lifestyle, they now were becoming equally enthralled with their family's various philanthropic activities as part of their "new life." The entire family's involvement with charity caused all of them to reconsider their excessive and lavish spending habits in other areas, especially as the children became aware that not everyone in the world was a millionaire. They learned that, in fact, some people were destitute.

There has been a clear change of direction in this family. This shift has not only benefited their community but has also benefited their children who were clearly headed in the wrong direction. Now, both the Roes and their children are finding true joy and significance in life.

Brian and Mandy Brayton

One realization that Brian and Mandy made during our Client Retreat was that their son Seth's life was stalled. Seth had been a perpetual student. He had been working on his Ph.D. dissertation for eight years and just could not get it completed.

Brian was beside himself with frustration that Seth was wasting time, getting nowhere fast. We asked Brian if he would be willing to spend some of Seth's inheritance now to help him get his dissertation done and get on with his life. He was not sure what we meant, but we had his attention.

We suggested that the Braytons set up a family foundation and fund it with one million dollars. They could use the foundation to fund the research that Seth needed to have done to complete his dissertation. The lights went on for Brian, and he now saw a way to help his son get this project done without continuing to nag him about it.

The Braytons set up a family foundation. They contacted Seth and told him what they had done. They suggested that Seth and his father could work together on the research projects he needed to get his dissertation done.

Their relationship changed almost overnight. Now instead of being a "lazy" son and a "nagging" father, they were a team of researchers working side by side. The dissertation was finally completed. Seth took a teaching post at a school. Seth's life was changed dramatically because his father decided to get involved in his son's life in a meaningful and loving way. Brian's influence in Seth's life continues to this day.

Conclusion

As long as you are on "this side of the grass," it is never too late to influence your adult children. They, like all of us, are still works in progress. They can still be changed and molded. But it must be done with authority and influence—not power and control. It may surprise many parents to learn that most adult children want the loving and supportive influence of their parents in their lives.

If your children have veered off course in life, there may still be time to try to bring them back. If they are financially incompetent or excessive, you can still provide them the knowledge and experience they need to make wise financial choices. We would even go so far as to suggest that no one is better suited to have this influence in a child's life than their own parents.

It may not happen instantly. It may take time to re-establish (or establish for the first time) a loving, trusting and accepting relationship filled with good communication. However, with desire, determination and consistency, parents can have a profound influence in the lives of their adult children.

CHAPTER 15

Assembling an Effective Planning Team

One of the greatest challenges for wealthy families is successfully putting together both a competent and complementary planning team. This challenge is much the same as putting together a champion sports team. Clients want the best players that money can buy, or at least that their money can buy. The personalities of the team members, their respective egos, their strengths and weaknesses all come into play as a group of talented individuals merges into a team that can effectively work together.

The similarities to a sports team are striking. Sports team members are highly compensated professionals who are very good at what they do. These professionals often believe their individual contribution to the team's success is the most important and that all the other players on the team are to merely support the "star." They often think that they know best what needs to be done to bring home a championship—know even more than the coach and the owner.

Like professional athletes, some advisors may be prima donnas. They already think they know it all and can do it all. They do not think they need anyone else telling them what to do and, consequently, are not coachable. Professional sports are full of players like this. It is tough enough to coach one of these players on a team, but how would anyone like to have an entire team of them? Time and time again, we have seen the highest paid teams be far less successful during a season than lower paid teams. Many times these high-profile teams do not even make the playoffs. The reason is simple. Individual ability and performance does not automatically translate into team success.

In order for a team to be successful, the players must play well together. A team full of superstars not playing well together will not be a winning team, or at least will seldom become champions. They must learn to respect the other team members' abilities. They must trust each team member to do the job for which they are most skilled. They must believe that each team member is committed to doing the best job they can for the client.

One problem that teams occasionally have is when everyone on the team wants to be the captain or the quarterback. They want to call the signals, run the plays and tell everyone else on the team what they should do. They want to be the team member who is in charge of all the others. A team made up of only quarterbacks is going to have little success out on the playing field.

In this chapter, we discuss the various "players" needed on a client's planning team. We will suggest ways to avoid the professional jealousies and infighting that often sabotage the planning process. Finally, we offer some guidelines on how to get the best possible results from your advisors.

Players Needed for a
Championship Advisory Team

We begin by emphasizing that we believe it is no longer possible for any one professional to have all the knowledge needed to create a flawless life and tax plan. There is simply too much to know, too many options and too many regulations.

One of our first rules for selecting team members is: If a professional advisor ever suggests that he or she can do the entire planning job, that advisor should not be on the planning team. This advisor would have to be either terribly naïve as to the sophistication and complexity of the planning process or have a greatly inflated ego to believe he or she could do it all. Either way, this advisor would be dangerous.

A championship planning team must have the highest levels of expertise in estate, gift, generation skipping, capital gains and income tax law, accounting, legal drafting, insurance, investments, money management, philanthropic alternatives and strategies, trust law, business succession, intergenerational family coaching, and mission statement development. No one on the face of the earth is the consummate expert in all of these areas. A person could not live long enough to learn and practice it all.

There is another reason why you want to have a team of advisors and not simply one professional. Advisors have a way of seeing everyone through their own professional biases and preferences. We briefly mentioned this problem in chapter 6. Advisors become comfortable with a particular tool, strategy or product, and then all of their plans for clients seem to incorporate that particular preference.

If you were to look at ten estate plans designed by a given attorney, you would most likely find them to be very similar in their design. If you looked at ten estate plans of an insurance professional, they would probably all be essentially the same. This would be fine if the clients involved were essentially the same. But their families are certainly not the same, nor are their life-purposes the same.

Recently, we were visiting with a wealthy couple. We asked, "If the names on your balance sheet and legal documents were changed and given back to your advisor, would your advisor's plan be any different than it is now?"

The husband thought for a moment and said, "Probably not."

We asked, "Why do you think that."

He answered, "Because he only asked me two questions. One, did I love my wife and did I think our marriage was going to last? I told him that we had been married for thirty-eight years, and I thought it would last. Two, did I have any problem kids? I told him we had one who was. He nodded knowingly and said, 'Okay, we can take care of that.' And that was about it. Then they went to work drawing up the documents for me to sign."

We then asked him, "Does it not make you feel a little uncomfortable that the plan designed for you is basically a boilerplate plan?"

Not surprisingly, it did.

You do not want to allow yourself to be limited to only one advisor's brilliance, comfort level or mode of operation. A customized plan requires a customized process. We see this all the time in our work. Each advisor is expert in one or two areas or tools. Their expertise drops off precipitously after that. It is when you bring the combined expertise of many advisors into a common planning process that you begin "thinking beyond the nine dots" and achieving the highest levels of creativity and planning.

The level of collective knowledge needed to do this kind of planning makes it incredibly easy to overlook a minor miscalculation that could produce a devastatingly negative impact on a plan's performance. We see this happen on many occasions as we review our clients' current plans. They are disasters waiting to happen, but no one ever caught the problem before the plans were originally implemented.

That is why you need more than one player on your team. You need and should want multiple reviews from multiple financial disciplines, ensuring that some issue has not been overlooked and that some innovative planning option has not been neglected. The old saying that there is safety in numbers applies. A team of advisors provides maximum protection and maximum creativity.

Having said all this, let us look at the players we need for a "championship" planning team. We list the individual players in alphabetical order, not by order of importance. Some of these players' roles can and often do overlap, so it may not be essential that a separate person carry out each role.

The Accountant

A qualified tax accountant, an expert in cash flows and number crunching, is a critically important player. Massive amounts of tax calculations and cash flows need to be run and evaluated, and accuracy and appropriateness must be confirmed. Once we get to the bottom line, the accountant is the one responsible for the accuracy of the numbers.

Often, we find that the accountant knows more about the client's financial affairs than any other advisor. They routinely file tax returns and prepare financial statements for their clients' businesses. For this reason, accountants often spend large amounts of time with their clients. Accountants are viewed as the most ethical advisors in business practices. For these reasons, the accountant is a vital player on the team.

The Appraiser

The appraiser is an important player on the team because most wealthy families have hard-to-value assets. The plans may require new valuations to be made after the assets have been repositioned into new ownership entities. The valuation expert will determine the amount of the adjustment of the asset(s) that has been moved.

The appraiser may be needed to value a specific asset to determine the amount of an income tax deduction that will be generated as a result of a charitable gift. If the hard-to-value asset is going to be sold, an appropriate sales price must be determined. Determining these values is critical in the planning process.

If the accounting firm has experience in this area, it may be able to provide appraisal services. If not, there are a number of highly competent national valuation companies that specialize in this service.

The Attorney

Competent estate planning attorneys are absolutely essential to the planning team. Their contributions are critical in a number of key areas. Their knowledge of the various planning tools and the underlying legal issues they are built upon is key to designing a plan that will stand up to the closest scrutiny.

Attorneys are at their best when they are critiquing a proposed plan design. Their input is usually invaluable. Their observations are astute, and their attention to detail is always important. As a player in the design and evaluation phases of the planning process, they bring much value to the table.

Of course, once all the advisors and the client have approved the plan design, the attorney is needed for the plan's implementation. Undoubtedly, legal documents will need to be drafted. Whether your local attorneys actually draft these documents or the team chooses to bring in a specialist to serve as co-counsel, their involvement is essential.

The Family Wealth Counselor

The Family Wealth Counselor is a relatively new player on the planning team. The role, however, is just as critical as the accountant's and the attorney's, but for very different reasons.

The Family Wealth Counselor brings to the table an overall planning process. This process integrates all three of the needed phases—counseling, planning and implementation—and creates a common platform that allows all the advisors to produce the best possible result for the team's owner.

The unique role that a Family Wealth Counselor plays on a planning team is vital. The following hypothetical story should illustrate the value and importance of a Family Wealth Counselor's presence on the team.

Imagine that you wish to visit a foreign country called "Gardenia" that is world-famous for its spectacular natural wonders. Gardenia, however, is strikingly different from America in a number of ways.

An example is how Gardenians greet one another. In our country, a handshake is the customary greeting between strangers. In Gardenia, if you greet a stranger with a handshake, you are expressing that you find him or her offensive and wish to challenge that person to a duel to the death. Their greeting is to put one hand on either side of the stranger's head and kiss the stranger on the forehead.

There is also a major difference in their language. No one in Gardenia speaks English. In fact, their language is considered by most linguists to be the most complex and difficult language in the world to understand and speak. Even if you could get a dictionary of the language, you would find it nearly impossible to say the words because the language requires you to articulate sounds that you have never learned to make.

Then there is Gardenia's economic system. In America, we have been taught to negotiate with people to get the best prices. In Gardenia, sellers set prices too low. The buyer is expected, as a show of generosity and kindness, to negotiate the price up to ensure that the seller will make enough money to stay in business. To try to negotiate the price down, or to not negotiate the price up, is the ultimate insult and a violation of business ethics. You could alienate yourself from the business community overnight. The country is very small, and word of your offense would spread quickly. In a very short time, you would not be welcome in any business establishment, including restaurants and inns.

There are hundreds of other cultural differences. If you do not know these differences in advance, your trip could prove to be disastrous, if not fatal.

Now, if you were planning a trip to Gardenia, would you want to solely use a travel agent or would you prefer a tour guide for this trip as well? A travel agent will buy your airline tickets, make your reservations at the appropriate inns, get your reservation for a car rental and possibly get you a road map of the country indicating some of the better sights—things that are all vitally important for a successful trip.

A tour guide, however, will go with you on your trip as your personal escort. The guide may or may not buy your airline tickets, or make inn and car reservations, but he or she will be right by your side on the entire trip. Your tour guide has been to Gardenia many times, speaks fluent Gardenian and intimately knows all the unusual cultural differences. The guide will also be able to show you all the sights and experiences that uninitiated tourists will never see or find, because only the locals and seasoned tour guides know about these incredible sights and adventures.

Would you prefer to use only a travel agent for the trip or would a tour guide be a valuable addition? Most people would much prefer to have experienced experts take them on this trip rather than brave it alone or with only the help of someone who has bought the tickets and made the reservations and sent you on your way.

The same is true with planning for your family's wealth. Do you want to use only people who can tell you how to get there but leave you on your own to figure out exactly what should be your ultimate destination and how best to make the trip? Or would you prefer to use someone who will carefully walk you through the entire planning process? How about a professional who has been there personally and has taken many others there before, someone who can explain all the options?

A Family Wealth Counselor can show you ideas and possibilities that other experts have not considered.

You need someone on your planning team who will ask you the critical life questions that must be answered to best plan for your family's wealth. You need someone who can help you reduce the answers to these questions to a written Family Wealth Letter of Intent (family mission statement). You need someone who knows how to put everything together into a tight, efficient and fulfilling plan that allows you to leverage your remaining time, unique talent and accumulated treasures to everyone's benefit. You need someone who can then help you choose just the right planning tools and techniques to achieve the highest and best good for you, your heirs and your fellow human beings.

We would suggest that there should always be a chair at every wealthy family's planning table for a Family Wealth Counselor—the family tour guide.

The Insurance Advisor

The insurance advisor may be an optional player. Most wealthy families do not have an intimate relationship with an insurance advisor. Seldom is the insurance advisor a regular member of the planning team. The planning team may elect to bring in an insurance advisor to offer a quote if the planning team has determined there is a need for life insurance.

As the insurance industry continues to merge into the financial services industry, we are finding that more and more attorneys, accountants and banks are licensed to sell life insurance products. The need for an advisor to serve solely in this capacity is decreasing. A seasoned life underwriter, however, may have innovative ideas on the use of life insurance and the kinds of products that would be best suited in your particular planning situation. Just because someone is licensed to sell insurance products does not make him or her knowledgeable or competent in this field.

Generally, if life insurance does prove to be advantageous, having a highly competent professional life underwriter on your planning team will be a decided advantage.

The Money Manager

Most wealthy families already have a money manager. In fact, they often have millions of dollars of assets under management. We have observed, however, that the money manager is seldom part of the clients' regular planning team. Money managers are seen in much the same way as the life insurance agents, as vendors who have something to sell. They are called upon when families want to buy something. Otherwise, they are kept on the fringes.

In contrast, with the sophistication of the planning strategies and the nature of the trusts that we often incorporate in our plans, specialized investment management expertise is required to produce optimal results. For this reason, the money manager needs to understand the financial objectives of the plan design and be able to provide input on whether the needed returns are achievable.

For example, why would we want to design an investment portfolio for total return for a charitable trust that is required to distribute an annual income? Understanding the overall-planning objective will help the money manager understand the rationale behind the investment strategy.

Their input as to investment yield potential is also helpful. They must understand the underlying purpose behind the estimated investment assumptions. Money managers are seldom proactive members of the planning team, but they are vital team members when it comes to effective implementation and ongoing management. Therefore, we believe there always ought to be a seat for them around the planning table.

The Trustee/Administrator

Often, complex trusts are established to help the family fulfill their Family Wealth Letter of

Intent. Consequently, there may be a number of trusts that need trustees. Depending on which tool it is, bank trustees, private administration companies or even children may serve on the planning team as trustees.

Trustees/Administrators are also not proactive members of the planning team, but they are vitally important supporting members. The selection of the trustees of these various trusts is not an insignificant matter and must be addressed with the same care as other aspects of the plan. The more input the trustee/administrator can provide during the planning and implementation phases, the better.

Getting the Team To Work as a Team

Building a successful planning team has three primary elements: (1) The client is clear about what he or she wants done, (2) Team members are clear in what their respective roles and duties are, and (3) There is a mutual respect of each team member's expertise. When all three of these are present, the results are impressive. When one or more of them is not, it results in what we call planning paralysis—nothing happens and the opportunities are lost.

The Client Is Clear about What Is To Be Done

The greatest conflicts among team members come when the client is not clear about what is to be accomplished. When the team members sense that the client is unsure, advisors begin to promote their favorite planning strategies or tools.

It would be like a football game, late in the fourth quarter. Your team is down by two points on the opponent's thirty-eight-yard line. It is fourth down and two. The coach (the client) calls a time-out to discuss the options. The offensive line wants the fullback to run right up the middle to get the needed yardage. The tight end and the halfback want to sweep around the end. The wide receivers want to go for broke and surprise them with a bomb. The punter wants to punt and pin them to the goal line. The place kicker wants to try a fifty-five-yard field goal.

Any one of these play options may get you where you want to go. But who must make the decision? The coach. Until the coach is clear on what is to be done, disagreements and debate will divide the team.

Once the coach decides what the team will do, the team members focus their energies on executing the coach's play. If the client (or coach) cannot articulate clearly what he or she wants, the planning team will flounder. They will debate what really is important to the client. They will question the client's motives. They will debate which planning strategy is best. Without clarity on the part of the coach, planning paralysis will result.

Each Team Member Knows Own Role/Duties

Another issue that creates conflicts among team members is poorly defined roles and unclear duties. If the team members are not clear about what position they are playing, the team is going to be very inefficient. Can you imagine two guards

255

and the center standing at the line of scrimmage arguing over who is supposed to snap the ball? That team is going to lose every game.

A meeting of the advisors must be held to determine who will do what based upon their expertise and their abilities. A team with all quarterbacks will be a team that loses every game. Somebody has to block, and somebody else has to carry the ball. All have important, yet different, roles. All the advisors must set aside their egos for the good of the team and the success of the owner.

When each member of the planning team is clear on the goals, what is being done and who is going to be doing it, a synergy develops among the members. They stop competing and start complementing one another.

Mutual Respect of Team Members' Expertise

Sometimes, there is a lack of respect among the team members. The attorneys may not think the Family Wealth Counselors know anything because they are not attorneys. The accountants may think the insurance professionals are only concerned about making a commission and do not have the clients' best interests in mind. We have seen team members from larger firms look down their noses at team members from smaller firms. The larger firms think the smaller firms are less competent because of their size.

One of the best ways to eliminate this kind of professional posturing is for the clients to make it clear that this is their team, and they expect them to work together as a team. Many times, the

Family Wealth Counselors are among the last advisors named to the team. Often, other advisors have been there for years. Now, all of a sudden, the original group finds there is a new player on the team. The team may feel threatened or fearful of what the new player is there to do. They might think they are being replaced or relegated to less active roles. They may fear that the new advisor is going to make them look bad in front of the clients. These are all very common fears and concerns. Clients must address this matter in a straightforward way by sending each current team member a letter introducing the Family Wealth Counselor and directing the team to work together.

The following is a sample letter that clients would send out to the team of advisors introducing Family Wealth Counselors to the planning team members. The letter dispels their fears and sets the stage for peer respect for all members of the team.

Dear {Advisory Team Member},

My wife and I have recently retained {Family Wealth Counselors' firm} to take us through their Family Wealth Counseling process. Although our current advisory team and we have accomplished much, we believe this firm brings unique creativity and skills in a number of significant areas to the entire planning process. We believe adding them to our advisory team will enable us to maximize our time, talents and accumulated wealth for everyone's benefit.

I have asked the firm's president, {name of Family Wealth Counselor}, to give you a call to introduce the firm, personally introduce himself (or herself) to you and learn of your role on the planning team. Once you see what they do, I think you will understand why we are so excited about adding them to our planning team.

This letter serves as my authorization for you to provide {Family Wealth Counselors' firm} and its members with whatever information, documentation or explanation they may need from you. Please assist them in any way possible as we proceed through this Family Wealth Planning process. I appreciate your cooperation in this matter.

I want to add that {Family Wealth Counselors' firm} has not been brought in to replace any of our current advisors. We believe that his (or her) firm brings unique talents, perspective and knowledge that will only complement our present advisory team. They will serve as a valuable addition to our team. Your continued active involvement in this process is absolutely essential.

Thank you in advance for your cooperation. Please call me if you have any questions or concerns.

Getting Successful Results from Your Planning Team

We have seen and been involved in situations where the client sets the planning team up to fail in its task. The clients sabotage the team by making choices that created the very problems they wanted to avoid. The following are our five rules for getting winning results from a team of advisors. When our clients follow these five rules, we always design and implement a plan successfully.

Rule #1 – Include all planning team members in the process from the beginning

Some time ago, we worked on a case where the clients, Joe and Cathy, told us that they wanted to get a different attorney for their planning than the one they were using for the business. We offered the names of some of the most competent counsel we had worked with for them to choose a different attorney. Joe told us to go ahead and proceed with the planning. They would choose an attorney soon. We proceeded unaware of what we had just allowed to happen.

Our Family Wealth Plan presentation was perfect. The plan accomplished everything Joe and Cathy desired. They were thrilled that we had kept their complex plan understandable. They were eager to proceed with the steps suggested for implementation. Knowing they were pleased with our referrals to competent legal counsel, we asked if they had selected their new attorney yet. Joe replied, "Oh, I forgot to tell you, we have decided to stay with our same attorney." Our worst nightmare had become a reality.

The attorney was very threatened when he saw all the work that had been done without him. He was protective, defensive and very adversarial. Who could blame him? He was not included in the planning loop from the beginning. He began a long, frustrating delaying tactic.

If the owner wants to design and implement a plan, the decision-making advisors must be included on the planning team from the very beginning. To work on a case, we now insist on it.

Rule #2 – Permit your advisors to openly communicate with one another whenever needed

We had the opportunity to work with a wealthy couple some years ago, Lester and Virginia, who had an extremely high net worth. It was a perfect situation for Family Wealth Counseling, or so we thought.

The fly in the ointment was that Lester refused to give us the name of his estate planning attorney. Lester said he wanted us to take them through the process, and then he would take the plan to his attorney for his review. We could see so much potential benefit for the family and for charity that, against our better judgment, we agreed to take the case and ignored the arrangement's inherent dangers. All we knew about this attorney was that he was considered the brightest and most creative estate planning attorney in this particular major U.S. city.

We went to work reviewing their current plan. Lester and Virginia were planning to gift specific assets to their private foundation upon Lester's death. The plan was to use the income from these assets to make annual gifts to charity. The problem was that a private foundation is not permitted to hold these kinds of assets. The result of this planning mistake was that his business partner would end up paying an additional $1.4 million in income taxes annually. This had been a major oversight.

Normally, we would go privately to the advisor who drafted the plan to discuss this problem, so he or she could address it with the client directly. But since we were not allowed to talk to the clients' advisor who drafted the plan, we had no choice except to point this out to the clients. Of course, the clients took it to their attorney. The attorney from that point forward became our adversary. We had been forced to violate one of our own cardinal rules: Never take another advisor's mistake to the client. Allow that advisor to address mistakes directly with the client.

Either in spite of or because of finding this mistake, Lester and Virginia retained us to design a new plan. The plan we designed produced substantial increased leverage in this family's ability to give to charity by eliminating substantial income taxes, all capital gains taxes and all estate taxes. We redirected that money to charitable causes. Lester's attorney had never even heard of one of our creative planning strategies.

When the attorney saw the plan, he felt threatened by us. We had shown this top attorney's clients a strategy that he did not know about, and his pride was damaged. We had been forced to educate him in front of one of his best clients rather than in private. Not a good thing.

We knew better than to enter into this kind of a "restricted" relationship, but, in our excitement to help this family, we let the client bring the seeds of dissension into the process by not letting all advisory planning team members have open communication with one another. Today, if the clients insist on this kind of arrangement, we simply refuse to work on the case. We already know disaster looms ahead.

One of our many positive examples of the success of keeping this rule came when Ethan referred us to his parents. Steve and Jennie were in their sixties. When Ethan's parents heard our story, they elected to engage us to take them through the process. The first step was setting the date for the Client Retreat. Although Steve and Jennie thought their objectives were simple and they were clear on them, we encouraged them to complete the counseling phase and experience all of the benefits. They were absolutely astounded by the power and clarity they gained in the counseling process. The resulting plan was equally amazing, and they were very happy with the cooperation among their advisors.

Their accountant provided tax returns for the prior three years. They provided a detailed list of assets with copies of all documents representing ownership. Their lawyer provided the wills and trusts that had been executed previously. Their insurance advisor provided insurance contracts, dates, cash values, death benefits, and ownership and beneficiary designations. All of this was accomplished within one week.

The communication and cooperation among the planning team members was extensive and complete from the very beginning of the planning phase. The result was a unique design that met all of the clients' objectives. They chose to fully implement the plan as their team had designed it. The process was successful because the cooperation was genuine and client centered.

Obviously, complete cooperation among the team of professional advisors is of paramount importance. Experience, knowledge and a full commitment to the clients' objectives as determined during the Client Retreat should be a requirement of any team member participating in the Family Wealth Counseling process.

Rule #3 – Do not pit your advisors against one another

We often find our fiercely-independent-entrepreneur-type clients almost enjoy the idea of pitting their advisors against one another, thinking that in doing so they will get more objective analyses of a plan design and will keep everyone honest. We have found that just the opposite is true. Emotions, egos, personalities and preferences get in the way of the planning process when this happens.

The client will get an idea, strategy or product that one advisor is recommending and then take it to the other advisors for their evaluation. The client is not able to explain adequately the rationale for the recommendation and cannot answer the other advisors' questions. The other advisors will reject the idea because they either do not understand it fully, or they may question the competency of the advisors recommending it. Either way, everybody loses.

After these barriers are constructed, when, or if, advisors do finally get together you can almost cut the air with a knife because the tension is so high. What ends up happening in these situations is nothing. The client gets frustrated, confused or scared and at best postpones any action until later or decides to forget the whole thing.

If you want to have success in planning, you must eliminate everything that would pit advisors against one another. They should not have to defend their competency, integrity or motives to the other advisors on the planning team. It does not work in sports, and it does not work here either.

Rule #4 – Insist on consensus from your planning team

When anyone gets a group of knowledgeable experts together, conflicts and differences of opinion are inevitable. This is not a bad thing. In fact, it is very good. As long as there is mutual respect of each member's expertise, it is good to let these advisors spar with one another as long as it does not get personal. One of the advantages of having broad professional diversification of knowledge and experience on the team is the creativity and insights that the team members can bring to the table.

However, what can and does happen is advisors may become so enamored with their own creativity that they dig in their heels and insist on it being their way no matter what the other team members say. They think they are right, or their way is best, and that is the end of the discussion. The other advisors do not agree, and the team finds itself in an intractable situation. The only thing we know for sure is that the clients are not going to move forward with this major roadblock among their trusted advisors.

We had a situation once where the clients simply forced their advisors to go back to the conference room and stay there until they came out with a consensus on a plan design. They all reviewed the Family Wealth Letter of Intent once again to make sure everyone was clear in what the clients wanted. The advisors then went to the conference room.

Three hours later, the team emerged with consensus. That plan was implemented immediately with everyone's support and agreement.

—————◦◦◦—————

Another example of the power of consensus was evident when an elderly couple, Fred and Anna, retained us to take them through the Family Wealth Counseling process and to become a key member of their planning team. The team spent the next three months working together to learn more of the intricacies of this family's financial and legal situation. Most of the advisors were receptive to having us on the team. They were cooperative and helpful in the process.

Early in the process, the accountant determined that the existing law firm did not have the expertise we would need to accomplish what was necessary to get the job done. At the direction of Fred, we began a search for a law firm who specialized in this kind of planning and who could serve as co-counsel to the family's current lawyer. This attorney was very valuable as a member of the planning team because he was a trusted advisor with a great deal of history with the family as well as knowledge of what would and would not work from a practical perspective for this family.

After several interviews of our suggested legal experts, the client added a new member to the planning team. The team was very pleased to have him on board.

As we progressed, the accountant gave the team additional insights about how our client made decisions and how he liked to work with advisors. On many different occasions, since we were introducing new concepts and ways of thinking, Fred looked to the accountant and his trusted attorney for interpretation and confidence that good decisions were being made. Their nod of approval carried the day.

Over a two-month period of time, a final plan design was developed. The final design was a comprehensive family wealth plan that succeeded in transferring more than fifteen million dollars to their newly developed family foundation. The benefits of this transfer included a net increase in their after tax income along with a two-million-dollar increase to the inheritances for each of their five children.

Upon the presentation of the team's final plan, Fred and Anna were very pleased. However, they wanted to shift some of the increased income that was created for them in this process to several of their children who they felt needed the income today. With this change in mind, we began implementation of the plan.

Legal documents were drafted, proofed and reviewed by each advisor to assure consistency with the plan design. A bank trustee was brought in to oversee a gifting strategy and to serve as a back up to trusted family members who were serving as trustees.

The Family Wealth Counseling process worked well because the planning team worked well together. We talked together. We planned together. We presented together. We implemented together. Everyone was happy with the result.

Rule #5 – Assume a leadership role on your planning team

One of the biggest mistakes that clients make is allowing their advisors to control the planning process. Clients must assume the leadership position. We often have clients ask how they can take control of the planning team, when they do not know anything about planning.

Our answer is simple. You do not need to know anything about planning to assume leadership of the planning team.

When generals order their divisions to advance to a certain point, there are a myriad of logistical matters that must be addressed to facilitate such a movement of thousands of troops, equipment and supplies. That is what colonels, majors, captains, lieutenants and sergeants do. The job of the general is to make the big decisions, to set the direction, to determine the objective and then give the orders to make it happen. When generals' orders are not carried out, they expect to know why.

Generals may not know how to fix a Jeep, service a cannon or cook for ten thousand soldiers, but they do not need such knowledge. It is not the job of a general to carry out those duties.

Likewise, clients do not need to know all the technical details of designing a plan. They simply need to tell their advisors what they want to do and determine if the plan design accomplishes their directives. That is why the Family Wealth Letter of Intent is so critical. It is the written directive from the commanders-in-chief. Remember our example of the Robinsons' plan in chapter 8? When the advisors began to experience discord, Mr. Robinson was able to bring the team back together by giving directives that were first outlined in the Robinson Family Wealth Letter of Intent. All other discussions were over. In short order, the plan was approved and the assignments made.

That is the kind of leadership we are referencing. The client does not need to know much about estate planning, but he or she certainly needs to know the desired goals and be able to express those goals clearly and confidently to the team of advisors.

Conclusion

When any aspect of this chapter is ignored, the clients will sooner or later have a problem. On the contrary, when a client follows these five rules (restated below), the entire Family Wealth Counseling process proceeds with incredible smoothness and efficiency, and everyone is happy with the results.

Rule #1: Include all planning team members in the process from the beginning

Rule #2: Permit your advisors to openly communicate with one another whenever needed

Rule #3: Do not pit your advisors against one another

Rule #4: Insist on consensus from your planning team

Rule #5: Assume a leadership role on your planning team

SECTION IV

THE UNIQUE PHILANTHROPIC PLANNING
ISSUES ADDRESSED IN FAMILY
WEALTH COUNSELING

CHAPTER 16

Building Bridges Instead of Walls

Many wealthy people who have been successful financially can and often do find themselves in a rather unfortunate circumstance later in life—waiting to die in luxury. The statement may seem harsh, but we have seen this reality many times. Their businesses have been sold. They have more time and money than they will ever need, and they have nothing in particular to do. They kick back and focus virtually all their time and energy on playing, having a good time and making themselves comfortable. All the while, they are moving closer and closer to the end of their days. They are, in fact, waiting to die in luxury.

In addition, many affluent people, particularly men, live much of their lives having created few, intimate, personal relationships. Their wealth and the power that comes from that wealth create walls between them and the rest of the world. Their wealth intimidates those who have little in comparison. Their wealth also makes them ripe targets for anyone who is trying to sell anything. They must endure a never-ending stream of vendors hawking their wares.

Instead of looking to close friends and family to help them, these overachievers can simply rely on their wealth's purchasing power to buy the needed services, allowing or possibly forcing them to keep personal intimacy with these hirelings at a safe distance.

What looks to outsiders like a life of ease is often a life of emptiness and loneliness. A wealthy person seldom would recognize or admit this because generally their materialistic abundance keeps them emotionally and mentally occupied. They seldom, if ever, consciously feel the emptiness. It is true that there are golf buddies and bridge club friends, but rarely are these relationships intensely close and caring. These relationships, more often than not, are merely superficial social interactions with other wealthy people. They talk about their latest travels or their most recent financial conquests, but sadly they never feel completely free to come out from behind their walls of wealth to be open, honest and real with each other.

Buying that next new car or that new vacation home, flying to Florida in their new jet or taking another cruise may be fun, but these activities are not deeply satisfying. They may be entertaining for a while, but as with most toys, people tire of them and go on to other newer, often more expensive toys for the next round of entertainment. As they repeat this sequence, only rarely do they recognize that they are in a disappointingly hollow pursuit.

In contrast, let us imagine the possibilities if we engaged these affluent movers and shakers and offered them an opportunity that would not only touch the world where they live, but also whatever other part of the world they choose to touch. Imagine the power that could be harnessed if these empire builders could catch a vision that would re-energize their creativity, experience and motivation? If someone could show the wealthy how to retain control of all their Social Capital (chap. 2) and self-direct that latent wealth to dearly held and passionately supported causes, an army of sleeping giants would be awakened.

Until now, the wealthy and their advisors have largely ignored the whole idea of Social Capital and have seen it as the enemy (taxes)—something to be minimized. They focus all their planning decisions strictly on what produces the most financial benefit to the family. Often, no one has explained the other option, giving their Social Capital away to charity. Why? Because planning is typically done in a financial vacuum ignoring the spiritual, emotional and social components of a person's life (chap. 1).

Since Social Capital does not help the wealthy family directly, but rather it is restricted to helping our society at large, many of these families and their advisors have not conducted any serious discussions about the use and distribution of their Social Capital. The wealthy couple might be offered some vague, general question from one of their advisors about whether they have any interest in giving some of their wealth to charity. But there is usually little meaningful conversation about the possibilities, much less any direct challenge to make a personal investment in any significant social outcome. It is presented as just one of many possible transactions, an optional expenditure. It is just one of the many questions on the advisors' list that must be asked before moving on to the really important things.

Rush and Ginger Saylor

We were having our meeting to begin the Family Wealth Counseling process with the Saylors. Rush mentioned that he had spoken with his attorney about some of the charitable planning strategies and tools that he heard in the Maximum Wealth Control Strategies private briefing he had attended. The Saylors' attorneys reminded Rush that they had discussed these tools with him previously, and the Saylors were not interested in any of them.

Rush confided, "I do not remember discussing any of these planning strategies or tools with my attorneys."

We do not doubt that some discussion of this type occurred between the Saylors and their attorneys. But the discussion was so routine, so forgettable, that the Saylors did not even recall it. We find it fascinating that these exact same planning opportunities now had captured Rush's imagination and so excited him that he retained us to take his family through the Family Wealth Counseling process.

Was this change in their attitude about these powerful and effective planning options due to a major change in their financial situation? Was it that they had recently developed a major philanthropic interest that was not there before? Was it that they had developed several new estate planning goals that made these tools more appealing? The answer is no to all of these.

What made the difference? They had heard the same story in a new and refreshing way. The first time they discussed charitable giving with their attorneys, nothing captured their imagination or interest, which is exactly why they could not recall the discussion. When they heard the story from us, they were challenged and intrigued by the innovations they had heard about in our private briefing.

We believe it is absolutely critical that advisors spend a substantial amount of time with wealthy people to find out where their passions are and what is really important to them. Advisors must help their clients think through the Primary Virtues upon which they have built their lives, what Core Values they might like to transfer to future generations and how they might effectively do that. Family Wealth Counselors assist individuals and families to discover and then fulfill their true life-purposes. Family Wealth Counselors show individuals and families how they can change the world in significant ways by effectively concentrating their remaining time, unique talents and accumulated treasures in areas that are important to them. These changes are far beyond anything they ever imagined possible.

To do this, their advisors must discuss things beyond financial statements and legal documents. Advisors must discuss the human side of the equation. The clients must talk about their hearts, souls, dreams and desires. Their advisors must help them leverage their untapped resources to make a difference—a difference that can last far beyond their lifetimes—impacting generations to come.

This is what happens in our Client Retreat (chap. 5). We ask questions that no one else has ever asked these individuals—the hard and important questions of life (chap. 6). These questions help identify what it is that they really care about by finding those places in their lives where they have been touched deeply, where help or influence has come from when needed.

We do not believe it is possible to have grown up in America and not have been served in some way by charitable organizations. We encourage our clients to take some time to think about the charitable organizations that have touched their lives from earliest childhood until today. Most people, once they begin to make a list, are amazed at just how many charitable organizations have actually impacted their lives and their family's lives over the years. Upon reflection, they are grateful that the charities were there for them, and they begin to explore how to support and sustain those same causes so that others will be helped in the future as they were in the past.

A metamorphosis takes place. New opportunities arise to enjoy life to its fullest, to create new meaning and to find new richness. Pretense disappears. Masks are gladly dropped. An open hand and a loving heart replace them.

The walls of wealth that once protected and insulated the wealthy from the rest of the world are now intentionally dismantled. With those same building materials, bridges can be constructed to reach out to those who are in need. These bridges can produce substantial and meaningful relationships with people who have needs that are both real and often desperate. Knowing that now something will remain, prosper, grow and endure creates an explosion of energy, a sense of renewed vitality and passionate urgency for those who contemplate the possibilities. Now, instead of simply marking time, waiting to die in luxury, wealthy people find themselves making time. Their energies are directed to new, creative challenges that feed both body and soul, and life takes on new meaning.

Rodney and Brooke Sizemore

We met Rodney Sizemore and his son Adam at a briefing in Central Florida. In a brief conversation, Rodney said he was interested in our services and had a current pressing need—the transfer of the family business to his two sons, Adam and Phil. Both sons were very active in the business, and Rodney volunteered that the sons were responsible for most of the growth of the business in the last few years.

We scheduled a time for the Client Retreat. They wanted to have Adam and Phil in the retreat as well. At that retreat, we shared in the joy of a family discovering their true calling.

279

"What do you most want to accomplish through this planning process?" we asked. At first, we received some of the basic issues any planner would expect: successful transfer of the business to the sons, providing equitability for other children, no decrease in income and avoidance of all estate taxes.

Brooke sat quietly while these objectives were discussed, but then she volunteered one thing that was important to her. She wanted to be sure they had enough income to continue their efforts to reach out to people around them. "That is the big one," Rodney agreed.

Since we were unsure what those efforts were, we asked for more information. The answer to this short question lasted more than an hour.

For many years, Rodney and Brooke had been reaching out to those who were down on their luck or stressed out from life. Even though they had a multimillion-dollar net worth, few knew they were "the millionaires next door." When they became aware of people in need, they took them out to dinner, coffee or some other activity that would take them away from their troubles. Brooke's concern was that in the process of avoiding taxes and passing the business on to the boys they would limit their income in a way that would stop them from providing this ministry to their friends and acquaintances.

As we explored, we learned this was a couple who had spent many years going out of their way to promote family values and to build bonds between the parents and children of other families. Their first such effort was the Sizemore Park and Pavilion. Rodney and Brooke purchased five and a half acres of land in the early part of their marriage as an investment. Their investment produced unique fruit when they decided to build a pavilion on the property.

Rodney and Brooke were concerned about the kind of friends who associated with their five children. They wanted a safe place for their children to play and have fun with their friends. The project soon grew in scope to include others. In addition to the pavilion, there is now a swimming pool, a fishing pond, a stable with a horse and a pony, shuffleboard, a basketball court, volleyball nets and other wonderful facilities. The pavilion over the years has been enclosed and equipped with air conditioning, fireplace, full kitchen, television and VCR, so it is usable at anytime of year or in any type of weather.

The property is now used at little or no cost by church groups, Boys and Girls Clubs, family reunions and a score of other groups. Each Halloween, they sponsor a bus that picks up children from the inner city of the community in which they live, and they hold a party on the grounds of the park with hot dogs and fun.

The Sizemores wanted to create an environment where families and organizations could focus on relationships and not on the logistical details of the event. It was evident the planning for this facility had been a family effort and central to many of the decisions they made. The result was a top-notch facility.

In spite of all the family effort in their mission to help other families, Rodney and Brooke sheepishly admitted they had never planned for the day that was now upon them—their own retirement. They wanted to turn their business over to their sons, but they were also very concerned about the ability of the business to support the retired owners and how that drain might hamper continued growth.

Adam and Phil now chimed in for the first time. They let their parents know that their only concern was having control of the business. All the other family assets could go to their siblings. They also said that any growth or financial struggle ahead was their responsibility, not their parents'. "If we are not prepared at our age, we will never be ready," said Adam.

Phil said he had seen and felt the benefit of his parents' efforts to reach out to others. He emphasized that the weight of continuing this legacy should be shouldered by the next generation as much as it had been by their parents.

As their Family Wealth Counselors, it was fascinating to watch a family discover that their true mission was this service to other families and not the family business. This work had burned in the family and the flames had spread to the children by practice, not teaching. Rodney did not say much, but the look of pride on his beaming face said it all as he watched his children taking on the family's mission.

The Sizemore family has now gone so far in their efforts that they have built a retreat home to share with others. Over the last three years, they have blasted out a building site on the side of the Cherokee Mountains. There sits a three-story retreat center with all the comforts of civilization, but with the feel of a cabin. They have built a series of steps and landings down to a gently flowing river at the bottom of a ravine. They are building a large gazebo for children to camp out in while they fish and enjoy the great outdoors.

The next major project at the site is a park at the end of the logging road to make the site more comfortable to families with young children. The site will have swings and a large wooden play area for the children. A launching area for canoes will also be added to enjoy the river without having to hike down from the house.

The Sizemores use this home in many ways. It is a central location for several extended family members to meet. They will often invite friends who are going through difficult times to spend a weekend. It allows their friends to escape their troubles for a short time, to allow wounds to heal and to gain a new perspective.

The sacrifice of the Sizemore family's time pales in comparison to the love they receive from their friends and acquaintances by sharing their wealth. They have indeed used their wealth to build bridges to others, and everyone's lives are being blessed.

Calvin and Maurine Hill

Calvin and Maurine Hill had no children. They had been married for forty-six years and had accumulated a very substantial fortune over the years. Their concern was that they had no one to leave their wealth to. They had a couple of nieces to whom they wanted to leave a small inheritance, but that was it. The problem for the Hills was what they should do with their accumulated wealth.

In the Client Retreat, we began to explore the possibility of adopting some "philanthropic" children since they had no biological children. Their first reaction was negative, but as they began to think about it they became more open to the idea.

We began researching local charitable organizations that served children. They found one they were particularly interested in. We scheduled a site visit to one of the organization's children's homes. The experience changed this couple forever.

As they got out of the car, they looked closely at the facilities. They were adequate, but needed painting and general maintenance. Just at that moment, a kickball came rolling toward our car followed by three children. Calvin reached down and picked up the ball. When the three children came racing up, they came to an abrupt stop and looked into Calvin's eyes. For that split second, time stopped. It seemed as if minutes passed with Calvin looking at these children when it was actually only a split second. When Calvin turned back to us, his eyes were filled with tears. It was then that we learned that Calvin had grown up in an orphanage himself.

The director of the children's home arrived and took us on a tour of the facility. The walls in the dining room were cracked. The basketball court was dirt. The playground was very tiny. The little pool had been closed for a lack of funds to maintain it. The dorm rooms had bare steel beds with lumpy mattresses.

Calvin asked the director how many of these children go to college. The answer was virtually none. They simply did not have the resources to get a college education. The laundry facility was antiquated, as was the infirmary. But, for these fifty-six children, it was home.

During the drive home, there was an intense silence. Calvin and Maurine said little. We knew this was the kind of silence that they needed then. When we arrived back at their home, they invited us in. They wanted to talk.

What happened next was moving beyond words. Calvin looked at Maurine and said, "You know, Honey, we have been planning to move off this farm and get a home in town. What would you think about turning our homestead into a home for those kids?"

Maurine responded, "We could convert this house into the main building and then build some smaller homes around the property for the children to live in. We could put a dock at the pond and make it into a swimming area." The dreams were flowing from them, and the energy and intensity of their excitement grew as they spoke.

They decided that they wanted to go back to the children's home. This time, their visit was not to see the building, it was to see the children. Calvin and Maurine spent the day with the children. They watched them play games, and they ate lunch with them. They began to learn their names.

They went back again. And again. Each time, they brought little goodies and occasionally a new outfit for Mary or a new ball glove for Tommy. The kids started calling Calvin and Maurine "Grandma and Grandpa." For all of them, their lives were richer and fuller.

Calvin and Maurine donated their homestead property to the children's home. They donated enough to build the needed buildings and to endow the maintenance of the entire property from their foundation. They also set up a scholarship program for the children from this home. Each year any child who graduates from high school with better than a B average receives a full four-year scholarship to the local state college from the foundation.

Once the children's home was relocated to the Hills' old homestead, they would drive out to eat dinner each evening with the children who now lived where they had lived for the past forty-six years. Calvin and Maurine knew each child's name.

One day during a visit to the home, Maurine looked at us and said, "Thank you for giving us such a wonderful family to leave our wealth to. We could not be happier if they were truly our own children."

That night, the board of directors hosted a dinner in honor of the Hills. When they were introduced, the children all spontaneously jumped up and cheered. Susie, a seven-year-old, ran over and climbed up in Calvin's lap and hugged him. Calvin kissed her on the forehead and then began to openly sob with joy as he held little Suzie in his lap. The entire room was moved to tears at the scene. It was an evening never to be forgotten.

Calvin and Maurine had torn down their walls of wealth and used those same materials to build bridges to the lives of these precious and helpless children. They changed these children's lives forever. But the children were not the only ones whose lives were changed forever. The Hills now had a family. They were no longer simply waiting to die in luxury. They had a purpose. They had a life. They were making a difference.

Conclusion

Addressing these social, spiritual and emotional aspects of a family's wealth must come first —before the financial aspect. Wealthy people must answer the question *why* before they can answer the *what* or the *how*.

Asking why opens up a whole world. It is a world where the heart is—where meaning and fulfillment are found. It is a world full of bridges instead of walls. It is a world that sees caring, open hands reaching out to help. It is a world where most of us would prefer to live, a world where we meet real life face to face, a world where we find the deepest sense of personal significance and life's highest levels of meaning. It is good!

CHAPTER 17

Casting a Shadow beyond the Grave

Mankind is mortal. Our Creator has granted us a certain number of days to dwell upon this earth. For some, it may be only days. For others, it may be tens of thousands of days. No matter what our number is, there will come a time for all of us when our last day will arrive. Our lives will be over.

At that point, who we were and what we did in our lives will be permanently fixed in the minds of those who knew us. There will be no additions to those memories. No corrections. No modifications. Our relationships with people, our actions, what was important to us, how we lived our lives and how we used our resources will be etched unchangeably in the memories of all those who knew us. The final paragraph of the final chapter of our book will have been written, and the indelible ink will have dried.

How fondly will those who knew you remember you? Will you be someone people will even want to remember? Will you be someone people will be glad to forget? Most of us hope that someone will remember us with gratitude and affection. We hope that something of what we have done in our lives will survive us and serve to one degree or another as a meaningful monument to our brief time on this planet.

The Day of Your Funeral Has Arrived

None of us will get a preview at what we will leave behind so that we can see how our lives impacted others. But, to gain a sense of what shadows you may be casting, consider the following imaginary exercise.

You have just died. (Sorry, but it is going to eventually happen to all of us.) What is different about your death, however, is that you are going to have the rare privilege of attending your own funeral service. No one will know that you are there or that you are listening to everything that is being said. Everyone believes that you are dead and gone.

What makes your funeral so interesting for you is looking over the crowd and noticing the people there, and maybe even more telling, mentally noting those who are not there. Funerals are crisis events. People take time off from their jobs, rearrange their schedules, cancel trips and dip into savings to get there. Funerals are never timed conveniently for anyone.

The funeral is about to begin. Your casket is in the front of the room. Friends, associates and family have gathered to pay their last respects. Your funeral service includes a series of eulogies offered by those who knew you best. After the opening strains of music conclude, your spouse shares what was really important to you during your lifetime. Then your children take their turns recounting to the audience what kind of a parent you were to them and what they saw as your life-priorities during the years they were growing up. They also share how you influenced and impacted them once they became adults.

After your family, some of your key employees take the platform to relate what kind of an employer you were and how working for you impacted their lives. One of your business associates describes what kind of a businessperson you were and the standards you lived by in conducting your business.

Then, your next-door neighbors stand to share with the audience what kind of a neighbor you were to them. A representative of the local charities then steps forward to tell of the role you played in helping the local nonprofit organizations fulfill their charitable missions. Finally, a city official enumerates how your life, your influence and your wealth made a difference in the local community.

The funeral concludes. You are buried. For those who survive you, life goes on.

For this little exercise to be helpful, it is important to reflect, "If I were to die tomorrow, how will people remember me and what would they say about me?"

Would you enjoy attending your funeral, or would it be painful? If what they would say about you is not how you want to be remembered, we have good news. You still have time to change what those eulogies would include.

One of the best examples of a man who changed his eulogy was Alfred Nobel. That name immediately brings to mind the Nobel Peace Prize. But that is only the second half of this man's story.

Alfred Nobel was a Swedish chemist who made a fortune inventing dynamite and several other explosives used for weapons of war. Years after his world-renowned developments, Nobel's brother died. The local newspaper mistakenly thought that it was Alfred Nobel who had died.

The next morning, Alfred Nobel arose to read his own eulogy in the paper. He was described as the man who became very wealthy enabling people to kill one another in unprecedented quantities. Nobel was stunned and shaken at what he read. He made the decision to use his accumulated wealth to honor people and accomplishments that benefited mankind. He created the Nobel Peace Prize, and you know the rest of the story.

Casting a Shadow for the Long Term

Being fondly remembered and having a long-term, positive impact on those with whom a person has lived and worked is a serious challenge. An even greater challenge presents itself in trying to cast a meaningful shadow on family and people yet unborn—generations yet to come.

To illustrate this challenge, can you remember your great-grandmother's name on your mother's side of the family?

Often people do not think about it, but it is likely that their great-grandmothers were alive when they were born. Yet very, very few people can even remember their names, much less even one personal detail in the lives of their great-grandmothers. If you do not remember her name, your great-grandmother's shadow never reached you. In truth, many people's shadows are short, and quickly we forget those who have gone before us. It is not that people mean to be forgotten, it was that they did little to lengthen their shadows during their lifetimes.

You Cannot Cast a Shadow on Yourself

The fact is that you cannot cast a shadow on yourself. Try it some time. It cannot be done. If the sun is perfectly overhead, a person casts no shadow at all. If the idea of casting a shadow represents having an impact on others, your shadow must fall upon the lives of others. If a person's life and pursuits all revolve around the self—what is in it for me—that person will likely cast a very short shadow, if any at all.

The question is, How I can cast a shadow that will stretch beyond my lifetime? Can I be certain I will continue to have an impact on the world even after I am dead and gone? How can I end up with more than a headstone over my grave as a remembrance that I was here? Will my great grandchildren even remember my name, much less what I stood for and cared about? Will I inspire and motivate others who survive me through the life I lived?

No one asks these important questions at a birth. But they do ask them at a funeral. A birth is a time of joy and happiness—a time of hope and great expectations. A funeral, on the other hand, is a time of reflection and being reminded of our own mortality.

Funerals often lead us to evaluate our life-priorities. We may more clearly distinguish between the tyranny of the urgent and the priority of the important. Funerals help us to look anew at the direction of our lives. We can then decide if this course will take us where we want to end up.

Those Who Consciously Try to Cast a Shadow During this Life and Beyond

We meet many wealthy people who concentrate on making a difference with their remaining time, their unique talents and their accumulated treasures. Yet, there is no way to fully comprehend the length and breadth of the shadow a person will cast. Often, what we give of ourselves to others ends up getting passed around to still others and may end up impacting the lives of countless people we will never get a chance to meet.

If we are going to cast a shadow beyond our own days, we must invest in things and people outside of ourselves. Keep in mind, you will not be remembered by what you have kept for yourself. You will only be remembered by what you have given to others.

We have seen wonderful examples of how wealthy people have used their lives and possessions to cast a shadow on future generations of their family as well as on future generations of their community. Here is just a sampling:

- A gift to a local university to build a twelve-thousand-seat pavilion to house future sporting events, concerts and shows.

- Setting up and running the first Special Olympics program in the family's community and then sponsoring it annually thereafter through an endowment.

- The creation of a family foundation funded with stock to produce annual grants for education, protection of the environment and scientific research projects.

- Grandparents taking their grandchildren with them to deliver fresh produce to needy families in the inner city each Saturday morning during the summer.

- A family undertaking the fund-raising for the restoration of a landmark community theater that had deteriorated and subsequently closed. The theater has been re-opened and completely restored to its original beauty. Each chair in the theater contains a plate naming the donor who gave to the restoration project.

- A gift to a university to build a new business school that will forever carry the family's name.

- A gift to the local YMCA endowment fund for scholarships to allow underprivileged children in the community to participate in YMCA activities and to advance the YMCA slogan: "We promote the building of strong kids, strong families, strong communities."

- An endowment that provides food for a local rescue mission. Each month the entire family goes to the mission to serve a meal to the homeless in their community. It is the highlight of the family's entire month.

- A major planned gift to a museum that records the history of the Jewish people during the holocaust.

- A gift to the local Boys and Girls Club for college scholarships for high school graduates who were active in the Boys and Girls Club.

- A gift made by a congregation member to help acquire property and build a new church building.

- A gift to a local museum to educate visitors on the community's history and the arts. A plaque honoring the donor's parents who lived and raised their families in the community.

- The creation of a charitable organization in the name of two families. The organization will create a habitat restoration project and education facility to teach visitors about the area's history, habitat and ecosystem.

- A major gift to the local hospital to build a new wing. At the entrance to the new wing a plaque will forever display the family name as a major contributor to the new wing.

- A public city park named after the family as well as an endowment to underwrite the park's maintenance.

- The largest private gift ever made to a local cancer institute for research and development of a cure for cancer.

- Creating a professionally produced videotape of the parents sharing their life-virtues and core values with their family for all future family generations to know and remember the founders of the family fortune.

- Building an educational building on the campus of the university the donor attended. It is a great joy to witness the donor's enthusiasm as he takes friends on a tour of his building while visiting the campus.

- Establishing scholarships for deserving students to attend the donor's alma mater. The family meets each year to decide who will receive their family's scholarships for that year.

- A family donating their second home for a crisis pregnancy center in their town and setting up a matching grant for its annual funding.

You can see that all of these examples demonstrate a focus on giving to others—casting a shadow both now and beyond their lifetimes to help make a difference in the lives of others. Further, did you notice how many of these simultaneously encompassed both family and others at the same time?

Ellen and Sandy Perry

Megan introduced us to her mother and grandmother. Both had accumulated very substantial wealth. They decided it would be beneficial from an intergenerational perspective to coordinate as much of the family planning as possible.

Therefore, Ellen (Megan's grandmother, age 85) and Sandy (Megan's mother, age 63) agreed to visit with us. Ellen and Sandy were leading quiet lives typical of women who were born from 1900 to 1930 in a small Midwestern town. Although they had significant family wealth, neither of them had fully explored this wealth's potential.

Documents that were drafted as a result of closed-door conversations between their now-deceased husbands and attorneys had largely been dormant for thirty years or more. In spite of the fact that their assets represented a significant holding to the local bank which serves as trustee, the women had been left out of all discussions which were supposedly being made on their behalf.

We shared with them the concept of virtues-based life planning and showed them how they could align their personal virtues and core values with their financial assets to create more meaning for their lives through the legacy they would one day leave. They were eager to begin, stating that no one had ever talked with them this way before and that this process was exactly what they had been looking for and needed. They completed the questionnaires, which helped us get in touch with who they were and what they held most dear.

Ellen and Sandy's primary virtues and core values were honesty, responsibility, sharing and family unity. Both quoted "do unto others as you would have done unto you" as a part of their cherished foundational beliefs. Ellen and Sandy believed passionately in preserving their wealth for the future because they felt an obligation to future generations to pass along a meaningful family legacy. As those who had gone before them had been helpful to them, they wanted this legacy of helping others to continue. Stewardship of the family heritage was a sacred trust for them.

As Ellen and Sandy began to get more in touch with the strength of their feelings and more clear about what was really important to them, they chose to replace their original wills with new ones representing their beliefs. They definitely wanted documents containing strategies that would incorporate their family mission into the planning process.

They chose to establish a family foundation that would carry on the legacy of sharing and being responsible stewards of their assets forever. Ellen was especially delighted to know that her grandchildren and great-grandchildren would have the opportunity and privilege to share wealth that had originated with Ellen and her husband. She said, "I will go to my grave knowing that I have done the right thing with our wealth. Thank you for giving me this gift of peace of mind."

When the strategies encompassed in each of their plans were in place and the final documents signed, Ellen and Sandy requested that we come to their lakefront cottage, which had been the cornerstone of some of the planning. They wanted to keep this cottage in the family, so future generations could enjoy the shared family experiences that only result when families take the time to be together, without the pressure of busy agendas. The entire family came, and we talked about the planning that had been done, how it was done and why. Although a part of their inheritances was given to others, each adult child came to us and said, "Thank you for creating such a special plan for my family. Thank you for explaining it to us so that I can plan for my own life now that I know how this will impact me."

Truly, now, their masterpiece is complete. As the family dreams live on and resonate through future generations, income from grandfather, father and husband will flow to grandmother, daughter, wife, children, grandchildren, great grandchildren and beyond as the family foundation continues to carry this family's values to the community and the world. This is the right way to cast a shadow beyond the grave!

Conclusion

No one wants to be forgotten. No one wants to feel like his or her life might prove to have been smaller than it could or should have been. We all want to think that how we have spent our lives has been a good investment for more than just our own creature comforts and sense of worldly success—that others will enjoy the fruits of our investments as well.

For this to happen, we must focus not on what we make, but what we give; not on how comfortable we can make ourselves, but on how comfortable we can make others; not on how much wealth we can accumulate for ourselves, but on how much wealth we can distribute to others.

In the 1800s Andrew Carnegie, businessman turned philanthropist, may have said it best in his book, *The Gospel of Wealth*. Carnegie, a dyed-in-the-wool capitalist, challenged the wealthy of his day with these provocative words:

> An ideal State [is one] in which the *surplus wealth* of the few will become . . . the property of the many . . . administered for the common good. The public verdict will then be: "The man who dies rich . . . dies disgraced." (emphasis added)

Andrew Carnegie still lives today. His life and influence continue to cast a shadow on us. Carnegie is remembered not because of his riches, but because of his generosity. Remember, you cannot cast a shadow on yourself.

CHAPTER 18

Building Family Unity through Philanthropy

The role philanthropy can play in a family's life is like looking at a prism. Depending on the shape of the prism and the precise angle of the light, you may see entirely different spectrums of beauty and color each time you look. In chapter 12, we discussed how philanthropy creates an ideal platform for helping children overcome common dysfunctions caused by inherited wealth. In this chapter, we want to explore another way in which philanthropy can actually benefit families—how to use philanthropy to build (or in some cases, rebuild) family unity.

Parents in this century face a very significant dilemma that most past generations did not face. Children and their families are scattered all over the country geographically, pursuing widely different careers and personal interests. How can parents successfully keep their families socially and emotionally together in this incredibly mobile and diversified society?

This splintering of the family unit can be even more pronounced if there are broken or damaged relationships added to the adult children naturally going their own ways in life. It is hard enough to stay in touch when all relationships are whole and healthy. It is almost impossible when there is bitterness and broken fellowship among family members (chap. 11).

Without some overriding purpose or commonality, family members can and often do go for extended periods of time, even years, never visiting or even communicating with one another through a phone call or letter. Socially, emotionally and spiritually, they become virtual strangers to one another in later years. Clearly, this is not an outcome that makes the parents feel good about the condition of their family. To the contrary, we find it usually brings great sadness and disappointment.

For families that have succeeded in remaining emotionally if not geographically close over the years, introducing a philanthropic mission to the family can catapult it to even higher levels of unity, cooperation and meaningful fellowship.

We know of no other aspect of family wealth that has more positive impacts and fewer negative consequences than actively working together in a shared philanthropic family mission. This is just another angle of the philanthropic prism that adds a strikingly brilliant new spectrum of light and beauty to the life of a family. We have discovered three critical ways in which philanthropy can rebuild unity and cooperation even in fragmented families.

1. External Family Focus

Often the children of wealthy parents have a myopic and egocentric view of life. Generally, their material desires are all met, and they see the world through the rose-colored glasses of wealth.

A shared philanthropic mission is the single most effective way to help a family overcome this myopia and egocentrism. The key is to recast the individual family members from a self-focus on their personal agendas, their private records of past family offenses or omissions, and/or their self-serving attitudes of "what is in it for me" to a focus on others. Now, by concentrating on the lives and needs of others, the entire family is elevated to something much higher, more noble and much more powerful that can survive over multiple generations.

As one teenager asked his mother recently, "Why should I get good grades and get a good education when I am going to be rich anyway?" This is, to say the least, a very troubling but logical conclusion. These children of wealth believe their "tickets have already been punched." Why get good grades? Why work hard? Why get a good job? They can already have whatever they want. They can go wherever they want. They can do whatever they want. For children of affluent parents this attitude reflects their perception of "real life."

Jeffrey and Colonie Fisher

Jeffrey and Colonie were extremely wealthy and enjoyed the fruits of their labor. They had a palatial home and all that accompanies it. Their children had grown accustomed to the finer things in life. It was obvious from our conversations with them that they were completely unaware of how the rest of the world lives.

We asked them, "Do you know that there are people living within one-hundred-fifty miles of you that are still living as primitively today as Americans were when this country was founded? Did you know that many of these people may be living in conditions that would rival living in Third World countries?"

Our revelation was a shock to both them and their children. Keep in mind, the family lived in one of the most exclusive residential estates of this major city. They had a chauffeur and housekeepers. The children all attended the most exclusive private schools. Their vacations included places like the beaches of the Riviera, the ruins of Greece and the ski slopes of Switzerland. They never stayed in anything less than five-star hotels, and they ate at only five-star restaurants. They had their own jet and full-time pilot.

This family was so insulated from the real world by their wealth that even when they saw a picture of a starving child in Africa, it did not seem real. It was more like a Hollywood movie plot. The children were following in their parents' footsteps in every way.

As part of our work with this family, we decided a site visit for the entire family was in order, and they agreed. We spent considerable time with the family preparing them for what they were about to see. We explained that they would witness the way much of the population of the world lives. We asked them to observe what they saw with their hearts and not just their minds.

The day came, and we all traveled to a remote location in one of the most impoverished mountain areas. The director of a charity who worked to help the people in this poor region accompanied us. Before we even got to the site, the sobering scenes we passed on our way already had begun to take a toll on this family.

During the trip the director explained to the family what was happening in these mountains, why things were the way they were and what his organization and others like his were doing to try to help. When we finally arrived at our destination, the family was as fully prepared to embrace what they saw as possible.

The poverty was beyond anything they had ever seen. It almost took their breath away. The homes were ramshackle huts with outhouses and no running water. People were cooking over open fires. What little paint was on these people's homes was peeling off. One home's front porch had all but collapsed. The few sticks of furniture were handmade and very primitive. Little children were running around in the dirt, wearing tattered clothes and only a few had shoes. The sight left the entire family both numb and speechless. They had no idea people so close to their home actually lived in such squalor and poverty. It was heart-wrenching.

Then the director took them down the road a short way to show them a new home that had been built by volunteers who wanted to help these poor families. It was incredibly modest and looked more like a tool shed than a home. But it was the nicest home they would see. The director pointed out a few families working in their gardens, using very nice tools that had been donated to help these people raise their own food.

Another location showed the Fishers how some other concerned people had stepped in and were showing the people of this area how to make country crafts that could be sold in the novelty shops in the cities for a very good price.

As the Fishers talked with the genuine and sincerely friendly people, the culture shock slowly wore off. The family members talked about what they might do to help Shorty, Anna, Burnadette, Ernest and the others in this village to make a better life. They began asking more and more questions of the director about his charity's plans to continue helping these people. They were absolutely shocked when they discovered how far so little money would go in helping the people in this poverty-stricken area.

The entire family began to get excited about the potential of their financial capacity to transform the lives of entire towns in this impoverished part of their own state. The site visit was an incredible success. For the first time in the Fishers' lives, they had a focus on something and someone other than themselves. Their "family" had just gotten a lot bigger.

Many meetings followed as the whole family began focusing on helping others instead of simply helping themselves. The Fishers now have a new focus that has brought a new excitement and a new unity to their family. It has given them something meaningful to talk about and to do as a family. For that, the entire family is deeply grateful.

A Common Family Mission

Part of the unifying process of philanthropy is the creation of a master plan that everyone in the family can truly buy into and be an active part of as the family works together toward one or more common philanthropic causes or activities.

We met a couple who had set up individual foundations for each of their three children. Each child could do exactly what he or she wanted with his or her own foundation's money without having to deal with the other siblings. This may be acceptable for the purpose of helping charities, but how will this approach help the family's siblings work together and be united as a family? They have all but guaranteed that this will be just another way in which each child can be isolated, never to be seen or heard from again except possibly at weddings and funerals.

The personal missions of different members of a family may be as diversified as anyone could imagine. But the philanthropic mission of the family can still be the glue that holds the family together from generation to generation and the lens that keeps them focused on a central, common family goal. As time passes, each senior generation is required to mentor and coach the younger generation to receive the family philanthropic mantle to continue on with the family legacy that was begun by the founder of the family fortune.

Adam and Stephanie McKinley

Adam and Stephanie are in their late seventies. They have raised two children who are grown, married and living near where they were raised in New York. There are seven grandchildren, ages ten to twenty-seven. Adam and Stephanie have accumulated substantial wealth over the years through Adam's ownership in a business and his prudent investing.

Since they were very private about their financial affairs, their children did not know exactly how much Adam and Stephanie had. They did know that they were worth millions of dollars. Adam and Stephanie had more than enough to live on, plus substantial excess wealth.

Stephanie was active in the local museum and hospital charitable fundraisers. Both Adam and Stephanie had healthy relationships with their children. The children had finished college and were successful business people. Neither had any interest in the family business, so they sold it to a minority partner seven years ago.

Adam is very tough and independent, a classic

entrepreneur. Even at his age, Adam continued to manage all of his assets and investments. He was raised in a very poor home and consequently had developed the value of being very frugal with his money. He was not a particularly charitable individual. His modest annual contributions to various charities and Stephanie's time given to the hospital and museum were all he felt compelled to do.

One day their son, Bill, was exposed to some powerful concepts on charitable giving that, if employed, would cost the family none of their accumulated wealth but would create millions for charity. Bill spoke to Adam about these concepts, and the ideas were very appealing to Adam as well. He became particularly excited about the idea of setting up and running a family foundation.

As a result of this discussion and various meetings with his attorney and us, Adam set up the foundation and contributed well over two million dollars to his newly formed family foundation. He then called a meeting of all his children, their spouses and his grandchildren. At their first meeting, the main topic was, what should they do with the money? One of the problems for Adam was that, even though he felt he had raised his children with good values and they turned out to be responsible adults, he had some serious concerns that his grandchildren might not end up the same way.

It had been very difficult for Adam and Stephanie to find a common basis upon which to develop a meaningful relationship with their grandchildren because of the grandchildren's tremendous age differences and different perspectives on life. Nevertheless, Adam felt it was important that the grandchildren be involved in this meeting since they would ultimately be given the responsibility of running the family foundation. At the meeting Adam and Stephanie suggested giving five hundred thousand dollars initially to some worthwhile cause and then in the future giving the income from the balance on an annual basis. The meeting ended with each one assigned the task of returning for the next meeting with a presentation of where the five hundred thousand dollars should be contributed.

At the next meeting, one grandchild, Jeremy, age fifteen, made a presentation on why most of the money should be donated to the city's substance abuse center. Jeremy, who was seen by Adam and Stephanie as their most troubled grandchild, hung around a tough and rather unsavory crowd. Jeremy shared his reasoning. His best friend had spent eight months living there to go through rehabilitation. His friend had been released two months earlier, and the facility seemed to have made great changes in his life. Jeremy had noticed these changes and knew in his heart that this facility had saved his friend's life. Jeremy's friend told him about the facility's need for money. Jeremy made quite a compelling case for making the gift to the center, sharing with his family the details of his best friend's story.

Jeremy then asked the director from the center, whom he had invited to the meeting, to come into the room to make a presentation on how the money could be used. The center was in great need of repairs to the living quarters, and in particular it needed a new kitchen and dining facilities.

After everyone had given their presentations on where the money should be given, a discussion was held and a family vote taken. The whole family unanimously voted for Jeremy's project. They felt that the initial money going to this cause would have more impact than any other cause presented. Adam and Stephanie could not have been happier and more proud of their young grandson and the entire family's participation in the family foundation. For the first time, Adam and Stephanie had an open door of influence with Jeremy.

The common family mission of giving to the Drug and Alcohol Rehab Center brought a new sense of unity to all three generations of the McKinley family. For the first time, all three generations agreed on something extremely important. It was the beginning of a very dynamic ongoing interaction among the McKinley family that has improved communication, relationships and unity in the family.

The Joy of Giving

Giving is something learned. It is not a natural part of our human nature. You only need see a couple of small children quarreling over the same toy, both simultaneously shouting, "mine" and trying to rip it out of the other's hands to see this truth.

"Survival of the fittest" is another example of this take-and-keep-for-yourself mindset. The idea of finding joy in giving to others is counterintuitive. Yet, it is taught in every major world religion and in all the major cultures in history.

Why would a young man sacrifice his life in a war to allow people he does not even know to continue to live in freedom? Why would someone who has worked hard and paid a very high price to be financially independent turn around and give most, if not all, that money away to others? These and other similar questions cause us to consider the idea of giving to others.

Our natural inclinations tell us there is joy in keeping, but not giving. There is joy in spending money on myself, but not spending money on others. Ask most children what is most exciting about Christmas, and the answer will be the same —getting presents. When we hear that answer, we all smile and maybe even conjure up a few of our own memories.

But, there is a much deeper level of fulfillment in life than the simple joy children experience as they rip open countless brightly colored packages full of wondrous things just for them. May we suggest that the greatest fulfillment in life can be found in doing what is counterintuitive?

The deepest levels of life's joy are not found in what we get but in what we give. If you try to explain this concept to small children, they will stare at you with blank looks on their faces, amazed that anything could possibly provide more joy than receiving presents. But, as many know, there is no gift parents and grandparents could ever receive that exceeds the joy of watching the bubbling enthusiasm of their own children or grandchildren as they wildly tear open a box, squeal with glee as they discover its contents, jump to their feet, dash headlong toward the parent or grandparent for a big hug, and offer a thousand kisses and thank you's.

Why should it be any different now with accumulated wealth? Far too often, in our pursuit to build and control our own financial empires we find ourselves far more focused on what we are getting out of it all than what we could be giving. Often, we find ourselves unconsciously reverting back to a childlike attitude towards happiness: getting toys for ourselves. With this attitude, we sacrifice the deeper joy in life by neglecting the ancient truth that tells us, "It is more blessed to give than to receive."

When wealthy families do not focus solely on maximizing what they will keep for themselves and their families, but strive to address the deeper issues of life, they will find a depth of joy that almost defies description.

The joy of giving can only be learned through personal experience. It cannot be learned academically. In order to truly discover the joy of giving, you must make a gift, and the larger and more sacrificial the gift the more profound the joy. Giving is one of life's great immutable principles.

Giving can also become addictive. The more you give, the more giving you want to do. However, unlike most addictive behaviors, the more of this people indulge in, the healthier and happier they become.

For any of us to experience great happiness, we must learn three important truths: (1) We must work hard, (2) We must save/invest part of what we earn, and (3) We must give some of what we have to others. It is what we call the financial EKG —"Earning, Keeping, and Giving principle." Two out of three will not bring happiness. In fact, two out of three can lead people to high levels of stress or extreme levels of unhappiness.

For wealthy families, the first two purposes are well within their experience and knowledge. But how will wealthy parents teach their children and grandchildren the joy of giving? This requires a good bit more thought. How will they let them experience how it feels to show grace to someone who does not deserve it? How will they come to fully appreciate the power of living with open hands and an open heart? This is often new ground that many families have never plowed before.

Duane and Betsy Carr

Duane and Betsy recognized that even though they had been generous with their own wealth, they had never taught their children how to give joyfully. They decided this was a project they wanted to accomplish with the children and grandchildren before their lives were over.

During the next Thanksgiving family reunion, the Carrs began working on this long-overdue training. Duane got down on the floor with each of his young grandchildren, gave them each a twenty-dollar bill and told them that he was giving this to them to do good. He then asked them what "doing good" meant to each of them. For about twenty minutes, Duane sat on the floor and shared with each of his small grandchildren what it meant to do good with money. Before the conversation was over, the grandchildren decided what good they wanted to do with the money that Duane had given them.

He continued that practice each year with the grandchildren, increasing the amount he gave them as they grew older. It became a family tradition for Grandpa to get down on the floor at Thanksgiving time and talk about what it means to do good with money.

What a profound impact Duane has had on his grandchildren's perspective on the purpose of wealth with that simple annual exercise. Duane knew that experiencing the joy of giving could only be learned by doing it. Since his grandchildren did not have it to give, he provided the resource for the learning.

David and Rachel Griffin

The Griffins likewise made a conscious decision to begin instilling the joy of giving in their heirs' lives. They decided the best way to provide this experience was to set up a family foundation. They called a family meeting of all the children, spouses and grandchildren to announce their plans.

David and Rachel asked each of their children to be on the foundation board with them. They were making a substantial, initial gift to fund the foundation. The children were both surprised and honored to be brought into their parent's financial inner circle to share in their philanthropic efforts.

They also wanted to engage their grandchildren in this process. They began by allocating one hundred dollars for each year of each grandchild's age as their gift to charity this year. Dan was given $2,300 to give; Sarah, $2,000; Sherry, $1,700; Ann, $1,300; Dave, $1,000; Drew, $900.

Their mission was (with their parent's help if needed) to come up with a proposal on who would be the recipient of their gift from their family foundation. They presented their gift recommendations at the next family meeting. When that meeting ended, there was not a dry eye in the house as the children revealed their recipient choices and explained the reasons they wanted to give to those particular people and organizations.

Dan had just lost a friend in a car accident and wanted to offer a scholarship to the university music department in his deceased friend's memory. Sarah had a friend whose father had just died, and the family was really struggling to make ends meet. Sherry wanted to send the money to the children's hospital to help fund research on Sudden Infant Death Syndrome. Their next-door neighbors just lost their child a month earlier to SIDS. Ann wanted to give her money to the local Special Olympics. She was a very talented runner who held the state record in two track events for her age group. She thought children less gifted than she should also be given a chance to compete. Dave wanted to give his money to the local youth camp because it needed new boats. Drew loved animals, and he wanted to give his money to the local animal shelter to help find good homes for "lost and lonely animals."

To see the depth of feeling and compassion of these grandchildren was deeply moving for David and Rachel—more so than anything they could have imagined. They were very pleased with the first phase of the grandchildren's training.

The next phase was to create a junior board on the foundation and appoint the grandchildren to be that board. They were given twenty-five thousand dollars and told to find one worthy cause that they wanted to support. The decision had to be unanimous. The older grandchildren got on the Internet and began looking for causes they were interested in. The junior board finally whittled it down to one project. It was a medical clinic project in Guatemala. The junior board requested of the grandparents an additional one thousand dollars for the oldest grandson Dan to make a site visit and talk with the organization that was raising funds for the clinic.

When the junior board made its report to their parents and grandparents, they had a twenty-five-page report including site pictures, sketches of the clinic, financial breakdowns and estimated times for the completion of the project. The grant was approved unanimously by the foundation board, and the twenty-five thousand dollars was sent to the organization with instructions to start on the project immediately.

What was really exciting for David and Rachel was that their two oldest grandchildren decided to go to Guatemala during their summer break and help with the construction of the clinic themselves. They raised their own money for this trip.

All of their grandchildren caught the philanthropic fever. The first topic of discussion at family get-togethers is the family's current charitable projects or new projects that they have encountered. The entire family is experiencing the blessings of having an external focus, a common family mission and the joy of giving to help others.

Conclusion

These moving examples of families that have proactively worked to bring their families together, use their wealth as a tool to build family unity and allow their family to experience the joy of giving cannot be minimized. The stories are compelling. The results are undeniable and profound. Little time and money is needed to get this kind of family-building experience started.

What makes the idea of including family philanthropy as a critical component of a master family plan so powerful is that it produces so many individual and collective benefits without any adverse side effects. The heirs are able to overcome many of the emotional problems inherited wealth carries with it (chap. 12). Multiple family generations can bond together in ways that would be impossible to achieve otherwise. The entire family learns the delicate balance between, "What my wealth can do for me and what my wealth can do for others." This knowledge and wisdom leads to happy, content lives full of meaning and joy for every member of the family.

Parents have everything to gain and nothing to lose by beginning this process with their own families. Again, the process takes little time and relatively little money to get started. What is required, however, is desire—desire to maintain a close-knit, unified family that loves and talks and works together in meaningful ways on meaningful projects outside of themselves.

In this situation, our counsel is the same as the famous Nike commercial, "Just do it!"

CHAPTER 19

Changing the World—One Life at a Time

The desperate needs of so many people in the world can be overwhelming. Even billions of dollars invested in helping them can produce little noticeable relief from a worldwide perspective. The sheer size of the world's needs is so staggering that people become discouraged because their "little bit" (even though it may be tens of millions of dollars) will not make a significant difference.

But do you know how to eat an elephant? The answer is very helpful in this discussion. You eat an elephant one bite at a time. If you think about eating an entire elephant in one big bite, it seems impossible and more than a little ludicrous. But when you break the task down to "bite-size" steps and then go after it, eventually the elephant will be eaten. If eating the elephant one bite at a time takes too long, then you can ask others to join you, provide them with forks and let them help you eat away. The more people you involve in the task, the easier and sooner it is achieved. Before you know it, you have accomplished something very significant that many would have deemed impossible—you have eaten an elephant.

———⯈◆⯇———

Early one morning, a man was walking down the beach. He noticed a very strange phenomenon. Up ahead of him, the beach was covered with starfish, thousands of starfish. The tide had washed them ashore during the night. Walking among the starfish was a beachcomber, picking up one starfish at a time and throwing it back into the ocean.

When the man came close enough to talk to the beachcomber, he chided him in a condescending way, "With thousands of starfish lining this beach, you really do not think what you are doing will make a difference, do you?"

The beachcomber picked up another starfish and flung it back into the sea. He then replied, "I made a difference for that starfish, didn't I?"

This is our point. Even if individuals gave all they had, all their remaining time, all their unique talents and all their accumulated treasures, to meet the needs of the world, the gestures would make little difference globally. The efforts and wealth would be spread too thinly over too many people to do much good for anyone. But just as the beachcomber understood that even though he could not save all the starfish, he *could* save some of them. He had accepted the task of making a difference to the extent he could with the time and resources he had.

We cannot help everyone, but we can help someone. We cannot do everything, but we can do something. We cannot change the entire world, but we can change some small part of it.

We all need to have a global awareness, but we need to have a local focus—hence the title of this chapter, "Changing the world—one life at a time:" changing the world (global awareness), one life at a time (local focus).

Even the longest trip begins with the first step. The task for each of us is to decide which lives in this world we want to change and how we want those lives to be changed.

Deciding a course of action is both a thrill and a very serious challenge. Even contemplating the myriad possibilities of what could be done to help others has left many somewhat baffled. This is not a new situation. It has perplexed and frustrated wealthy people for centuries. Aristotle recognized the difficulty of effective philanthropy:

> To give money away is an easy matter and within any man's power. But to decide to whom to give it, and how large and when, and for what purpose and how, is neither in every man's power—nor an easy matter. Hence it is that such excellence is rare, praiseworthy and noble.

Morris Cook

A client of ours, a banker, shared with us the story of Morris Cook. Morris was a retired business owner and a widower. He was eighty-six years old and had no surviving children. His net worth was more than eleven million dollars. He had four nieces and nephews whom he did not care for at all. He did not want to leave them any of his wealth. He decided to give all he owned away to charity when he died.

Morris went to his attorney and announced his plans. The attorney told him that he must decide to which charities he wanted to leave his wealth. Morris had not considered a beneficiary. He had only thought about the people he did not want to have as beneficiaries. He told the attorney, "I will have to give that some thought. I will get back with you."

About two weeks passed, and the attorney called Morris to see if he had made a decision. Morris replied, "No, I am still thinking about it. This is a tougher decision than I thought. I will let you know as soon as I decide."

After three months, the attorney called Morris again. He told Morris he needed to know which charities he would be naming, so he could get the legal documents executed.

"Well, I am still not sure, but it is on my mind a lot. I will be deciding here before too long," Morris assured his attorney.

A year had passed since Morris' first meeting

with his attorney, and still he had not decided upon a charitable beneficiary.

Then, one morning the attorney opened his morning paper and read, "Prominent retired businessman dies at eighty-seven." It was Morris Cook.

Morris died before making his decision. Do you know who ended up with his wealth? Tragically, his nieces, nephews and the federal government got it all. Charity got nothing. Those he did not want to get anything, got it all. Those he wanted to benefit, got nothing. Why? Because Morris could not make a final decision on the important questions—how, when, what and to whom he wanted to give his wealth. Many wealthy families we work with struggle with this difficult challenge. Here is another story with a happier ending.

Ted and Kate Bonifay

We were introduced to Ted and Kate by their accountant. They were eighty-three and eighty-two, respectively. They had amassed wealth of approximately fourteen million dollars and did not have any direct heirs. However, they had already directed approximately seventy percent to their friends, nieces and nephews. The remaining thirty percent was going to charitable causes. They felt they had done all of the planning that could be done.

We had reviewed the Family Wealth Counseling methodology previously with their accountant, and he was intrigued. He asked if we would be willing to speak with the Bonifays about our process.

327

During the course of our first interview, we discovered a number of interesting facts about their financial life as well as their desire to assist charitable causes whose value systems they supported. They had previously created a small charitable trust. The trust was generating a small amount of income to them that they did not need. They had in excess of $1.2 million of annual income, generated mostly by their investment portfolio. They needed three hundred thousand dollars per year to maintain their lifestyle. Kate was severely disabled and needed twenty-four-hour care.

Due to the clients' advanced ages, we conducted the Client Retreat in four separate segments, each approximately three hours long. We spent a good deal of the time clarifying why they had chosen to assist the particular charities listed as beneficiaries in a testamentary bequest of thirty percent of their estate. We learned that prior to Kate's disability she had significant interest in these charities, and Ted wanted to make certain that her wishes were carried out after their passing.

We explored whether he would like to leave even more to charity and whether they realized that, if they made the gifts now as opposed to after their deaths, they could also obtain a current income-tax deduction as well as estate-tax savings. They told us that they did not realize this but that it was an intriguing concept. Over the course of the next couple of months, we prepared a number of discussion drafts before finalizing our planning.

One of their preferences involved the changing of the eventual beneficiary of their current charitable trust to a family foundation. They were concerned that charities' initial missions and focuses might change somewhere along the line to perhaps no longer reflect the donors' original intent. Had the donors known these changes were going to take place, they perhaps may not have continued to give them additional contributions. They also noted that using a charitable foundation rather than testamentary lump sum gifts to charity would perpetuate their family name. More importantly, they could hold the charities of their choosing accountable annually. In other words, the trustees would be instructed to continue making annual contributions to the particular charities as long as their missions met with the family's standards.

Next, Ted was concerned with their ability to make current charitable gifts. We assured him that our cash-flow analysis would deal with not only affordability but also his comfort zone. On that basis, the Bonifays agreed to proceed and gave us the authority to create a plan utilizing $2.5 million of their tax-free bond portfolio.

The first stage of our planning involved the conversion of $2.5 million of their tax-free bond portfolio. The innovative planning strategy we used more than tripled their current net, after-tax cash flow. This additional cash flow allowed us to utilize another planning strategy that would almost quadruple the inheritance to their heirs.

Ted was amazed that this could be done. In fact, he was so amazed that he determined that this was too much to leave his heirs and asked whether there was some way that they could make an additional gift to charity. We answered in the affirmative, and he determined what portion of that excess income could be contributed annually to their newly created family foundation, which would in turn invest the money. The end result of this phase of the planning was that the Bonifays' heirs received substantially more than they would have received with the old plan, and charity received almost three million dollars more as well.

On the way back from his attorney's office after executing all the necessary documents, Ted asked us, "Now you did tell me I could do more of this if I wanted to, is that right?" We assured him that he was correct, and he said that he would like to discuss some ideas that he had at a later time.

Approximately one month later, Ted called his accountant and told him that he would like to meet with us again. We set up the meeting and were pleased to hear that Ted and Kate were not only extremely excited with what we accomplished so far, they wanted to explore accelerating significantly their charitable gifts. They gave us the following parameters:

1. Contribute an additional four hundred thousand dollars annually to the family foundation without having to pay capital gains tax on the sale of the appreciated portfolio.

2. Create a mechanism whereby the foundation could remain in perpetuity.

3. Have no effect on their lifestyle and little, if any, effect on their cash flow.

It was obvious that the Bonifays had gotten the message. They understood that by making current, as opposed to testamentary, gifts they could actually increase the amount of money that went to charity as well as to their heirs.

The Bonifays have given five million dollars more to their heirs and four million dollars more to charity. They have created a mechanism for their family name and value systems to be perpetuated through eternity, all under the family's control.

Ted could not stop shaking his head. He just kept repeating, "I cannot believe that we will be able to accomplish so much with so little and that my accountant and attorney not only agreed with but endorsed the process. We will be grateful to you forever."

In the twilight of their lives, this couple discovered several powerful new ways to change their world. In fact, they will never know in this life the countless people who will be blessed by their deep desire to make a difference. The Family Wealth Counseling process equipped them with planning strategies that allowed them to have a greater impact in the world than they ever dreamed possible. And for the Bonifays, their lives are richer and fuller than ever before.

Strong Desire + Great Capacity = Phenomenal Impact

We have met many people who have a strong desire to make a significant difference in the lives of others—to change the world. But, typically, these extraordinary people have ordinary capacity with which to fund their extraordinary dreams. Most charitable organizations are founded by those who have created a nonprofit organization in an attempt to raise funds from the general public in order to transform their grand vision for changing the world into reality. These individuals have strong desire, but limited financial capacity. Their overall social impact is hindered by their financial shortfall. Almost every charity in America would tell you that if they had more funding the charity could do more good and have a greater impact on the world. *Strong Desire + Limited Capacity = Reduced Impact*

Then, there are many affluent families in our country who have incredible financial capacity, but for whatever the reason, have limited desire to reach out and make a difference in the world. Many times, they are so focused on the demands and interests of their own lives that they seldom have time to take a look at what is going on in the rest of the world. These well-to-do families have incredible capacity to change the world, but they have limited desire to do so, at least in any meaningful way. The result is that they do dramatically less good than they could. *Weak Desire + Great Capacity = Reduced Impact*

But when a wealthy family develops a strong

desire, coupled with their great financial capacity, the impact this family can have in the world jumps off the charts. These families are able to fund their own vision. They do not need to go out and raise funds to make it happen. They have the resources within their own possession. The problem is that they do not know how to unlock these treasures to fund their vision. This is why our role as Family Wealth Counselors becomes so critical. We help our wealthy clients discover their life-purpose, cast their philanthropic vision for changing the world and then help them fund it from their own accumulated wealth. *Strong Desire + Great Capacity = Phenomenal Impact*

To follow are some exciting stories of people who were able to put it all together.

Jean Woods

Jean is a very successful business owner. She operates the business with her two children. When we first met with Jean, she had a very traditional estate plan. She was an active spokesperson for Al-Anon and had speaking engagements all over the United States. We asked her about her dreams, goals and objectives. She shared that she would like to help make sure the organization had ongoing funds after her death. She had never felt like she could give big sums of money away because her assets were tied up in a closely held company.

We shared with Jean the Family Wealth Counseling process and how our objective is to help her fulfill her dreams—not only for her family, but also for the organizations that have helped mold her family. She told us that she does not know where she would be today without Al-Anon. She grew up in a situation with alcoholic parents. She was aware of the abuse coming from that environment.

She said, "Al-Anon has helped me with my personal faith. It has helped me raise good kids who do not drink, and they have raised good grandkids. I do not know where I would be without that organization."

We took her through the entire Family Wealth Counseling process and showed her that by using a combination of tools and strategies she could pass substantial assets to charity without disrupting or reducing the business cash flow. The design zeroed out her estate taxes. We then showed her how she could give the amount that would normally have gone to taxes to her newly established foundation.

Jean commented, "I cannot believe how happy I feel. I was worried about this process. Now I am going to be a philanthropist, and my kids are going to be philanthropists, too. We want to give back to those organizations that have meant so much to us."

Through this planning, Jean was able to increase by millions her current giving and the amount of funding she would now be directing to Al-Anon instead of the federal government. What a life-changing thrill for Jean to know she is going to change a small part of her world through creative planning. *Strong Desire + Great Capacity = Phenomenal Impact*

Kyle and Kay Baker

Those who have known Kyle and Kay Baker are well acquainted with their extraordinary compassion and caring, especially for children. Kyle and Kay are two remarkable individuals who exemplify the very spirit of philanthropy—their generosity comes from the heart.

Through their personal involvement and philanthropy, they have left a significant mark on their community. Through twenty-two years of personal, hands-on involvement with charity and their philanthropic gifts, they have given generously of themselves.

Some twenty years ago, Kyle and Kay had extra money, and they decided to set up the Kyle and Kay Baker Foundation. Initially, they decided to contribute to ten organizations. However, as they began listing organizations they were interested in giving to, they realized how many more causes and organizations they would like to support. Their list grew to twenty, thirty and then forty organizations that they wanted to include. Their philosophy is to give smaller gifts to many organizations instead of a few large gifts. As new programs or problems surface, Kyle and Kay are often the first to step forward with their financial support.

"There are some people who have a great deal of wealth, and they buy more things," Kay says, "but I cannot turn my back on these problems." The programs that the Baker Foundation has supported have been very significant with benefits to many. They include starting up and then enlarging the mental health department at the children's hospital in their town. Kay feels that mental health does not get noticed nearly as much as physical health. "It is a shame," she says. "Kyle and I want to support mental health because there is little mental health care available."

Kyle and Kay, however, are also concerned about physical health. They were the first to put videoscopic and laser surgery in the hospital in their town. In addition to the mental health unit at the children's hospital, the Baker Foundation is now funding a family library. They established a heart unit at the local university hospital and a cancer unit at a hospital in another state. "Now, people do not have to come to our hometown for their cancer treatments," Kay says.

Once, while reading the morning paper, Kyle noticed a picture of himself and Kay at a charity function. The caption referred to Kay wearing the same old dress. Kay responded that if she could send children to Easter Seals Camp instead of buying a new dress, she would rather do so. The Baker Foundation continues to pay for twenty-five children to attend Easter Seals Camp each year. "Many of their children are handicapped and never get out," she said. "This is the one day a year they get to feel really special."

The beauty of a charitable foundation such as Kyle and Kay's is that it can exist in perpetuity. Katherine Abernathy, Kay's daughter, has been active in the foundation for several years. Kyle trained her. When she asked her father what she needed to be successful in running a foundation, her father responded, "A heart." Katherine will continue running the foundation, even after her mother is no longer involved.

The foundation is hands-on. Kay and Katherine always visit the programs and charities they are funding. If they see room for improvement, they will make suggestions. "Kay always brings a special warmth and love to the children she visits at our children's hospital," says Tonya Hall, director of planned gifts, "The children respond beautifully to her gentle, caring manner." *Strong Desire + Great Capacity = Phenomenal Impact*

The Bakers are indeed changing the world— one life at a time.

Craig Goodman

Craig Goodman's life is proof that one person can change the world through building on a foundation of personal integrity and an unwavering commitment to excellence. While Craig is widely recognized for his extraordinary accomplishments in industry, his interests and commitments go beyond the world of business. He is a man who cares greatly about his community, his country and society.

He has given back to the community in many ways as evidenced by his contributions to countless charities, assistance to former convicts and support of financial-education programs for youth. During the past decade, he has also donated twenty-two million dollars to a local university business school, now his namesake despite his considerable reluctance to permit the naming of any institution in his honor. Craig Goodman's lifework has enhanced the community both economically and philanthropically.

Through charitable donations, sponsorship of educational programs and institutions, and other civic-minded endeavors, Craig has interwoven his industry stature with his humanitarianism. For his many philanthropic activities, the local university honored him with a Doctor of Humanities degree.

Through advertising campaigns and by example, Craig has urged members of his industry to give back to their communities. They have heard his message. Always a spokesman for the industry, he commissioned a study in 1990 to assess the industry's philanthropic contributions. The report concluded that, to date, his industry had donated approximately $5.5 billion to charitable organizations, disaster victims and municipalities throughout the country.

Craig has combined his passion for sports and flying with some of his philanthropic endeavors. For example, he sponsored a former convict for the heavyweight boxing championship. Through his personal efforts, Craig has helped numerous other former inmates find jobs and stay out of trouble. He also helped found a nonprofit rehabilitation center for drug addicts, alcoholics and people with behavioral problems.

More recently, Craig combined flying with fundraising when he sponsored a flight in 1996 to set a new speed record for business jets. The flight not only set a world record, but also it raised three hundred thousand dollars for charity.

Craig's most notable philanthropic projects have been his pioneering efforts in education through a bank he created at the local university.

Recognizing the value of learning financial responsibility at a young age, Craig founded the bank in 1987 to provide a full range of banking services to children and young adults. The bank provides hands-on learning experiences in financial management. It now has thirty thousand customers under the age of twenty-two in all fifty states and ten other countries. Craig invested millions to establish the bank.

In November 1988, Craig presented the university with a multimillion-dollar matching grant, the largest in the school's history. By stressing ethics, integrity, communication skills, community service and other socially valuable qualities, the resulting MBA program prepares students to be enlightened industry and civic leaders. In 1995, he presented the Goodman College of Business at the university with another multimillion-dollar gift for constructing new facilities. *Strong Desire + Great Capacity = Phenomenal Impact*

Can you even imagine the number of lives that Craig has and will continue to impact as he tries to change his part of the world—one life at a time?

Boyd and Elizabeth Berry

Boyd and Elizabeth Berry are helping to prove that people can honor their roots and give back to the communities in which they live.

The Berrys, who met and grew up in a city in Ohio, now live in another major city farther west.

"When we grew up, the inner city was the place to be; it was where everyone grew up," says Boyd. "However, as in many other cities, people migrated to the suburbs, but we knew the schools in the area were a valuable asset."

The Berrys wanted to support the educational experiences of inner-city youth in the town where they grew up. Grants from the Boyd and Elizabeth Berry Family Foundation have helped create the Pacesetter Program. The program provides students with scholarships for private elementary schools and high schools in their hometown, and for college at a university in Cincinnati.

The Berrys also invested in athletic facilities at Central Catholic High School. "We learned that if you invest in the facilities and the people it creates a synergy," they said.

Improving the high school was part of an area-wide redevelopment, including the hospital next door. Together, the projects have revitalized the entire neighborhood.

In the town where the Berrys now live, they are helping to revitalize the river valley by investing in one of the area's valuable assets—a world-class aquarium that brings the magic of the ocean and the tropical rainforest to the heart of the state. The aquarium has sparked a community resurgence that began before it even opened its doors.

The entire Berry family shares a sense of giving back to the community and many members serve on the Berry Foundation Board. "We are glad to have a vehicle for giving that lets us help in all of

our areas of interest," says Boyd. *Strong Desire +*
Great Capacity = Phenomenal Impact

The Berrys caught the vision to change their
world—one life at a time. They had the desire and
they had the capacity and countless lives have
been blessed because of their vision and caring.

Sonny Parter

The degree of Elaine (Sonny) Parter's generosity was not known to many. "She gave without
strings. She never expected to get anything back,"
said the pastor at her church, where Sonny
worked as secretary during the week and played
piano Sunday mornings.

Recipients of Sonny's estate include a Christian liberal arts university, a Christian school, two
Christian homes for abused children, a national
Jewish medical and research center, a local university's department of orthopedics, a children's
hospital and her church. She also helped put several students through college.

Collin Errel, who received one thousand dollars from Sonny for an overseas foreign exchange
program, remembered the woman for her "quiet
wealth." "She provided the church with an awful
lot of support—by building things and giving to
needy individuals, too," said Collin.

Sonny "adopted" Collin's family when they
moved to town, treating him and his siblings like
the grandchildren she never had. She always considered her wealth a gift and a responsibility. She
felt she was in a stewardship position, meaning

that she was obligated to preserve and use her resources wisely.

Sonny lived with her parents in a modest home for much of her life. She was married but divorced quickly and returned to her parents' home. She never remarried. Her father made products for veterinarians. A corporation that eventually became a Fortune 500 company bought his company. Sonny's father kept the stock and left it to his daughter.

The organizations she chose to give to expressed her passions. She was never able to have children of her own, but she loved children and loved helping. For example, during her childhood, Sonny and her mother visited a Christian home, then an orphanage, to read to the children. Decades later she continued to visit the home, reciting from memory the same Bible stories she had read with her mother.

She donated the largest share of her estate to that home. Each day, elementary school children gather in a classroom named for her. The children know about Sonny and how she contributed to their education and treatment. An endowment was set up at the Christian home on her behalf to be used to support the children perpetually.

Through her donations, she will be remembered for generations to come, in ways she could not have imagined. Sonny's generosity has made a difference in many lives. She greatly believed in the importance of her charitable work and provided gifts of health, hope and joy to the children and families of her community. *Strong Desire + Great Capacity = Phenomenal Impact*

Changing the world one life at a time—that was the story of Sonny's life.

Conclusion

You cannot help everyone, but you can help someone. You cannot do everything, but you can do something. You cannot change the entire world, but you can change some small part of it.

It all begins with contemplating: Do you really care? Do you really want to make a difference? Do you really want to change the world in some meaningful way?

The world should always be a better place because a man has lived. Is the world going to be a better place because you have lived? With the remaining time, the unique talents and the accumulated wealth that you have, will you invest yourself in changing the world—one life at a time?

Will those who survive you be able to say truly that the world is a better place because you lived?

ADDENDA

Addendum one

REVIEWS OF
RECOMMENDED READING

REVIEWS OF RECOMMENDED READING

BOOKS ON EFFECTIVE PERSONAL LIVING

Halftime

Bob Buford

Halftime is an inspirational and compelling introduction of a concept that conflicts with society's perception of a mid-life crisis.

Bob Buford addresses that time of life when someone has experienced success and then has a hard realization. What once was thought would satisfy only leaves the successful wanting more. Buford proposes "changing your game plan from success to significance." By using the talents, experience and abilities developed in the first half of life and coupling them with the time and financial resources afforded with success, you can maximize fulfillment in life.

Buford's style of sharing his personal renaissance makes him unquestionably qualified to motivate the reader. His stories call us to discover how we are uniquely created. He relates how we can maximize our enjoyment of our special blessings and multiply them through a process of giving them back in service to others.

Buford, Bob. *Halftime: Changing Your Game Plan from Success to Significance*. Grand Rapids: Zondervan Publishing House, 1994. ISBN: 0-310-37540-1

The Seven Habits of Highly Effective People
Stephen R. Covey

We invite you to share the positive ideas found in Stephen R. Covey's book, *The Seven Habits of Highly Effective People*. You will find this book extremely thought provoking. It is the equivalent of an entire library for improving your personal effectiveness and strengthening your personal and professional relations. Covey offers insight to a balanced life with eternal principles for happiness and success. Covey asserts there is no better investment than self-growth. This book offers the confidence that your steps are in the right direction. Effective communication habits are taught in an easy-to-understand method.

The most powerful of the Seven Habits is to *seek first to understand before you seek to be understood*. The greatest need of a human being is to be understood, to be affirmed and to be validated. This can only occur through communication, not through assumptions.

This is the foundation of Family Wealth Counseling, to be an empathetic listener. As the book teaches, we have learned the skills of empathetic listening which inspires openness and trust. Our goal is listening to understand. Learn first to see problems from the other point of view and then give expression to the needs and concerns of the other parties.

The principles taught in this book are enlightening. This powerful read can open the door to positive change. Again, we invite you to read this book and have the opportunities to live the positive ideas it expresses.

Covey, Stephen R. *The Seven Habits of Highly Effective People.* New York: Simon & Schuster, 1990. ISBN: 0-671-70863-5

Make a Life: Not Just a Living
Dr. Ron Jenson

Ron Jenson researched the lives of leaders from around the world to find out what enabled them to make not only a great living, but also to have a significant life. In his book, *Make a Life: Not Just a Living*, he describes ten life skills that will maximize our real net worth. He challenges us to determine our own concept of success. This progressive realization causes us to be all that we were meant to be and do all that we were meant to do. Action steps are suggested at the end of each chapter, and these steps aid us in becoming aware of our root attitudes, in acting out our root beliefs and in processing externally our root commitments.

The author's ability to illustrate each principle

with his own past personal experiences or those of world leaders makes it hard to put the book down.

Jenson, Ron. *Make A Life: Not Just a Living.* Nashville: Broadman & Holman Publishers, Inc., 1998. ISBN: 0-808-541196-8

The Power of Purpose
Richard Leider

If you could live your life over again, what would you do differently?

The answers to this critical question given to author Richard Leider from adults over age sixty-five created three themes that form the core of this profound book. The three themes are:

Be more reflective,

Be more courageous, and

Be clear earlier about my purpose.

The *Power of Purpose* is based on the premise that purpose is already within us waiting to be discovered. Intuition is that sixth sense independent of conscious reasoning, which allows us to invite purpose (residing deep inside the human soul) into our daily life. For this to happen, we must trust our intuition. Courage and reflection are also critical to the disciplined practice of living our purpose daily.

The book is a compilation of inspirational stories, timeless quotes and interactive questionnaires designed to help readers overcome obstacles to discover and live their life purposes.

Its teachings are equally effective for those who are still seeking to begin living their life-purpose, those who are afraid they may have missed it, and for people who are on track yet desire to focus more clearly on how they are to contribute in this life.

Leider does a magnificent job of integrating life and work in this practically written book about discovering one's life calling.

> Leider, Richard J. *The Power of Purpose: Creating Meaning in Your Life and Work.* San Francisco: Berrett-Koehler Publishers, Inc., 1997. telephone 415-288-0260. ISBN: 1-57675-021-3

INSPIRATIONAL BOOKS ON THE LIVES OF REAL PEOPLE

The Soul of a Business

Managing for Profit and the Common Good

Tom Chappell

In his book, *The Soul of a Business: Managing for Profit and the Common Good,* Tom Chappell has taken a surprisingly different approach. Chappell is the CEO of Tom's of Maine, a manufacturer of all-natural personal care products with environmentally sensitive packaging. We see in his story of success a different avenue. Sensing an empty feeling in his life, he enrolled in the Harvard Divinity School to rediscover his values. The experience ultimately became one entrepreneur's search for his own soul only to find the soul of his business.

In the process of identifying his values, he discovered that the same set of values could be used in his business. Treating others with respect, inspiring employees to exercise their creativity and building a sense of community became the primary values in his company. The result was the transformation of Tom's of Maine into a company that works for the common good. Tom's is about injecting personal values into business planning. "Human beings and nature have inherent worth and deserve respect" and "to be a profitable and successful company, while acting in a socially responsible manner" became the watchwords throughout the company. The result is a company that continues its innovative growth, averaging fifteen percent to twenty-five percent every year and anticipating sales of one hundred million dollars in the near future.

We found the book and the story it told to be good, light-hearted reading.

Chappell, Tom. *The Soul of a Business, Managing for the Common Good.* New York: Bantam Doubleday Dell Publishing Group, Inc., 1993. Book available at your local bookstore. ISBN: 0-553-37415-X

Paul J. Meyer and the Art of Giving
John Edmund Haggai

Author John Edmund Haggai wrote about Paul J. Meyer in order to share with the world a role model for the art of giving. Meyer desires to inspire the world and believes Christian stewardship and financial success go hand in hand. He believes giving is fun and strives to be Christlike in all that he does. He has created a giving system. He believes giving to others makes you a whole person and sets high stewardship targets. A critical aspect of his plan is long-range thinking and a commitment to relationships.

Another aspect of his plan is taking risks in order to make an impact on your community. Without taking risks, you have no opportunity to succeed. Taking risks also means being willing to fail, because you tried. Meyer believes failing is an excellent educational experience. Haggai uses other philanthropic examples throughout the book, such as George Eastman who believed it is more fun giving money than willing money.

We encourage you to give this book to your entire business and personal network. Meyer's philanthropic example is a refreshing selfless approach of how any person, no matter how small their monetary contribution, can be a whole person, have a happy life and make a difference in this world.

Haggai, John Edmund. *Paul J. Meyer and the Art of Giving*. Atlanta: Kobrey Press, 1994. Book available from author at 770-449-8869, address: Dr. John Edmund Haggai, Haggai Institute, PO Box 13, Atlanta, Georgia, 30370. The book is free, but a donation is appreciated.

Renewing American Compassion
Marvin Olasky

Marvin Olasky outlines a compelling vision of a real alternative to failed efforts to "institutionalize" compassion. He calls for action that is counterintuitive to many but is the essence of true compassion, *suffering with* our neighbors. This "new" definition of compassion was actually the philosophy that dominated the first 250 years of charitable giving on this continent.

Olasky demonstrates that most of the current welfare-reform programs are just aims at including conservative-sounding objectives in traditional big-money, feel-good programs. This system is not capable of reformation and is in need of replacement altogether. If there is a rally cry implied in the book, it is "Changed hearts are the key to renewal." Moral corruption and not problematic social circumstance is the root issue. Olasky understands that real change is internal and expressed in external betterment. He questions our commitment—is it to systems, or people? Olasky asserts that charity, in the form of handouts, does nothing but prolong and deepen the problem. Judicious, responsible giving is necessary while the opposite is immoral.

We heartily recommend this book to all who are considering their roles as philanthropists with compassion.

Olasky, Marvin. *Renewing American Compassion: How compassion for the needy can turn ordinary citizens into heroes.* New York: Simon & Schuster Inc., 1996. ISBN: 0-684-83000-0

Courage is Contagious
John Kasich

Congressman John Kasich believes in the glorious promise of America. After eight terms in Congress, he also believes the power—and the responsibility—to fulfill that promise lies within the hearts and minds of the American people, not the American government.

Courage is Contagious is Kasich's salute to and celebration of an inspiring and growing movement of ordinary individuals doing extraordinary things to change the face of America. The "ordinary heroes" he profiles—and he says there are millions among us—did not set out to move mountains. They simply refused to sit passively by and do nothing when they saw others in need.

They made a sandwich for the hungry, donated a shoeshine-tip fundraiser to a children's hospital, tutored an at-risk youth from the inner city or held a dying hand, and incredible things began to happen. One by one these agents of change have quietly transformed lives, neighborhoods, communities and ultimately the face of this country.

Many felt they had little to offer, but they did something anyway. Slowly but surely, their idealism, determination and courage is building the America of our dreams.

Kasich's goal is not to solicit our applause for these merchants of hope. Rather, his book is a call to action to join them. By introducing us to these ordinary heroes, Kasich inspires us to summon the courage to do our own heroic deeds. In doing so, he tells us we will not only shape a brighter future for our children; we will discover that what you give does not begin to compare with what you receive back.

Kasich, John. *Courage is Contagious: Ordinary People Doing Extraordinary Things to Change the Face of America.* New York: Doubleday, 1998. ISBN: 0-385-49147-6

Building Family Unity Through Giving
The Story of the Namaste Foundation
Deanne Stone

By following the establishment and development of the Namaste Foundation founded by Bob and Wendy Graham, Deanne Stone offers insight into how one family addresses dysfunctional actions, makes appropriate compromises and grows in their philanthropic wisdom.

It was Bob Namaste's hope that bringing the children into the family foundation would pass on his personal philanthropic interests and develop a program through which his children would be educated in the management and use of money. Stone traces this process, including the education of children, the evolution of a philosophy, the shaping of family values and, ultimately, the planning and establishment of the family foundation. In a well thought out manner, Bob identifies his parental responsibilities as being those of promoting self-esteem, teaching responsible management of money and facilitating his children's learning about responsible uses of money. In the early stages of developing the family foundation, Bob employs the services of a family coach.

Stone follows the family as they learn the art of giving and set aside personal agendas for the good of the causes the foundation is chartered to support. Their success is best expressed in the words of Bob, who says, "Our culture does a woefully inadequate job of exposing children to the ideals of philanthropy. If parents want to instill a service ethic in their children they have to take charge of educating them while they are young." His best piece of advice is "just get started; you'll have to revise your plan somewhere down the line anyway. So why not have the satisfaction now of helping others and, at the same time, give your family the opportunity to grow and discover the pleasures of working together democratically?"

We would recommend this book to anyone considering a family foundation that brings family on as members of the board.

Stone, Deanne. *Building Family Unity Through Giving: The Story of the Namaste Foundation*. San Francisco: The Whitman Institute, 1992. Book available at The Whitman Institute: 415-982-0386.

PRACTICAL BOOKS ON FAMILY WEALTH ISSUES AND STRATEGIES

Beyond the Grave:

The Right Way and the Wrong Way of Leaving Money to Your Children (and Others)

Gerald M. Condon, Esq. and Jeffrey L. Condon, Esq.

Do you plan to have heirs? If so, do not die without reading and following the advice of this book!

No book focuses on the interrelationships between the future deceased parents and their children as heirs as pointedly as this book by Condon and Condon, a father and son attorney team. Their mission is to focus on typical family conflicts and problems that arise when wealth passes to the next generation. The topics include the divisive consequences of the parents' planning or lack of appropriate planning. The Condons demonstrate how to keep your family and your assets together through life and death, using proper inheritance planning.

This book is very reader-friendly. The Condons have a true sense of humor and interject it throughout their cases as many of their scenarios combine both the psychological and emotional components of the problems and the solutions.

Do not allow your wealth to start out a blessing

and turn into a curse. Eliminate the family bickering, protect your child's inheritance from an ex-spouse or creditor, compel your children to share after you pass away, leave more to your family and less to Uncle Sam, and control how charities use your donations. This book is a must-read if you care about your family's future.

Condon, Gerald M., Esq. and Jeffery L. Condon, Esq. *Beyond the Grave: The Right Way and the Wrong Way of Leaving Money to Your Children (and Others)*. New York: Harper Business, 1995. ISBN: 0-887-30703-5

For Love and Money:

A Comprehensive Guide to the Successful Generational Transfer of Wealth

Roy O. Williams

Roy Williams' book is indeed "a comprehensive guide to the successful generational transfer of wealth" as its subtitle suggests.

Each chapter builds in a logical sequencing of ideas. Ideas are well developed, and themes are reinforced. Stories and anecdotes are used to personalize his material and help to expand his audience.

There is an effective use of easy-to-understand graphics that show how Williams' process develops along the three main areas of trust/communication, preparation and estate planning.

Williams describes in detail the important functions of a family coach. He asserts that a family coach integrates and articulates the family vision. Included is a discussion about educating and interacting with the children, choosing a mentor, and preparing the children for the future.

Williams continually offers clarifying summaries of ideas, including the need for formal family meetings. The author provides many helpful lists: seven levels of competence, six kinds of family power, eighteen preparations for wealth transfer, and fourteen reasons for inaction.

Williams explains the importance of the family having a network of resources, a unified mission statement, a long-term commitment to the process and a solid relationship within the family.

This book discusses the need for synergism, where all members of the team have the same information. The family coach, with his/her broad experience, can translate family values and goals into a successfully integrated wealth transfer plan.

Williams, Roy O. *For Love and Money: A Comprehensive Guide to the Successful Generational Transfer of Wealth.* Marina, CA: Monterey Institute, 1997. Available at: 888-467-5310, fax: 209-951-9232, or mail: Accents/Bookminders, PO Box 70344, Stockton, CA 95267. ISBN 1-880710-01-3

The Golden Ghetto

Jessie O'Neill

The *Golden Ghetto* provides an insightful look at "affluenza," a dysfunctional relationship with money that can be manifested in a variety of destructive behavior patterns. Having suffered from affluenza herself, author Jessie O'Neill exposes the common misconception that money is the ultimate source of happiness.

She identifies numerous ideas that lay the groundwork for understanding the psychology of affluence and for finding a way out of the golden ghetto. She notes that affluenza is generational and is set in motion by a patriarch and matriarch who are often isolated from the family. The absence of parents in the children's lives creates abandonment and trust issues for the children of affluence that follow them into adulthood.

O'Neill also notes that inherited or sudden wealth can create a false sense of entitlement, a loss of future motivation and an inability to delay gratification and tolerate frustration. The behavior that heirs often exhibit in society creates a highly ambivalent attitude toward the wealthy among the less fortunate public that often manifests as reverse snobbery or "wealthism." The fallout for the children of the affluent is often damaged self-esteem, self-worth and self-confidence.

Is there a way out of the unhappiness that strikes so many at the top of the economic pyramid? One example that O'Neill gives is of the founder of the Harley Davidson motorcycle empire. On his son's thirty-fifth birthday, the father turned over the balance of the son's trust fund, along with advice that he "enjoy the money, use (his) talents wisely and be charitable to others."

The author recommends a variety of measures, including some therapies specifically designed to address these issues. As a practicing

362

therapist who went through many of the issues she describes, O'Neill is uniquely positioned to offer useful commentary. I would recommend this book to anyone who wants to understand the unique mindset and issues involved in accumulating large amounts of wealth in America.

O'Neill, Jessie H. *The Golden Ghetto: The Psychology of Affluence.* Minnesota: Hazelden, 1997. ISBN: 1-56838-1199-0

Children of Paradise

Successful Parenting for Prosperous Families

Lee Hausner, Ph.D.

Lee Hausner's *Children of Paradise* is one of the finest books on the special problems faced by affluent parents we have found. Although this book was originally released in 1990 (before the recent explosion of newly affluent stock option recipients), the majority of the advice is applicable to virtually all affluent households. Hausner's background as a Ph.D. and psychologist for the Beverly Hills School District gives her a unique perspective on both the problems faced by affluent parents and some potential solutions.

After laying out the various challenges faced by affluent parents, Hausner discusses several steps parents can take to raise effective children in this special environment. These steps include the following:

1. Developing your child's self-esteem

2. Making the most of the limited time you have available to spend with your children

3. Raising a self-motivated and competent child

4. Learning how to listen and talk to your children

5. Brat-proofing your children

6. Teaching children the value of money

7. Practicing effective discipline

As a whole, we believe this is an excellent manuscript to help overextended affluent parents attempt to have the same successes in parenting that they have experienced elsewhere in life.

> Hausner, Lee, Ph.D. *Children of Paradise.* New York: St. Martin's Press, 1990. Book is out of print; however, Amazon.com will query their network of used bookstores and send an update within a week.

Technical Books on Planning Tools and Strategies

Wealth Preservation for Closely-held Business Owners (and Others)

Jonathan G. Blattmachr

In this treatise of 657 pages, there is much more than we might expect from a volume on traditional estate planning. We learn from his extensive treatment of the frequent questions: Do we need a will? Should I avoid probate? How do we save estate and related taxes with the use of trusts? Whom do we choose as executors and trustees? and How do we gain protection against credit claims?

Leading to his very useful insights, we study the beginning and more fundamental bases of why we bother to plan. Here we see that our methodical planning for business contributes to our understanding that similar careful planning for our estates and financial affairs benefits our businesses, our employers, our families, our communities and ourselves. We learn that it is best when a business plan is integrated with an estate and financial plan as early as possible. The discussion of diversifying wealth has thoughtful applications not only with business types and industry cycles, but also with the impact of our growth, smooth or cyclical, on our family and community. Blattmachr relates the importance of appropriate qualities of senior management and the value of choosing to train a successor early, before planning to step down. Other valuable areas of discussion about the business include: What about kids in . . .? How to keep employees in . . . after I am gone; How to prepare to get out of (sell) . . .; and also, How to prevent the business from being sold.

Next to the estate and related tax discussions, the most extensive parts deal with acquiring life insurance and how to plan for retirement. One of the strong reasons for the length of these discussions is the complexity of the tax implications and benefits of the various planned structures for maximum use. From his use of more descriptive terms to rename conventional tools, we gain an ability to present them to clients more clearly and, thus, to make more extensive use of these methods and techniques than traditional estate planners.

Blattmachr, Jonathon G. *Wealth Preservation and Protection for Closely-held Business Owners (and Others)*. Washington, D.C.: Libey Publishing Incorporated, 1993. Order from author at 212-530-5066

The Rich Die Richer and You Can Too
William D. Zabel

When looking for gifts for your attorney, accountant and other family wealth counseling team members, this is the book! Encourage them to read it once a year and keep it in their libraries.

The author, leading estate and tax attorney William D. Zabel, shares his experiences dealing with the concerns of many of his trust and estate clients and provides his solutions for their various specific problems. Each chapter focuses on educational and historical background materials on the estate and tax topics and is then followed by short case studies. The topics include selecting fiduciaries, gifting, asset protection, estate and gift tax saving strategies, the right to die, pre- and post-nuptial agreements, creditors, expatriation, compensating lawyers, heirs, spouses, health care and living wills.

We can all learn from the strategies the author shares on how the rich die richer and adapt them to fit our unique situations. Acting on these money-saving techniques of the rich will assure the readers of an enrichment and growth of not only their own estates, but also those of their clients.

Zabel, William D. *The Rich Die Richer and You Can Too.* New York: William Morrow and Company, Inc., 1995 – ISBN: 0-688-123503

BOOKS ON RESEARCH CONCERNING FAMILIES OF WEALTH

The Achievers

The study of motivation analyst and styles of leadership

Dr. Gerald D. Bell

In his psychological studies, Dr. Gerald D. Bell has identified six styles of leadership that have combined a need to avoid failure with a need for achievement.

Bell identifies the first style as the need to command. Commanders need to control whatever situation they confront and to dominate every group they are in. They live an orderly and systematic life.

The second style is identified by the need to attack. <u>Attackers</u> need to release their hostilities without accepting responsibility or acknowledging their dependence on others.

The third style is the avoider. <u>Avoiders</u> need to avoid failure. Their goal in life is to hide. They want to stay out of trouble and depend on others to lead. They possess little self-confidence.

The fourth style is the need to please. <u>Pleasers</u> need to make others like and approve of them. They seek to gain acceptance from those they associate with by being pliable, kind and generous. They would rather make friends than perform a task well.

The psychological need to perform gives rise to the fifth style. <u>Performers</u> need to gain prestige and recognition. They try to manipulate others and make favorable impressions.

The sixth leadership style is the achiever. <u>Achievers</u> need to maximize their potential, achieving the highest levels of confidence. They are problem-centered, goal-oriented and self-reliant. The achiever is self-fulfilled, warm, spontaneous, flexible and open to ideas.

These six personality styles are pure classical personality models.

Achievers may ask themselves, "How meaningful are the things I am doing? How significant are the results of my efforts?" They have deep genuine human relationships because of their self-acceptance.

In studies where over 3,000 individuals were asked to identify the most effective leaders or managers they have ever known and write a detailed description of that person, giving examples of behavior and key characteristics, almost eighty-five percent described achievers as the most effective leaders.

Bell, Gerald D. *The Achievers: Six Styles of Personality and Leadership.* Chapel Hill: Preston-Hill, Inc., 1997. Order from: Bell Leadership, P.O. Box 572, Chapel Hill, NC 27514. ISBN: 0-91461-600-5

The Millionaire Next Door
Thomas J. Stanley, Ph.D. & William D. Danko, Ph.D.

The old adage, "Don't judge a book by its cover," resonates throughout this book. Of all U.S. households, 3.5 percent have a net worth of one million dollars or more. We live in a consumption-based society in which everyone is more concerned with what they make and own, rather than what they keep! This everyday consumption must be planned and controlled in order to accumulate wealth.

We have encounters everyday with people who are millionaires. We assume this by their possessions. We do not fully realize that the majority of these people are living well beyond their means. Also, most wealth, contrary to a widespread belief, is not inherited. Most millionaires today are first-generation. They are self-made, and the majority are self-employed business owners and entrepreneurs. However, the book goes on to imply that anybody who has steady employment and reasonable income levels can become wealthy. They, too, can become wealthy by planning and sacrifice.

Some keys to financial fitness are as follows:

1. Set goals.

2. Set a budget and visualize the long-term benefits.

3. Be frugal—live below your means.

4. Devote the time it takes to develop a proper financial plan.

5. Make a decision to accumulate wealth versus just being "better off."

All the millionaires interviewed already knew where they were going. In addition to the above, they consistently kept their domestic overhead low. The key is to allocate time, energy and money efficiently in ways conducive to building wealth (chap. 3).

Lastly, we learn from this book that the number one income-consuming category among the affluent is income tax. The very wealthy, on average, have total realized income of 6.7 percent of their net worth. People accumulate significant wealth by minimizing their realized/taxable income and maximizing their unrealized/non-taxable income.

Stanley, Thomas J., and William D. Danko. *The Millionaire Next Door: The Surprising Secrets of America's Wealthy.* Atlanta: Longstreet Press, 1996. ISBN: 1-56352-330-2

Beyond Death and Taxes

Greg Englund

Greg Englund does a superb job in illustrating how the integration of a complex, well-designed estate plan can be used as a tool for good family communication and as an educational foundation from which to train future generations.

Englund also translates many advanced planning strategies into easy-to-understand terms and flow charts that make this publication an excellent resource for someone who would like to better understand some of the tools and techniques that could be considered in the creation of a total wealth-control plan.

Englund, Gregory J. *Beyond Death & Taxes: A Guide to Total Wealth Control.* Second ed. Boston: Estate Planning Press, 1993. Order from publisher at 617-451-5057

CERTIFIED FAMILY WEALTH COUNSELOR™ TRAINING REQUIREMENTS

CERTIFIED FAMILY WEALTH COUNSELOR™

Professional Designation Training Requirements

- Attend Professional Mentoring Program training and educational sessions [125+ classroom hours]

- Complete required course reading [16 books and booklets]

- Attend a minimum of 12 national educational teleconferences [minimum of 12 educational hours]

- Pass the comprehensive competency exam [10-12 hours to complete exam]

- Present two implemented cases with letters from each client stating the Family Wealth Counselor's personal and professional value and the value of the Family Wealth Counseling process [verifiable, successful field experience]

Continuing education requirements:

- Attend annually at least one of the National Association of Family Wealth Counselors' semiannual educational conferences [15 hours per year]

- Attend annually at least six Professional Mentoring Program national educational teleconferences [six hours per year]

Addendum three

ABOUT THE NATIONAL ASSOCIATION OF FAMILY WEALTH COUNSELORS

NATIONAL ASSOCIATION OF FAMILY WEALTH COUNSELORS™

All contributing authors of this book are members of The National Association of Family Wealth Counselors™ (NAFWC), the premiere nonprofit, member-run association for Family Wealth Counselors. These professionals come together to enhance their ongoing education. Authors, researchers, Family Wealth Counselors and other national professionals present on topics currently impacting the Family Wealth Counseling field. NAFWC also provides its members with forums for national networking among the Family Wealth Counselors and other professionals adding value to the Family Wealth Counseling process.

NAFWC grants membership status to students entering the Professional Mentoring Program. To qualify as a Regular Member, individuals who are leading professionals in their own right must complete the intensive 125-hour, classroom training. All members are encouraged to qualify for the Certified Family Wealth Counselor designation (addendum 2).

The mission of Family Wealth Counseling is to help families seize their remaining time, employ their unique talents and mobilize their accumulated treasures to find fulfillment and significance as they discover and carry out their life purposes. Individually and collectively, we are making a positive difference in America and the world.

Addendum four

CONTRIBUTING AUTHORS

Contributors

All Contributors are Members of the
National Association of Family Wealth Counselors

Ralph Antolino, Jr.
Antolino & Associates, Inc.
3240 West Henderson Road
Columbus, OH 43221

Mitchell C. Barnes
Mitch Barnes Family Wealth Counseling, Inc.
800 Stonecreek Parkway, Suite 3
Louisville, KY 40223

Timothy N. Bearden
Strategic Family Wealth Counselors
32255 Northwestern Hwy
Suite 205
Farmington Hills, MI 48334

Norman H. Bevan
First Financial Resources
2777 Allen Parkway
Suite 1122
Houston, TX 77019

David R. Breuer
Mennonite Mutual Aid
1110 N. Main St.
P.O. Box 483
Goshen, IN 46527

Paul H. Brock
Allmerica Financial
4 Greenleaf Woods Dr.
Suite 301
Portsmouth, NH 03801

Stephen E. Capizzi
Core Financial Advisors, Inc.
3700 Mansell Road
Suite 220
Alpharetta, GA 30022

David R. Chepauskas
The Institute for Family Wealth Counseling, LLC
Victoria Plaza
615 Hope Road, Building 5A
Eatontown, NJ 07724

Earl G. Chesson
Hill, Chesson and Associates
213 Providence Road
Chapel Hill, NC 27514

Barbara A. Culver
Resonate, Inc.
4750 Ashwood Drive
Cincinnati, OH 45241

Thomas E. Dundorf
Charlotte Financial Concepts
230 S. Tryon
Suite 1400
Charlotte, NC 28202

Stephanie V. Enright
Enright Financial Consultants, Inc.
21515 Hawthorne Blvd.
Suite 1050
Torrance, CA 90503

Kenneth Chaim Fink
Family Wealth Counselors, LLC
3100 West Lake Street
Suite 420
Minneapolis, MN 55416

David L. Geller

Geller Financial Advisors
1777 Northeast Expressway N.E.
Suite 100
Atlanta, GA 30329-2440

Joanne Grant

Exeter Trust Company
6099 Riverside Drive
Suite 207
Dublin, OH 43017

Victor M. Harbachow

The Harbachow Companies
333 Albert Street
Suite 202
East Lansing, MI 48823

Donald B. Harris

Beaird Harris & Co., P.C.
12377 Merit Drive
Suite 220
Dallas, TX 75251

Eddie F. Hearp

Family Wealth Counselors, Inc.
4401 Starkey Road
Roanoke, VA 24014

Steve Heckard

Family Wealth Counselors of South Carolina, Inc.
P.O. Box 11001
1230 Ebenezer Road
Rock Hill, SC 29731

George W. Hester

The Hester Group
104 E. Washington Street
P.O. Drawer 1199
Kosciusko, MS 39090

David F. Hokanson
Creative Planning, Inc.
5340 College Boulevard
Overland Park, KS 66211

N. Douglas Hostetler
Hostetler & Associates, LLC
10420 Little Patuxent Parkway
Suite 490
Columbia, MD 21044

George N. Justice
Justice & Associates, Inc./
Family Wealth Counselors
1500 2nd Ave. SE, Suite 212
Cedar Rapids, IA 52403

Thomas R. Kaplan
Bernstein, Kaplan & Krauss, LLC
1200 North Federal Highway
Suite 200
Boca Raton, FL 33432

William H. Koptis
The Koptis Organization
8180 Brecksville Road
Cleveland, OH 44141

Stephen C. Langhofer
Langhofer Financial Group
7570 West 21st Street North
Building 1050; Suite A
Wichita, KS 67205-1734

Marc Lewyn
Geller Financial Advisors
1777 Northeast Expressway NE
Suite 100
Atlanta, GA 30329-2440

E. G. "Jay" Link
Family Wealth Counselors of America, LLC
20 Circle Drive
Franklin, IN 46131

Carlos H. Lowenberg, Jr.
Covenant Wealth Management , Inc.
811 Barton Springs Road
Suite 200
Austin, TX 78704

William H. McGowen, III
Family Wealth Counselors, Inc.
924 Mont Clair Rd.
Suite 116
Birmingham, AL 35213

Don Mehlig
Family Wealth Counseling, Inc.
2790 Skypark Drive
Suite 203
Torrance, CA 90505

William R. Muench
Family Wealth Counselors of America, LLC
20 Circle Drive
Franklin, IN 46131

Jerry D. Nuerge
Financial Independence Group
127 West Berry Street
Suite 310
Ft. Wayne, IN 46802

Robert M. Oliver III
National Family Wealth Counseling, Inc.
201 Alhambra Circle
Suite 510
Coral Gables, FL 33134

Frank P. Orzel

Frank P. Orzel & Co.
208 South LaSalle St.
Suite 1320
Chicago, IL 60604

Judith M. Panos

PFC Planned Financial Concepts, Inc.
an affiliate of International Planning Alliance, LLC
65 Willowbrook Blvd., 1st Floor
Wayne, NJ 07470-7053

Arlin L. Penner

2011 N. Skyline Dr.
Fullerton, CA 92831

Clare C. Price

Family Wealth Consultants, Ltd.
3250 West Big Beaver Road
Suite 135
Troy, MI 48084-2902

C. Scott Rassler

Family Wealth Counselors, Inc.
600 Corporate Drive
Suite 310
Fort Lauderdale, FL 33334

Kurt Rauzi

Rauzi Retirement & Estate Planning
120 Montgomery Street
Suite 2190
San Francisco, CA 94104

Salvadore R. Salvo

The Institute for Family Wealth Counseling, LLC
4 Campus Dr.
Parsippany, NJ 07054-3644

Richard A. Schiendler
Newport Advisors, Inc.
4001 MacArthur Boulevard
Suite 200
Newport Beach, CA 92660

Sanford A. Schmidt
Schmidt Financial Group
5600 North River Road
Suite 740
Rosemont, IL 60018

Jon Emmett Shuler
Wealth Management Associates
311 East Main Street
Spartanburg, SC 29302

Simon Singer
First Financial Resources
4700 Topeka Drive
Tarzana, CA 91356

Joseph W. Spada
The Institute for Family Wealth Counseling, LLC
4 Campus Drive
Parsippany, NJ 07054

Brent W. Stephenson
Cornerstone Legacy Advisors, Ltd.
918 Fry Road
Suite C
Greenwood, IN 46142

John E. Sullivan
Heritage Wealth Counselors, LLC
115 Route 46
Suite B10
Mountain Lakes, NJ 07046

Peter Tedstrom

Brown & Tedstrom, Inc.
1700 Broadway
Suite 500
Denver, CO 80290

Jerome A. Timmermann

The Timmermann Group
P.O. Box 346
205 N. Main
Breese, IL 62230

Phyllis J. Wordhouse

Medallion Investment Advisors, LLC
42680 Ford Road
Canton, MI 48187

Richard Young

Family Heritage Resource, Inc.
205 Hudson Trace
Suite A
Augusta, GA 30907

FAMILY
WEALTH
COUNSELING

Getting to the Heart of the Matter

A revolution in estate planning
for wealthy families

In this supplement, the editors and contributors are not engaged in rendering legal, tax, accounting, financial planning, investment or similar professional advice or services for any specific individual or situation. Examples in this text are used for illustrative purposes only and do not represent recommendations. All stories in this supplement are based on actual experiences. In some cases, the names and details have been changed to protect the privacy of the people involved. Some material may be affected by changes in the laws or in the interpretations of such laws since the manuscript for this supplement was completed. For that reason, the accuracy and completeness of such information and the opinions based thereon are not guaranteed. In addition, state or local tax laws or procedural rules may have a material impact on the general recommendations made by the contributing authors, and the strategies outlined in this supplement may not be suitable for every individual. Anyone planning to take action in any of the areas this book describes should, of course, seek professional advice from Family Wealth Counselors, accountants, lawyers, tax and other advisors, as would be prudent and advisable under their given circumstances.

Supplement to ISBN 0-9674023-0-1
Library of Congress Catalog Card Number 99-066550

Technical Editor: William R. Muench JD, CPA
Substantive Editors: E.G. "Jay" Link and Paul H. Brock
Managing Editor: Sonya Hallett

Professional Mentoring Program
P.O. Box 697
Franklin, Indiana 46131
1-888-736-7201
www.fwc9dots.com

Contents

The Common Planning Tools and Techniques of Our Profession

Sample Case Studies

THE COMMON PLANNING TOOLS AND TECHNIQUES OF OUR PROFESSION

CLT with Shortened LE

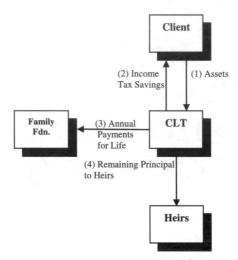

(1) Assets are transferred into the Charitable Lead Annuity Trust (CLT). The life expectancy of the grantor is taken from the IRS's tables to calculate the remainder interest. The remainder interest is calculated based on the number of years the average person of the grantor's age is expected to live. If the grantor person does not live to life expectancy, the trust will terminate and the beneficiaries will receive the remaining assets sooner than the table anticipates. The grantor has the flexibility to determine the amount of the contributions, the payout rate and the length of time the trust will be in existence. In this example, the trust was set up to remain in existence only while the grantor is alive.

(2) If this is a Grantor CLT, the contributions will generate an income tax deduction equal to the income interest. All income then earned during the term of the trust will be included as income on the personal income tax return of the grantor. If this were a Non-Grantor CLT, there would be no income tax deduction upon the contribution of assets, but no future income of the trust would be included on the personal income tax return of the grantor.

(3) The CLT will distribute an annual payment to the grantor's Family Foundation until the death of the grantor when the trust terminates.

(4) The heirs will receive the remaining principal of the trust upon the death of the grantor.

CRT WITH CLT

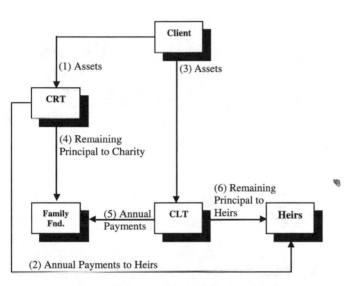

(1) A Charitable Remainder Trust (CRT) will be created under the terms of your Living Trust or Will upon your death. This CRT is a tax-exempt trust, meaning that the trust can trade securities in a tax-free environment. Because of the tax-exempt nature of the trust, this trust will be able to avoid any taxes on repositioning the portfolio to a new investment style.

(2) The CRT will provide a significant annual income to the heirs for the term of the trust.

(3) Also, upon the grantor's death, a Charitable Lead Annuity Trust (CLT) will be created under the terms of the Living Trust or Will. A formula contained in the Living Trust

or Will determines the percentage payout/length of years of this trust.

(4) At the end of the term of the CRT, the remaining value in the CRT will pass to the Family Foundation.

(5) The CLT will distribute a significant amount of money annually during the term of the trust to your Family Foundation.

(6) The heirs will receive the remaining balance in the CLT after the trust terminates.

CRT with GRAT

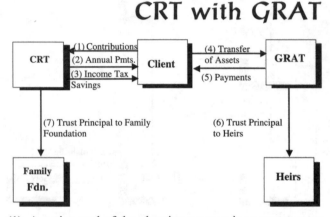

(1) A major goal of the planning process is to ensure your annual cash flow needed to maintain your lifestyle. You can generate a major portion of this income need by placing low yielding, highly appreciated securities into a Charitable Remainder Trust (CRT). Under special provisions of the Internal Revenue Code, this is a tax-exempt trust, meaning that the trust can sell stock or any other highly appreciated asset while incurring no current capital gains taxes and then reinvest in a diversified portfolio of securities. Either you, your spouse or both can serve as trustee(s) and delegate administrative and compliance duties to a third-party administrator. The trustee(s) will control all the investment decisions.

(2) The CRT will provide an annual income to you for your lifetime. Since there is no up-front capital gains tax paid to reduce the principal amount, this income stream is more than

you would have otherwise if you had paid the tax and invested the remainder. This trust can either be based on a term of years or a single or joint life expectancy.

(3) For making this contribution, you will enjoy a charitable income tax deduction. You can use this deduction up to an amount equal to 30 percent of your adjusted gross income. Any portion of the deduction exceeding this 30 percent limit may be carried over and used for an additional five years.

(4) Other assets are then transferred into a Grantor Retained Annuity Trust (GRAT). This trust is for a term of years. You have the flexibility to determine the amount of the contributions, the payout rate and the length of time the trust will be in existence. In order for this strategy to work effectively, the grantor must survive the term of the trust. If not, there will be estate inclusion for all or part of the remaining trust principal.

(5) The GRAT will distribute an amount of money annually during the term of the trust to you. This means a significant amount of money will be returned to you and/or your spouse during the term of the trust.

(6) The heirs will receive the remaining balance in the GRAT after the trust terminates.

(7) At the end of the term of the trust, the remaining value in the CRT will pass to your Family Foundation.

CRT with ILIT

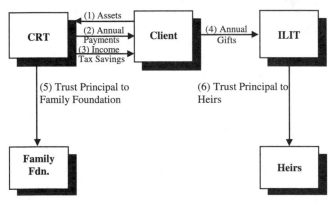

(1) A major goal of the planning process is to ensure the annual income you will need to maintain your lifestyle. You can generate a major portion of this income need by placing low yielding, highly appreciated securities into a Charitable Remainder Trust (CRT). Under special provisions of the Internal Revenue Code, this is a tax-exempt trust, meaning that the trust can sell stock or any other highly appreciated asset while incurring no capital gains tax and then reinvest in a diversified portfolio of securities. Either or both of you can serve as trustee(s) of this trust and delegate administrative and compliance duties to a third-party administrator. The trustees will control all the investment decisions.

(2) The CRT will provide an annual income to you for your lifetime. Since there was no up-front capital gains tax paid to reduce the principal amount, this income stream is more than you would have otherwise if you had paid the tax and invested the remainder. This trust can either be based on a single or joint life expectancy.

(3) For making this contribution, you will enjoy a charitable income tax deduction. You can use this deduction up to an amount equal to 30 percent of your adjusted gross income. Any portion of the deduction exceeding this 30 percent limit may be carried over and used for an additional five years.

(4) To ensure that the assets given away to charity will be adequately replaced for your heirs' inheritance, you could establish an Irrevocable Life Insurance Trust (ILIT) and immediately begin making annual gifts to the trust. These gifts could be made under the gift tax annual exclusion which permits each taxpayer to give away up to $10,000 per donee each year without any gift tax liability. These small gifts can result, over the course of several years, in a significant reduction in your gross estate and in your estate tax liability. If you wish to ensure your heirs' inheritance regardless of the year of your death, the trustee of this trust may then use those gifts to purchase a life insurance policy on your life or on the joint lives of you and your spouse. Alternately, you may prefer to have the trustee purchase investments if you are comfortable assuming you will live to normal life expectancy.

These trusts can be drafted with great flexibility. For example, the trust can allow income and principal to be used for a child's or grandchild's health, education, maintenance and support, and grant the child or grandchild the power to determine who among your descendants should receive the trust assets when the child or grandchild passes away. The child can even serve as a trustee of his or her trust, although it may also be appropriate for the child to serve as a co-trustee with an advisor.

To preserve this wealth for generations, we could make the trust a Dynasty Trust. Because the Dynasty Trust will continue for the benefit of your grandchildren and other descendants, it may be subject to the Generation Skipping Transfer Tax. However, each taxpayer is entitled to a Generation Skipping Tax exclusion of $1 million per tax-payer, which can be properly allocated to avoid this tax.

(5) At your death, the remaining value in the CRT will pass to your Family Foundation.

(6) At your death, the proceeds from the ILIT would be distributed to your children or grandchildren, or kept in trust for their benefit.

CHARITABLE STOCK
BAIL OUT PLAN

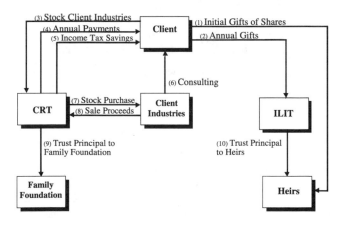

(1) The clients owned 100 percent of the stock in a closely held business worth approximately $5 million. The business was a C corporation. The first thing we recommended was a transfer of one percent of the company stock to the children working in the company. The parents retained 99 percent ownership.

(2) The family then established an Irrevocable Life Insurance Trust (ILIT), funded over the next three years. This funding was accomplished using only annual exclusion gifts. Three other children, not involved in the business, were the primary beneficiaries of this trust.

(3) The parents made annual transfers of company stock into a Charitable Remainder Trust (CRT) starting in the fourth year. From that point forward, there was an additional owner of the business—the CRT.

(4) Through a series of capital gains tax sheltered stock sales, the CRT will provide an annual income of approximately $5.4 million over the parents' lifetimes. This is $5.4 million of "new" income for the parents since the stock of the company was not paying dividends due to the adverse tax treatment. (Dividends are nondeductible to the corporation, so we find that most closely held C corporations are non-dividend paying for this reason.) In essence, we have turned non-income-producing assets into income producing ones when the stock is subsequently sold, without the adverse tax consequences usually required to do so.

(5) In addition, the transfers of company stock to the CRT over the next 25 years are going to save $480,000 in income taxes from the deductions as the stock is transferred.

(6) The parents contracted with the company to provide consulting services for an annual fee of $100,000 per year.

(7) Each year when the stock transfers into the CRT, the corporation can make a decision whether it wants to retire some outstanding stock. If it does, the corporation announces its interest in buying the outstanding shares of stock to all stockholders. The children would not typically be interested in selling their shares of stock. The parents would not sell any stock because of the capital gains taxes. The CRT, however, would sell its shares. The company buys the stock back and

8

retires it as treasury stock. This will continue to be done over the next 25 years. The ownership of the company will continually shift year by year to the children. In 16 years, the children will have voting control of the business. If the parents live to life expectancy, they will have transferred the entire value of the company to the two children. They will have paid no capital gains tax and no gift tax. They also will not have paid any estate tax at death, because the business is now outside of their estates.

(8) If the corporation put out an offer to buy, and the CRT decided to sell, the corporation would buy the stock for cash. The CRT would then reinvest those proceeds into a diversified portfolio.

(9) After both parents pass away, the CRT terminates. It funnels millions into the Family Foundation. The distribution privileges are with all five children. They play an equal role in philanthropy for their local community. We avoid the up-front capital gains taxes on the potential sale of the company. We also get the company to the children in the business without estate tax. Additionally, we increase the parents' income because non-income-producing assets are converted into income-producing ones.

(10) When both parents die, their remaining Unified Credit amounts go to the children not involved in the business. The ILIT will terminate and pass to the children not in the business income and estate tax free. All five children will have approximately $5 million each.

FLP with CLT

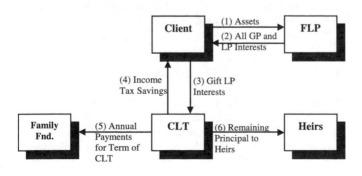

(1) You can fund this Family Limited Partnership (FLP) with cash, securities (marketable and nonmarketable), real estate and other assets. This partnership allows you to retain control over all income distributions from the partnership units, even if the Limited Partner (LP) units are given away to your heirs. You do this by acting as a controlling General Partner (GP) throughout your life. An FLP can also promote your family's ideals in important ways. In particular, your family can:

- Meet regularly to discuss how assets can be invested to further the family's purpose, virtues and values

- Jointly make investment decisions that maintain current income levels or improve returns generated by the assets

- Provide a large measure of immunization of your assets from the claims of future creditors and predators

- Keep control and ownership of assets within the family by preventing ownership from falling into the hands of in-laws upon the divorce or death of a child and from falling into the hands of any person outside the family

- Teach other family members fiscal and investment responsibility

- Amend or revoke the FLP more easily than other estate planning tools such as Irrevocable Trusts

(2) Because the LP interests in the FLP will have liquidity, marketability, and minority interest constraints, it is reasonable to assume there will be a valuation adjustment. A qualified appraiser must establish reasonable adjustments after evaluating the terms of the partnership agreement and assets used to fund the FLP. The value will likely be based in part on valuation adjustments applied to similar partnerships. After you establish and fund the FLP, you will receive GP and LP interests.

(3) The LP interests can then be transferred into a Charitable Lead Annuity Trust (CLT). The term of this trust could be either the life expectancy of the donor or a term of years. You have the flexibility to determine the amount of the contributions, the payout rate and the length of time the trust will be in existence. Due to the valuation adjustments, the payout rate of the CLT will be greater than the underlying

rate of return on the assets inside the FLP. An example is as follows: Assume a 25-percent valuation adjustment on the limited FLP interest and a six-percent rate of return on assets. An asset worth $100,000 will yield $6,000 annually. With that asset inside the FLP, the adjusted value will be $75,000. The $6,000 will then equate to an eight-percent yield ($6,000 ÷ $75,000) on that adjusted value. This will shorten the length of time that the CLT will have to be in existence.

(4) If this is a Grantor CLT, the contributions will generate an income tax deduction equal to the income interest. All income then earned during the term of the trust will be included as income on the personal income tax return of the grantor. If this is a Non-Grantor CLT, there will be no income tax deduction upon the contribution of assets, but no future income of the trust will be included on the personal income tax return of the grantor.

(5) The CLT will distribute an amount of money annually during the term of the trust to your Family Foundation. This could total a significant amount of money during the term of the trust that will be given to your Family Foundation.

(6) The heirs will receive the remaining balance in the CLT after the trust terminates.

FLP WITH CRT

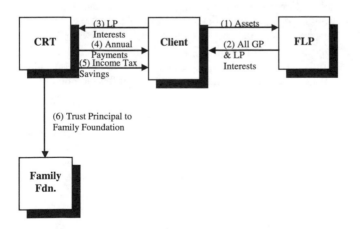

(1) See preceding technique (FLP with CLT), item (1), for explanation of FLP.

(2) Because the LP interests in the FLP will have liquidity, marketability and minority interest constraints, it is reasonable to assume there will be a valuation adjustment. A qualified appraiser must establish reasonable adjustments after evaluating the terms of the partnership agreement and assets used to fund the FLP. The value will likely be based in part on valuation adjustments applied to similar partnerships. After you establish and fund the FLP, you will receive GP and LP interests.

(3) A major goal of the planning process is to ensure the annual income you need to maintain your lifestyle. You can generate a portion of this income need by placing low yielding, highly appreciated securities into a Charitable Remainder Trust (CRT). This is a tax-exempt trust, meaning that the trust can sell stock or any other highly appreciated asset while incurring no capital gains taxes and then reinvest in a diversified portfolio of securities. Administrative and compliance duties can be delegated to a third-party administrator.

By structuring this CRT as a Net Income Make-up Charitable Remainder Unitrust (NIMCRUT), you create maximum control over taxable income in the account. The FLP structure gives you the ability to recognize or not recognize income depending on your needs. If you choose not to draw the income during your life, the tax dollars that would ordinarily have been paid will instead compound tax-deferred and pass to your family foundation or preferred charities at your death. These charities will reflect your family's mission and virtues. The uniqueness of this plan design, in essence, is that you can control the income.

(4) The CRT will provide an annual income to you for your lifetime. Since there was no up-front capital gains tax paid to reduce the principal amount, this income stream is more than you would have otherwise received had you paid the tax and invested the remainder. This trust can either be based on a term of years or a single or joint life expectancy.

(5) For making this contribution, you will enjoy a charitable income tax deduction. You can use this deduction up to an amount equal to 30 percent of your adjusted gross income. Any portion of the deduction exceeding this 30 percent limit may be carried over and used for an additional five years.

(6) At the end of the term of the trust, the remaining value in the CRT will pass to your Family Foundation.

FLP with GRAT

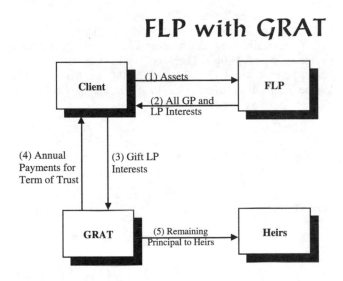

(1) See previous technique (FLP with CLT), item (1), for explanation of FLP.

(2) Because the LP interests in the FLP will have liquidity, marketability, and minority interest constraints, it is reasonable to assume there will be a valuation adjustment. A qualified appraiser will have to establish reasonable adjustments after evaluating the terms of the partnership agreement and assets used to fund the FLP. The value will likely be based in part on valuation adjustments applied to similar partnerships. After you establish and fund the FLP, you will receive GP and LP interests.

(3) The LP Interests are then transferred into a Grantor Retained Annuity Trust (GRAT). This trust is for a term of

years. You have the flexibility to determine the amount of the contributions, the payout rate and the length of time the trust will be in existence. In order for this strategy to work effectively, you must survive the term of the trust. If you do not, there will be estate inclusion for all or part of the remaining trust principal. Because of the valuation adjustments, the payout rate of the GRAT will be greater than the underlying rate of return on the assets inside the FLP. An example is as follows. Assume a 25-percent valuation adjustment on the limited FLP interest and a six-percent rate of return on assets. An asset worth $100,000 will yield $6,000 annually. With that asset inside the FLP, the adjusted value will be $75,000. The $6,000 will then equate to an eight-percent yield ($6,000 ÷ $75,000) on that adjusted value. This will shorten the length of time that the GRAT will have to be in existence.

(4) The GRAT will distribute an amount of money annually during the term of the trust to you. This could total a significant amount of money that will be returned to you and/or your spouse during the term of the trust.

(5) The heirs will receive the remaining balance in the GRAT after the trust terminates.

FLP with IDGT

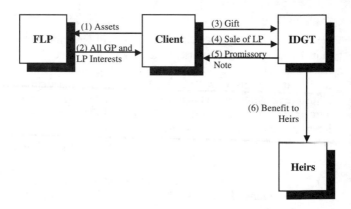

(1) See previous technique (FLP with CLT), item (1), for explanation of FLP.

(2) Because the LP interests in the FLP will have liquidity, marketability and minority interest constraints, it is reasonable to assume there will be a valuation adjustment. A qualified appraiser will have to establish reasonable adjustments after evaluating the terms of the partnership agreement and assets used to fund the FLP. The value will likely be based in part on valuation adjustments applied to similar partnerships. After you establish and fund the FLP, you will receive GP and LP interests.

(3) A gift should be made to a trust that is designed to be a Grantor Trust. An Intentionally Defective Grantor Trust (IDGT) is a trust that includes specific provisions designed to make the income of the trust taxable to the grantor. This is accomplished by allowing the grantor to retain certain administrative powers, such as the right "to reacquire the trust corpus by substituting other property of equivalent value" which, under the grantor trust rules in IRC Section 671-678, causes the grantor to be deemed the owner of the trust assets for income tax purposes. The idea is to include a provision that causes the trust to be a Grantor Trust for income tax purposes while still excluding the trust assets from the grantor's estate for estate tax purposes. This special feature makes it possible for the grantor to engage in income tax-free transactions with the trust.

(4) The grantor sells the LP interest to the IDGT for a promissory note. When you, as a grantor, sell an asset to your IDGT, it is treated as though you have sold it to yourself, and the transaction is ignored for federal capital gains and income tax purposes. Assuming the sale is at fair market value, there is no gift and no recognition of any gain or loss on this transaction. Likewise, the interest payments received by the grantor on the promissory note in connection with the asset purchase do not result in a tax deduction to the trust, nor do they constitute taxable income to the grantor. The grantor does, however, continue to pay tax on the income earned by the assets in the IDGT. This shift of the income tax liability from the trust and/or its beneficiaries back to the grantor results in the added benefit of reducing the grantor's estate

even further while enabling the assets in the IDGT to grow and have that appreciation excluded for estate tax purposes.

As long as the grantor does not retain any rights or powers that would otherwise cause inclusion under IRC Sections 2036 or 2038, then the trust assets will be excluded from his estate. Only the unpaid balance, if any, on the promissory note is included in the grantor's estate.

(5) In payment for the LP Units, the IDGT issues the grantor a fixed term promissory note bearing interest at the then current Applicable Federal Interest Rate. Over the term of the note, the grantor will receive principal and interest payments from the IDGT. As GPs of the FLP, you will have the flexibility to determine whether the FLP will distribute cash and/or in-kind portions of the underlying assets in the FLP to the IDGT to fund the note payments. If you continue to control the GP, you can continue to receive ongoing compensation from the FLP in payment for services as GP.

(6) At the end of the term of the trust, the remaining value in the IDGT will pass to the beneficiaries of the trust. After completion of the note term, you can terminate the grantor trust status and shift the income tax liability to the trust and/or its beneficiaries. You also have the ability to continue to receive ongoing compensation from the FLP in payment for services as GP.

LIFE ESTATE AGREEMENT

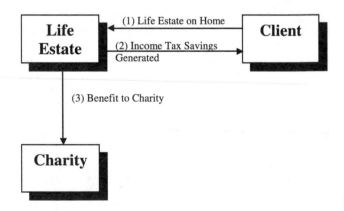

16

(1) In many cases it may make sense to contribute the remainder interest in your personal residence to your Family Foundation and retain a life estate interest in the residence over your and your spouse's lifetimes. This technique is termed "Life Estate Agreement." During your lifetime and the lifetime of the survivor, you continue to maintain your home and to pay the taxes and insurance. However, you get an up-front tax deduction today for a gift that will not be completed until the time of your death (or the sale of the property).

If you decide to sell the home, you and the Foundation can enter into a joint sale since the home is now owned partly by you (the lifetime interest) and partly by the Foundation (the remainder interest for which you received a tax deduction). The sale proceeds are divided among you and the Foundation based on your respective shares of ownership as determined using IRS actuarial tables. You also have flexibility with your retained lifetime interest. You can (1) give it away to charity or others, (2) transfer it to your CRT when you wish to sell it, or (3) later combine the Life Estate Agreement with other estate planning techniques such as a Qualified Personal Residence Trust.

You should be able to use the Life Estate Agreement technique for all residences. The term "personal residence" means any property used by its owner(s) as a personal residence, although such property need not be used as the principal residence [I.R.C. Section 170(f)(3)(B)(i) Treas. Reg. Section 1.170A-7(b)(3)]. Thus, a remainder interest in a taxpayer's vacation home that is used as a personal residence qualifies for the deduction [Treas. Reg. Sec. 1.170A-7(b)(3)].

(2) For your transfer of the remainder interest, you will receive an income tax deduction.

(3) The home will be distributed to the Family Foundation as per the Life Estate Agreement.

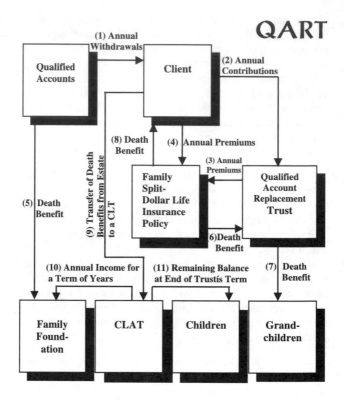

QART

(1) The clients' income exceeds their needs. Therefore, specific income amounts may be targeted for the Qualified Account Replacement Trust (QART) technique. Unneeded qualified accounts are an excellent source for this income, especially since required minimum distributions occur at age $70\frac{1}{2}$ and multiple levels of taxation (as high as 75%) are accessed on them at death.

(2) The clients gift the equivalent term cost of joint survivor life coverage (PS 38) on themselves to a QART. To the extent that it exceeds annual gifting exclusions, this transfer is subject to federal gift taxes.

(3) The QART enters into a split-dollar joint survivor life insurance contract with the clients. The QART pays the PS 38

cost and is designated as the beneficiary of the net death benefit (death benefit minus premiums loaned to date).

(4) The clients loan the remaining portion of the premiums due to the split-dollar policy. The total premium loans will be repaid either after a period of years or at the second death. The clients do not have collateral rights or cash value access to the policy during the split-dollar arrangement. Because it is a loan and not a gift, this portion of the premium is not subject to federal gift taxes.

(5) After the second death, the qualified account balance is directed to a charity, preferably a Family Foundation or a Donor Advised Fund (DAF) at a local community foundation.

(6) The split-dollar policy pays the net death benefit (death benefit minus premiums loaned to date) to the QART.

(7) The QART distributes the proceeds to its beneficiaries. Ideally, the proceeds will equal or exceed the balance of the qualified accounts, thus, "replacing" them. Because of life insurance's Generation Skipping Tax (GST) Exemption, designating grandchildren as beneficiaries can produce significant transfer leverage.

(8) The split-dollar policy returns the total amount of premiums loaned to the clients (if still living) or to the estate of the second spouse to die.

Optional:

(9) The executor of the clients' estate forwards the proceeds of the split-dollar policy to a Charitable Lead Annuity Trust (CLAT).

(10) The CLAT pays a set income to charity for a predetermined period of years. Again, the charity could be a Family Foundation or DAF. This illustration assumes the CLAT produces no remainder interest for tax purposes.

(11) After the term of the CLAT is complete, the assets flow to the heirs tax free. Because CLATs are not GST exempt, designating children, not grandchildren, as beneficiaries is recommended.

QRPT

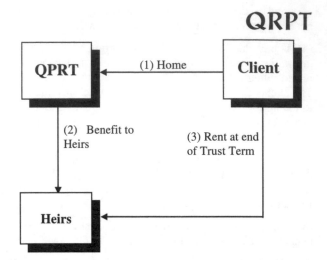

(1) You give your home to a Qualified Personal Residence Trust (QPRT) or a House GRIT [I.R.C. sec. 2702(a)(3)(A)(ii)]. Using this technique, you may transfer an asset of significant value to family members and incur little or no gift tax. (However, you must survive the term of the trust. If you do not, the asset is included in your estate at the value as of your date of death.)

To use this strategy, you create an Irrevocable QPRT and give your home to it while you retain the right to use the property for a specified number of years. This QPRT is a "Grantor Trust" and all income, if any, is taxable to the grantor(s).

During the term of the QPRT, you will have the right to continue to live in and use the house. You will pay all the costs of maintaining the house as you have always done.

(2) When the trust terminates, the home will be distributed to your heirs as per the terms of the trust.

(3) Since your heirs now own the home, you must pay rent to live in the home. This may or may not be income taxable to your heirs, depending on how this is structured. The additional benefit to this type of planning is the ability to get more money to your heirs, estate tax free, since rent payments are not subject to gift or estate tax.

TESTAMENTARY SALE OF BUSINESS/NOTE TO CLT

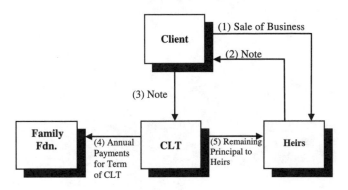

(1) Your estate will sell your business interest for a note upon your death. There will be no capital gains tax to pay on this transaction since the business received a step up in basis at your death. The sale price of the business must be for its appraised value.

(2) A note from the heirs to your estate will be executed. This note should bear a reasonable interest rate and maturity date given the market conditions at that time.

(3) A Charitable Lead Annuity Trust (CLT) will be created under the terms of your Living Trust or Will. A formula contained in your Living Trust or Will determines either the percentage payout or the length of years of this trust. The note can then be given to the trust and have no adverse tax consequences.

(4) The CLT will distribute an amount of money annually during the term of the trust to your Family Foundation. This could total a significant amount of money that will be given to your Family Foundation during the term of the trust.

(5) The heirs will receive the remaining balance in the CLT after the trust terminates.

Sample Case
Studies

Family Wealth Counseling
Case Study

Daniel and Cathy Carlson

Daniel and Cathy Carlson are in every sense philanthropic. Daniel, in his late 60s when we met, was a successful attorney. Cathy, in her mid-60s, was a devoted mother and homemaker. Daniel was slowing down in his profession and spending more time developing his philanthropic endeavors. Cathy was already involved with volunteer work and overseeing several philanthropic programs.

Over the years, Daniel had endowed a chair for approximately $1 million at his alma mater. He and Cathy were contributing approximately $250,000 a year to various charitable causes. They lived modestly and were very private individuals.

Daniel was doing a last-minute review of the family estate plan before he and Cathy were to leave on an extended vacation. Daniel was told the entire estate could be subject to as high as a 60% transfer tax should they both die.

The Carlsons were referred to us, and we showed them how our Family Wealth Counseling process would enable them to use their Social Capital (tax dollars) to perpetuate their family legacy by redirecting their taxes from the government to the causes they already supported.

One tax savings transaction they could make immediately was to change the beneficiary on Daniel's $2 million IRA account to a named charity. This account would suffer as much as an 85% tax bite if left in the estate.

While the Carlsons were completing the Life on Purpose Questionnaire, we analyzed their asset position and legal documents. We showed them exactly where they currently were in relation to where they said they wanted to be as outlined in their Family Wealth Letter of Intent. In the current plan, there was no mention of charity. As a result, their estate would be divided between their two children and the IRS.

Another immediate tax savings strategy they implemented immediately was to utilize both of their unified credits. Currently they were not each taking advantage of that opportunity. At that time, the credit allowed each individual to pass $600,000 in assets free of estate tax. One of the Carlsons' goals was to maximize the annual gifts they could give to their children, yet they were limiting themselves to only the $10,000 per person. We explained that each of the Carlsons could also pass $1 million to their grandchildren with no transfer tax, avoiding the 50% tax at the children's level. The Carlsons concluded that they wanted their children to have $5 million each and $2 million for the grandchildren.

Their current plan provided for the distribution to their children and grandchildren. However, the IRS would get as much as their children, and charity would lose. (See Fig. 1 and following explanation)

Current Plan Flowchart
(Fig. 1)

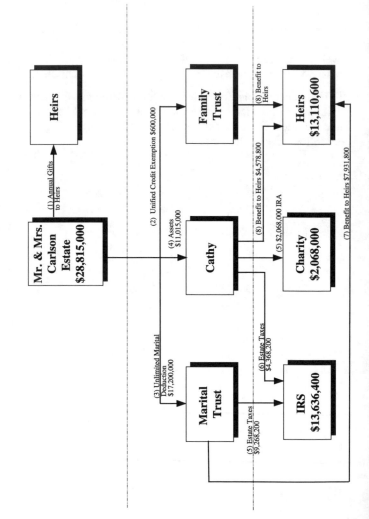

Explanation of Current
Estate Plan Flowchart (Fig. 1)

(Assumptions: All tax rates remain the same, both Carlsons live to their life expectancies, the growth of the estate keeps pace with inflation, no further amounts of either spouse's lifetime exclusion will be used up during the remainder of their lives. This plan was created before the increase of the Unified Credit. Therefore, we have assumed a $600,000 per person lifetime exclusion amount.)

What Happens While Both Are Alive

(1) During the remainder of their lives, they will continue to maximize the annual gifts to the children. These gifts are reinvested for the children. The interest, dividends and capital gains are taxable annually to the children. At the children's deaths, those assets would also be subject to 55% federal estate tax, assuming their estates are each worth more than $3-4 million.

What Will Happen at Daniel's
Death in 17 Years

(2) At Daniel's death, the remaining lifetime exclusion of $600,000 will be transferred to the Family Trust. This will be a tax-free transfer into that trust.

(3) The balance of Daniel's estate, $17.2 million, will pass tax free to the marital trust under the unlimited marital deduction.

(4) At Daniel's death, Cathy will receive other assets and the IRA via a beneficiary designation.

What Will Happen at Cathy's
Death in 17 Years

(5) At Cathy's death, this plan has the balance of Daniel's IRA transferred outright to charity. This transfer saves approximately $1.5 million in estate, income and excise taxes. The estate receives a 100% estate tax deduction for this gift.

(6) The IRS would receive approximately $13.5 million that is due and payable within nine months after Cathy's death. Over 50% of the portfolio would be lost forever.

(7) The children receive the balance of the assets in the Marital Trust with 50% of the principal distributed at age 25 and the balance at age 30.

(8) The balance of the Family Trust would pass tax free to the children.

Summary

As a result of the current estate plan, the Carlsons' heirs would receive approximately $13 million, the IRS would receive approximately $13.5 million and charity would receive the balance of the IRA, currently $2 million. The Carlsons are currently in a 55% estate tax bracket. As their net worth grows, the estate tax problem will get worse. As they continue to liquidate and reposition appreciated assets, additional capital gains tax will erode their principal.

Analysis of their mutual fund portfolio reflects high expenses associated with the management of the Class B shares. This in turn takes away from the overall performance. For example, our analysis reflects approximately $58,000 per year in extra costs simply because they held Class B shares over Class A shares for the same funds. That amount over a 5-to-6-year period equates to $300,000-$350,000 of excess expenses. Since the portfolio mirrors the S&P 500 and no special management was taking place, there seemed to be no reason for such high charges.

We Helped the Carlsons Determine Their Goals and Objectives:

❏ Eliminate all estate taxes on the transfer of our estate.

❏ Minimize capital gains taxes on asset sales.

❏ Reduce current income taxes through tax planning techniques.

❏ Secure a comfortable lifestyle with annual after-tax income of $250,000, all of which should come from investments after Daniel minimizes his wage income.

☐ Provide a safety net of asset reserves available for funding any long-term care needs not covered by the annual income provisions.

☐ Provide $5 million minimum to each of the children.

☐ Provide $1 million for each grandchild after the death of the grandparents. These funds should be controlled by each grandchild's parents until they determine when it is appropriate to pass a portion or all outright to the grandchild.

☐ Divert funds to charity that might otherwise have been used to pay unnecessary estate, capital gains, income, and excise taxes. Maintain annual charitable giving of $250,000 to $300,000.

☐ Create an investment environment that will allow for the tax-free growth of investments.

☐ Perpetuate intergenerational commitment to the causes of philanthropy supported by us.

The Carlsons' current plan did not fulfill their needs. In contrast, our proposed plan (Fig. 2) accomplished all of the Carlsons' planning goals and objectives.

Proposed Plan Flowchart
(Fig. 2)

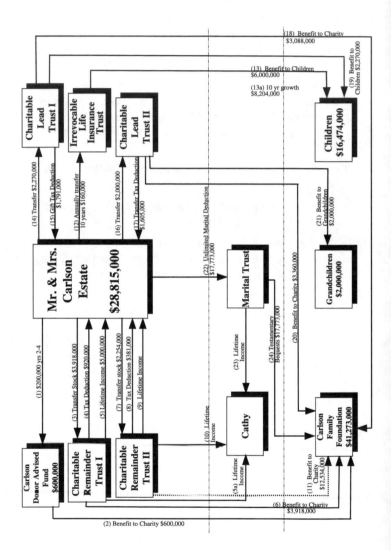

Explanation of Proposed
Family Wealth Plan Flowchart (Fig. 2)

(Assumptions: We must maintain after-tax income of at least $250,000 to $300,000 per year. We assume that both will live to their life expectancies of 17 years. We also assume that the Federal Estate Tax Rates remain unchanged. At the time of death, all parties take advantage of lifetime exclusions and other provisions of the 1997 Tax Law.)

What Happens While Both Are Still Alive

(1) Donate $200,000 per year for three years starting next year to the Carlson Donor Advised Fund (DAF). The existence of a DAF facilitates giving while we establish and wait for IRS approval of alternative philanthropic instruments, such as a public family foundation.

(2) The Carlsons can direct the DAF assets to a variety of philanthropic projects, or ultimately to the Family Foundation.

(3) Because their list of goals includes reduction of estate, capital gains, and income taxes, this Family Wealth Plan first proposes tools that will achieve all of these objectives. In particular, by transferring assets to two Charitable Remainder Trusts (CRTs), they can eliminate capital gains taxes, avoid transfer taxes, and generate retirement income streams that could be taxed at capital gains rather than ordinary income tax rates. To take advantage of these benefits, we recommended they move $3,918,000 of highly appreciated equities into a CRT, specifically a Standard Charitable Remainder Unitrust (SCRUT).

(4) Contributing assets to the SCRUT produces a tax deduction of $920,000 in the year of the transfer. We recommended they establish this charitable instrument at the end of this year. This allowed them to use the full amount of available charitable deductions limited to 30% of their Adjusted Gross Income. The portion of the tax deduction not used this year will be able to be carried forward for up to five additional years, if necessary.

Technical Memorandum: The IRS limits charitable deductions for gifts of appreciated securities to public charities to 30% of AGI. These limits apply when stocks are transferred to a CRT that passes all or part of the gift to a public family foundation when the Carlsons die. We recommend funding the SCRUT at the end of the year to avoid producing an unneeded income distribution this year. Because of the nature of the SCRUT accounting, the IRS will require a small income distribution this year. Because this may be for just one day, we have only shown a token amount in the cash flow projections for the current year.

(5) The SCRUT will generate income during their lifetimes at an 8% rate for a cumulative total of about $5 million.

Technical Memorandum: This Family Wealth Plan assumes that Daniel will predecease Cathy. Regardless, the survivor will continue to receive income distributions from the SCRUT for life.

(6) Upon the death of the Carlsons, the remaining balance of this Trust will pass to the Foundation.

(7) To receive greater tax benefits than those produced by the SCRUT, we recommended the Carlsons move $2,254,000 into a second CRT. The second CRT should be a Net Income Make-Up Charitable Remainder Unitrust (NIMCRUT). Unlike the first CRT, which produces income, the second CRT, properly invested, accumulates money in a make-up account. This account can be accessed throughout retirement years, fulfilling the goal of creating a safety net of substantial asset reserves.

(8) Contributing assets to a NIMCRUT with a 10% payout potential produces a tax deduction of $381,000 in the year of the transfer. We recommended that they establish this charitable instrument at the beginning of next year.

(9) The NIMCRUT is projected to grow throughout the lives of the Carlsons at a 10% rate. If this return is earned but not withdrawn, the earnings will accumulate in a make-up account. Based on this assumption, the NIMCRUT may accumulate more than $12.5 million of assets, a large portion of which can be accessed if necessary.

Technical Memorandum: Because the Carlsons will have substantial assets in CRT II, they can benefit greatly from maintaining an investment policy that maximizes returns.

Their current investment approach exposes them to the risks similar to owning growth stocks in a relatively undiversified portfolio. An expert in strategic asset allocation should analyze the portfolio and recommend how repositioning to different asset classes could help maintain current returns while reducing volatility and other risks. Moreover, through asset allocation, the Carlsons could increase the current cash flow from the portfolio without compromising total return. Furthermore, by using index funds or annuities, the Carlsons could avoid unnecessary taxes that result from turnover in the current portfolio. In short, a prudent asset allocation philosophy could maximize the after-tax, after-inflation, risk-adjusted return.

(10) Regardless of which spouse dies first, the survivor can continue to receive income distributions from both CRTs for life.

(11) Only after there is no longer a need for any money from the NIMCRUT, the remaining balance will pass to the Family Foundation. Because the Carlsons have so many cash flow sources in addition to the NIMCRUT make-up account, it is unlikely that they will need funds from this source during their lifetime. As a result, it is possible that the entire accumulated value will pass to charity. Assuming a 10% growth rate, we calculate the future value at $12,534,000.

(12) We recommended the Carlsons fund an Irrevocable Life Insurance Trust (ILIT). Proceeds from this trust will replace assets transferred to the CRTs and also give the children sufficient funds to purchase antiques or other sentimental assets transferred to the Family Foundation at death. Making annual gifts of $160,000 per year will fund the trust. As shown in the cash flow calculations, there should be excess income to pay for the annual gifts without compromising the Carlsons' lifestyle. Moreover, through prudent application of estate and transfer tax exemptions, the trust can be entirely funded without tax consequences. In particular, we recommended transferring $80,000 per year to the ILIT by utilizing the per donor per annum (PDPA) exclusions for each of the members in the immediate family. In addition to taking advantage of the PDPA amounts, $80,000 of the Unified Credit each year can be used.

(13) The ILIT will pay $6 million to the children after both Carlsons die.

Technical Memorandum: The results illustrated can be achieved by funding the ILIT with gifts of securities, assuming the Carlsons live to normal life expectancy. If the Carlsons wish to guarantee attainment of similar results regardless of year of death, then consideration should be given to using the stream of gifts to purchase a second-to-die life insurance policy on the lives of Mr. and Mrs. Carlson.

(13a) The Death Benefit is projected to increase to $14,204,182 over a 10-year period, based on an assumed return of 9%.

(14) We recommended they establish a Charitable Lead Annuity Trust (CLAT) with a transfer of $2,270,000. This CLAT provides significantly greater tax benefits than leaving assets in the Marital Trust. Consequently, a smaller portion of the assets in the trust ultimately go to the Treasury Department, and a much larger share of the assets will transfer to the children.

(15) Funding the CLAT produces a transfer tax deduction that offsets most of the gift tax. Nonetheless, the IRS tables show that a $2,270,375 CLAT with an 8% payout with a lifetime term (17 years) will still have a remainder interest of $479,830, which will be subject to gift taxes. Such taxes can be avoided by applying a portion of the Unified Credit against the taxable amount.

(16) In order to benefit the grandchildren by taking advantage of the Generation Skipping Tax Exemption (GSTE), we recommended they establish a Charitable Lead Unitrust (CLUT). By creating a CLUT, rather than a CLAT, we can determine in advance what the tax benefits will be. Therefore, even if the value of the assets grow, we need not worry that the taxable amount could exceed the $2 million of GSTE available.

Technical Memorandum: The Generation Skipping Trust (GST) can provide that income, and principal will initially flow to the children. As each child dies, the balance of his or her GST will pass to the grandchildren. If a grandchild has not yet reached an age of maturity, the assets will initially pass to the grandchild in trust. The Carlsons or their children can have greater control over the terms of the GST to ensure that the grandchildren will not have too much discretion over the use of funds in the GST.

(17) Creating the CLUT with assets of $2 million produces a transfer tax deduction of approximately $1,605,000. Consequently, the remainder interest subject to gift tax is approximately $395,000. Applying a portion of the Unified Credit as well as the GSTE can offset this gift tax.

Technical Memorandum: Most of the Carlsons' GST credit will be allocated to this trust to offset any taxes due on the eventual transfer to grandchildren. To avoid both estate taxes and generation skipping taxes, both Unified Credit and GST credits must be allocated to the trust.

What Happens at Daniel's Death in 17 Years

(18) Assuming that the CLAT is funded at the start of the plan or early in the next year, the trust will make annual distributions of $181,630 to the Family Foundation for 17 years beginning next year. Over their lifetimes, total transfers to the Foundation should total $3,088,000.

(19) At the end of the term of the CLAT, assets in the trust will pass to the children. This transfer produces $2,270,000 of their expected inheritance.

(20) Assuming that the CLUT is funded at the start of the plan or early in the next year, the trust will make annual distributions of approximately $160,000 to the Family Foundation for 21 years. Over the Carlsons' lifetimes, transfers from this trust to the Family Foundation should total $3,360,000.

(21) At the end of the term of CLUT, assets in the trust will pass to the grandchildren. This transfer produces $2 million of their expected inheritance.

(22) Assets in the estate not sheltered from transfer taxes by the various trusts and insurance will be sheltered from estate taxes at the first death by the Unlimited Marital Deduction. All assets will flow to a Marital Trust that will last throughout the life of Cathy.

(23) The Marital Trust will generate income for Cathy during her lifetime.

What Happens at Cathy's Death in 17 Years

(24) The balance of the assets in Cathy's estate passes to the Carlson Family Foundation at Cathy's death. This value is currently estimated to be approximately $18 million.

Technical Memorandum: We recommended they structure their foundation as a 509(a)(3) Supporting Organization.

Summary

As a result of the proposed Family Wealth Plan, the heirs (or trusts for their benefit) will inherit substantial assets. The plan also provides for substantial improvements in transfers to charity. Their current portfolio produced income that was subject to unnecessary taxes. Our alternative provided only the after-tax income needed and allowed investment earnings to accumulate tax deferred in the make-up account of a CRT. By adding the after-tax value of the make-up account amounts to their income, the present and potential income available during each year of their retirement exceeds what they had previously expected to have during their retirement years.

In short, the proposed plan outperforms the current plan by eliminating unnecessary transfer taxes, enhancing the inheritance for the heirs, augmenting funds available for charity, and improving access to a substantial after-tax income stream during the Carlsons' retirement years.

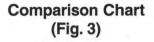

Comparison Chart
(Fig. 3)

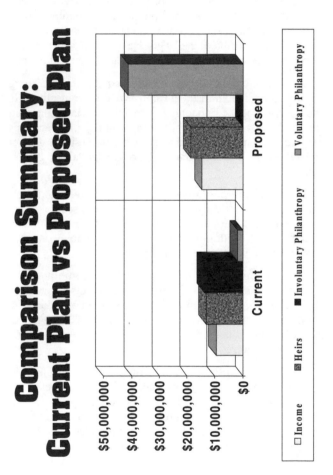

Family Wealth Counseling

CASE STUDY

DAVID AND MARGARET NOBLE

We were referred to the Nobles by a major law firm. Mr. Noble was 80, a self-made multimillionaire, an entrepreneur who started with a few thousand dollars. He had grown up during the depression of the 1930s. He now had a corporation worth millions of dollars, employing over a thousand people.

We spent four hours just getting acquainted and going through the principles used in Family Wealth Counseling. He had experienced the Economic/Financial Aspects of planning and had an excellent lawyer representing him and his corporation. Further, he had a charitable interest but did not realize how he could leverage his Social Capital for greater good.

The following day, we scheduled the Nobles and their daughter Annie for a Client Retreat. We spent several hours gaining insight into their feelings about their wealth and Social Capital. With our new insight, we commenced work on the Family Wealth Counseling process.

After many hours of analysis, we combined the economic/financial data with the social aspects to create a "before" and "after" blueprint. The uniqueness of linking the emotional/spiritual philosophies of David and Margaret to the economic issues and social issues made the planning process come alive.

Our responsibility was to complete the project in conjunction with the professional advisors (attorneys, tax advisors and trustees). The Nobles' estate prior to our involvement was valued at approximately $31 million. Based on the planning that had been done, the heirs would have received roughly $14.5 million and the government $16.5 million. Our challenge was to move the Social Capital to the causes the Nobles chose to support.

In the implementation stage, we used three very vital components to the planning process:

- Valuation adjustments to estate assets

- Charitable giving tools

- Financially leveraged insurance

We doubled the heirs' inheritance, reduced the government from $16.5 million to $2 million and gave the family $32 million for causes they wanted to support.

Our planning process actually increases their cash flow while they are alive, due primarily to additional tax deductions and higher payout rates on their charitable trusts.

Current Plan Flowchart
(Fig. 4)

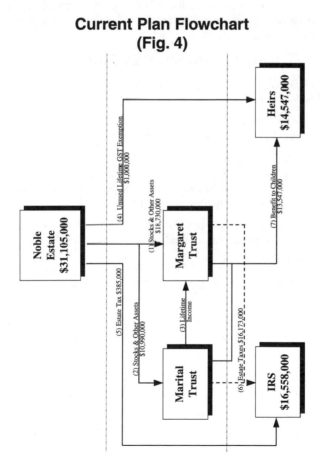

Explanation of the Current
Estate Plan Flowchart (Fig. 4)

(Assumptions: The current estate plan flowchart assumes that tax rates and the maximum lifetime exemptions remain unchanged.)

What Happens While Both Are Alive

As long as both are living, all of the income produced by the existing assets will be for the Nobles' personal benefit, and they may dispose of any of the assets they wish. However, since many of the assets are made up of highly appreciated stock, a significant capital gains tax will result upon the disposition of the assets.

What Will Happen at David's Death

(1) David's revocable trust gives Margaret his share of the residences and other collectively held property outright.

(2) The balance of David's revocable trust assets (less $1 million for the GST share) is distributed to the Marital Trust.

(3) The income from the Marital Trust is paid to Margaret quarterly and will pay principal to her as needed for her health and support. In addition, she may remove these assets from the trust at any time for any reason.

(4) The trust also establishes a Generation Skipping Exemption Share that is funded with the maximum amount of generation skipping credit available to David's estate. This amount is currently $1 million. This share is immediately distributed to the Heirs' Trust that is used to benefit the grandchildren.

(5) All of David's property passes to Margaret except for the $1 million. This will be the only amount that is subject to estate tax at David's death. The tax due is approximately $385,000.

What Will Happen at Margaret's Death

(6) At Margaret's death, the majority of the estate taxes will be paid. The total taxes paid will be approximately $16,173,000.

(7) The balance of Margaret's trust and the Marital Trust will pass to the heirs. This will be done both outright and through transfers in trust.

Summary

At David's death, the estate will pay approximately $385,000 in estate taxes. At Margaret's death, the estate will pay taxes of approximately $16,173,000. This does not include any settlement expenses. In addition to those taxes, if any appreciated assets are liquidated while they are living (i.e. stocks), capital gains taxes will be paid.

Finally, we would like to note that there are no provisions in the current estate plan for charitable gifts.

We Helped the Nobles Determine Their Goals and Objectives:

❐ Pass the full value of their estate to daughter Annie and her children.

❐ Continue current gifting to the grandchildren.

❐ Provide Annie with a current income equivalent to $80,000 per year.

❐ Keep all real estate currently owned in the family.

❐ Move the home to Annie as soon as possible.

❐ Eliminate estate taxes.

❐ Reduce current taxes if possible.

❐ Provide a legacy through the generations.

❐ Provide a lump sum to Annie and the grandchildren over time.

The Nobles' current plan did not fulfill their estate planning needs. In contrast, our proposed plan (Fig. 5) accomplished all of the Nobles' planning goals and objectives.

Proposed Plan Flowchart
(Fig. 5)

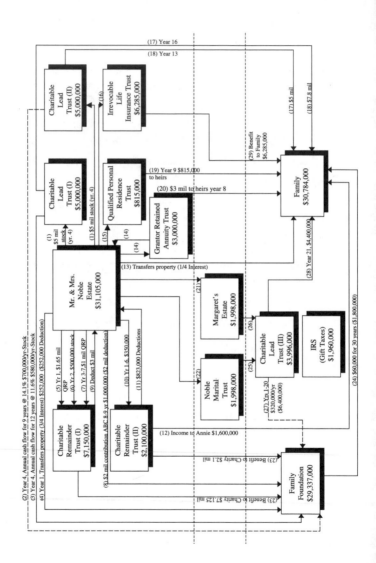

Explanation of the Proposed
Estate Plan Flowchart (Fig. 5)

(Assumptions: The proposed estate plan flowchart assumes that David predeceases Margaret. This proposed plan assumes that tax rates and the maximum lifetime exemption remain unchanged. Asset growth is assumed to keep pace with inflation unless otherwise noted.)

What Will Happen While Both Are Alive

(1) The estate is currently valued at approximately $31.1 million. The first step to providing distributions to Annie in lump sums and in later years will be to establish two Charitable Lead Trusts (CLTs). The CLTs will each be funded with $5 million of Qualified Replacement Property from the sale of the ABC Corporation Stock. The current plan is to sell this stock in the fourth year. The trusts will be funded when the stock is sold. The trusts will have terms allowing payouts in different years to Annie.

(2) CLT(II) will pay out to the Family Foundation approximately 14% of the initial funded balance for nine years ($700,000/year). Distributions may be in-kind (giving stock to the Foundation), particularly after the second year.

(3) CLT(I) will pay out to the Family Foundation approximately 11.6% ($580,000/year) for 12 years.

(4) The Nobles will transfer real estate that the family no longer uses to the Family Foundation and receive a tax deduction for the gift.

(5) In the first year, they contribute $1.65 million of Qualified Replacement Property to the Charitable Remainder Trust I [CRT(I)]. This trust will pay income to the Nobles for their lives.

(6) In the second year, they contribute $500,000 of existing stock portfolio to CRT(I).

(7) In years 3-7, they contribute $1 million of stock. The contribution will probably be Qualified Replacement Property. All contributions to CRT(I) will allow them to sell stock without upfront capital gains tax, and the trust will pay

43

income annually for both lives. The income will likely be capital gains income, taxed at 20%, depending on the investments selected after the original stock is sold.

(8) In years 8-9, $2 million of ABC Corporation stock ($1 million each year) can be directly contributed to the Family Foundation. This will provide an immediate income tax deduction that carries forward for the next five years. This will provide benefits to the Foundation and will help the estate to continue achieving significant tax deductions to offset costs throughout life expectancy. Caution should be used to relate tax deductions to adjusted gross income.

(9) The Nobles will receive a current tax deduction for contributions to CRT(I) equal to the contribution less the present value of the projected income that will be received by the Nobles from the trust in the future. This will total approximately $3 million of deductions, spread over the years of contribution.

(10) To meet the goal of getting Annie an immediate benefit, we recommend a second CRT [CRT(II)], funded by contributing $350,000 of Qualified Replacement Property per year for 6 years. A gift tax will be paid on each contribution. This trust will provide an annual income to Annie for a term of 14 years. By then, her salary from the Family Foundation will have increased, and she will have cash from her current options as well as assets from the CLT(II) and GRAT.

(11) The Nobles will receive a tax deduction for each gift with total deductions of approximately $823,000.

(12) Annie will receive approximately $1.6 million in income over the term of the trust.

(13) The Nobles may gift the remaining ¼ interest in their property to Annie at their discretion. There will be a minimal gift tax to pay with this transaction.

(14) The ABC stock they still hold is projected to grow at 16% or greater. Using this assumption, the Nobles can create a GRAT paying 16% annually of the initial funded balance for 8 years. Payments may be in cash or in-kind. The Nobles

will be responsible to pay taxes on any income earned by the trust. This will keep the family in control of ABC stock.

(15) This step will move the homes in Greenville and Oldport to a Qualified Personal Residence Trust. The trust will provide for the Nobles to live in the properties for 8 years. The properties would then pass to the designated beneficiary. The gift value of this is approximately $389,400. The Nobles may wait until the Unified Credit limit has been raised to offset this tax. (Note: Margaret must outlive the trust term to avoid the property being taxed in the total estate).

(16) Their existing life insurance of $300,000 will be transferred to the ILIT. This will remove the insurance proceeds from the taxable estate, so they will pass income and estate tax free to the beneficiaries of the trust. The Nobles have chosen to obtain an additional $6 million of life insurance to provide liquidity in order to meet their goals. We have assumed a joint second-to-die insurance policy for cost effectiveness. The additional liquidity needed will be funded with the assistance of the tax deductions from the CRT. This additional insurance will replace the value of the assets placed in the other trusts while providing liquidity in the event of premature death. The cost of the additional liquidity is approximately $280,000 and will be covered by income tax deductions.

(17) The remaining balance in CLT(I) passes outright to Annie. Based on current projections, this will occur in year 16.

(18) The remaining balance in CLT(II) passes outright to Annie. Based on current projections, this will occur in year 13.

(19) The properties in the Residence Trust will go outright to Annie in approximately year 9.

(20) The remaining balance in the GRAT will go outright to Annie in approximately year 8. Based on current assumptions, this will be about $3 million.

What Will Happen at David's Death

(21) At David's death, Margaret's assets will remain in her estate.

(22) David's assets will be transferred to the Noble Marital Trust.

What Will Happen at Margaret's Death

(23) At Margaret's death, the value of CRT(II) will move to the Family Foundation.

(24) The Family Foundation will pay an annual salary of approximately $60,000 per year for 30 years to Annie.

(25) Assets from the Noble Marital Trust will pass to CLT(III) to benefit the grandchildren.

(26) Assets from Margaret's estate will pass to CLT(III) to benefit the grandchildren. The remainder value of this trust (approx. $1 million or less) will pass to the grandchildren, and Margaret's estate will incur an estate tax on this amount.

(27) CLT(III) will pay 8% of the original value of the trust for 20 years to the Family Foundation. This provides additional funds to perpetuate the Nobles' legacy and provides additional assets for Annie to manage.

(28) After 20 years, the value of the trust will pass to the grandchildren. They will likely be in their late 40s to mid-50s. This can pass outright to the grandchildren or in a Dynasty Trust for their benefit for many years to come.

(29) The value of the ILIT will pass directly to their heirs—income, gift and estate tax free.

Summary

(1) Our plan allows the Nobles and their heirs the opportunity to self-direct their Social Capital to the Family Foundation so that it can be used to support charitable and civic organizations close to their hearts.

(2) The family will control and direct significantly more Social Capital.

(3) The family will receive a larger inheritance.

(4) The Nobles will receive more income during their lives.

In summary, the proposed plan took the Nobles' assets, philosophies and values and blended them in such a way as to meet all their goals and objectives.

Comparison Chart
(Fig. 6)

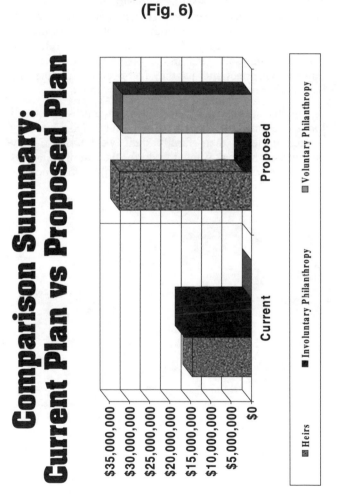

Family Wealth Counseling
Case Study

Dick and Lauren Graham

The Grahams were in their mid-60s. They had a publishing business as well as a construction business. The businesses produced a very good income, far more than they needed. Without solicitation, they were offered $10 million cash for their businesses. Four months after the offer, the businesses were sold. Their estate totaled approximately $12 million. When they met us, they had been holding the sale proceeds for more than a year, unsure how to move.

Through our Family Wealth Counseling process, Dick and Lauren became very clear as to how much and when they wanted to leave their family their wealth. Also, they discovered what they wanted to do for the rest of their lives and how they wanted to include their family in the process.

Current Plan Flowchart
(Fig. 7)

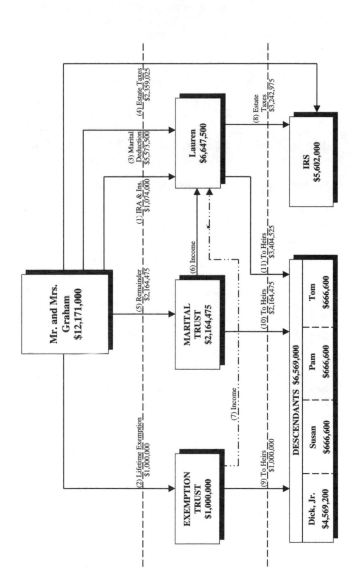

Explanation of Current
Estate Plan Flowchart (Fig. 7)

(Assumptions: The current estate plan flowchart assumes that Dick predeceases Lauren. It also assumes that both will live to their life expectancies of 14 years and 17 years, respectively. All tax rates will remain unchanged.)

What Happens While They Are Still Alive

The Grahams have traditional estate planning that includes a Revocable Living Trust (RLT). They are also making annual gifts to their children and grandchildren. In addition, they have set aside more than $91,000 in UGMA accounts for the education of their grandchildren.

What Happens at Dick's Death in 14 Years

(1) By virtue of the beneficiary designations, Lauren will be the recipient of the $677,000 in the IRAs and $397,000 of life insurance policies for a total of $1,074,000.

(2) The Exemption Trust will consist of the maximum amount that can pass free of estate tax. This amount is currently $650,000, but will be increasing to $1 million by the year 2006. The higher amount has been used for this illustration. This trust will pay income to Lauren for life, and pay principal to Lauren or Dick, Jr. if needed for their health, maintenance, or support.

(3) Lauren's share of the marital assets is $5,573,500 and it passes tax free to her by virtue of the unlimited marital deduction.

(4) Dick's share of the remaining property would also be $5,523,500. However, $1 million was left to the Exemption Trust, so his portion would normally be $4,523,500. Unfortunately, due to an error in the wording of the Marital Trust, it will not be eligible for the Marital Deduction at Dick's death and will pay $2,359,025 in estate taxes and settlement expenses.

Technical Memorandum: The Marital Trust in this case was flawed and did not qualify for the Marital Deduction at the death of the first-to-die. At the first death, the trust was to split into three shares. The Marital Trust is the balance of the first-to-die's assets less the Unified Credit amount allocated to the Exemption Trust. The obvious intent is to make the QTIP election on the Marital Trust and have it taxed at the survivor's death. Unfortunately, the Marital Trust does not qualify for the QTIP election because it fails one of the basic requirements: no one other than the spouse may have an interest in the trust during the survivor's life. In this case, page 10 of the trust allows principal to be distributed "to or for the benefit of any one of the beneficiaries."

The consequence of this error is much greater than the loss of $2,359,025. Assuming the lost principal generated 10% per year, the survivor of the couple would lose the potential income of $235,900 per year. This could amount to millions of dollars if either spouse were to die well before life expectancy.

(5) The Marital Trust will contain Dick's share of the remaining property, $2,164,475. ($5,523,500 less the $1 million Lifetime Exemption and the estate tax of $2,359,025)

(6) The Marital Trust may pay Lauren income for life.

(7) Lauren will be entitled to all of the income from the Exemption Trust.

What Happens at Lauren's Death in 17 Years

(8) The federal estate tax and settlement expenses due upon Lauren's death will be $3,242,975.

(9) The Exemption Trust, valued at $1 million, will pass to the descendants free of estate tax.

(10) The Marital Trust, valued at $2,164,475, will pass directly to the descendants free of additional estate tax.

(11) The balance of Lauren's assets, estimated at $3,404,525, will pass to the descendants.

The Balance of Lauren's assets, valued at $3,404,525, plus the Exemption Trust of $1 million and the Marital Trust of $2,164,475 will be divided. Dick, Jr. will receive $4,569,200, and Dick, Jr.'s children will share the remaining $1,999,800, or $666,600, per grandchild.

Summary

There are only three places that the Graham estate can go when death occurs: family, IRS and charity. The Grahams are facing maximum exposure to the government's system of Involuntary Philanthropy.

The following illustrates how the estate would be distributed under the current plan.

Beneficiary	Amount	% of Estate
Dick, Jr.	$4,569,200	38%
Grandchildren	$1,999,800	16%
IRS	$5,602,000	46%

We Helped the Grahams Determine Their Goals and Objectives:

❏ Eliminate estate taxes and effectively redirect Social Capital from the government to the Graham Family Foundation.

❏ Maintain their ideals and principles.

❏ Maintain ample liquidity and generate excess cash flow.

❏ Create observable and measurable standards for receiving an inheritance.

❏ Fund their grandchildren's educational expenses without gift taxes

The Grahams' current plan did not fulfill their estate planning needs. In contrast, our proposed plan (Fig. 8) accomplished all of the Grahams' planning goals and objectives.

Proposed Plan Flowchart
(Fig. 8)

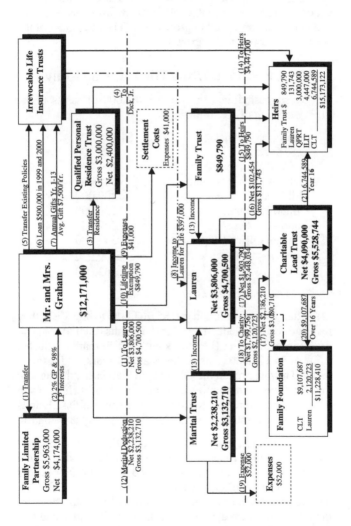

Explanation of the Proposed
Estate Plan Flowchart (Fig. 8)

(Assumptions: The Grahams both live to their life expectancies. The average income tax bracket is 42% and the capital gains rate is 27%, including state and federal. Estate tax rate remains at current level. Security investments, stocks and bonds, are projected to grow at 9%. The remainder of the estate is not estimated to grow.)

What Happens While They Are Still Alive

(1) We suggested they transfer $5,963,000 of assets to the FLP consisting of the following:

California Mutual	$4,179,000
U.S. Savings	25,000
Bank of York (cash)	106,000
Net Proceeds Bus. Sale	500,000
Hill Head	400,000
Condo-Kashmir	150,000
Land – 40 Acres	200,000
Graham Office Bldg.	343,000
County Property	60,000
Gross Value	$5,963,000
Adjusted Market Value	$4,174,000

(2) After the contribution of $5,963,000 to the FLP, they received two 1% General Partner (GP) units (total of 2%) and 98% Limited Partner (LP) units with a total market adjusted value of $4,174,000. This assumes a 30% market adjustment factor. They will retain the GP units in their estate throughout their lifetimes to maximize control over all of their assets in the FLP. They were able to discount the value of the LP units due to the constraints on marketability, liquidity and control.

(3) The home is owned jointly in the Graham Trust. Each of their community property interests should be transferred to a 10-year Qualified Personal Residence Trust (QPRT). Under the terms of the QPRT, if each of them survives the full 10-year term, 50% interest in the home will pass to Dick, Jr., including all future appreciation, free of gift and estate tax. Since the home cannot be sold without the agreement of the

owners of the separate trusts, an appraiser would assign a discount to the value. A 20% valuation adjustment was used.

The gift tax value of this transaction is $150,210 for Dick's interest and $139,661 for Lauren's interest. If either does not survive the term of the QPRT, the individual's share of the home will be included in the deceased's estate but would pass to the surviving spouse tax-free under the terms of the Unlimited Marital Deduction.

Technical memorandum: It is recommended that a certified appraisal on a property be made prior to the inclusion of a residence into a QPRT. Also, a longer term QPRT could have been used if the Grahams wanted to pass the ownership of the home more than 10 years later.

(4) At the end of the 10-year term of the QPRT, ownership of the property will pass to Dick, Jr. The Grahams can continue to live in the home but would be required to pay market rent to Dick, Jr. While at first glance this may seem to be a negative issue, many families view this as an opportunity to transfer additional assets without gift tax through the rent payments.

(5) We recommended they establish an Irrevocable Life Insurance Trust (ILIT). Initially, we recommended they transfer their existing life insurance policies to this trust. By transferring existing policies, they utilized $60,000 of their $80,000 annual gift exclusion as the cash value in the policies approximated $60,000. Additionally, they wanted the trust to acquire an additional $4 million of second-to-die life insurance for reasons discussed below. (Note: A different ILIT should hold the new insurance.)

(6) Utilizing a Family Split Dollar Agreement in conjunction with a Variable Life policy will fund the new $4 million policy. In 1999 and 2000, they will loan $500,000 per year to the trust for a total of $1 million over the 2-year period. At the end of 10 years, the loans will be repaid to them.

(7) Under the IRS regulations referring to split-dollar life insurance, the insureds are deemed to have made a taxable gift to the trust, computed using a government table (P.S. 38). Therefore, in years 1-13, taxable gifts will average

approximately $7,500. They have a reportable gift of $7,500 that they will have to contribute, in cash, to the trust each year.

What Happens at Dick's Death in 14 Years

(8) Upon Dick's death, Lauren will be entitled to receive the income from the $397,000 life insurance proceeds on Dick's life from his single life policies. At Lauren's option, she can waive the income and allow the interest to accumulate in the ILIT.

(9) Estimated final expenses are $41,000.

(10) Dick's lifetime exemption is projected to be $1 million. However, $150,210 was utilized when the QPRT was created. Therefore, $849,790 will pass directly to the Family Trust. (The current lifetime exemption is $650,000 and increases gradually to 2006, when it becomes $1 million.)

(11) Lauren will receive her half of the community property. Her half of the community property is as follows:

50% of the FLP – Adjusted Value	$2,087,000
50% of the cash	500,000
50% of marketable securities	187,000
50% of Dakota Road	300,000
50% of personal property	55,000
Total	3,129,000

Lauren will also receive Dick's IRA of $677,000. The total net value will be $3,806,000. The gross value of the underlying assets will be approximately $4,700,500.

(12) The remaining portion of Dick's half of the estate, with an adjusted value at $2,238,210 and a gross value at $3,132,710, flows into the Marital Trust.

(13) Lauren will have the right to all of the income from the Marital and the Family Trusts. She will also have the right to invade the principal to maintain her support, health and maintenance.

What Happens at Lauren's Death in 17 Years

(14) At Lauren's death, $4,447,000 of life insurance proceeds will pour into the trusts. The trustee can examine the total inheritances received by Dick, Jr. and the grandchildren before deciding what portion of the proceeds should be distributed to the heirs. This enables them to achieve their goal of maximizing their inheritance to their grandchildren.

(15) The Family Trust, valued at $849,790, will pass directly to the heirs.

(16) The balance of Lauren's lifetime exemption, $102,454, is left directly to the heirs. This should include any GP interest remaining in the estate. Either the heirs or the ILIT should purchase any GP interest not passed by the remaining lifetime exemption from the estate.

(17) The LP interests of the FLP that are valued at a total adjusted value of $4,090,000 will pass to a testamentary CLT. From the Marital Trust will come $2,186,210 and from Lauren's estate will come $1,903,790. The terms of the trust are designed to provide an estate tax charitable deduction large enough to eliminate any tax attributable to these assets.

(18) The rest of Lauren's assets will pass directly to the Graham Family Foundation.

(19) The estimated settlement expenses are $52,000.

(20) The testamentary CLT will make distributions to the Family Foundation for a period of 16 years following Lauren's death. The annual payments begin at $531,700. Due to the design of the trust, annual payments will increase to $608,283 in year 16. The total payments to the Graham Family Foundation will be $9,107,687.

(21) At the end of the term of the CLT, the balance of the LP interests with a discounted present value of $2,143,550 will go directly to the heirs. The underlying asset value will be approximately $6,744,589.

Summary

The proposed plan has created substantial advantages for the Grahams, their family and our country. The Grahams' heirs inherit substantially more of the estate, and the inheritance to the grandchildren will be spread out in the manner the Grahams' directed.

In addition, the Graham family will be able to direct 100% of their Social Capital. They have gained substantial leverage that will make a difference in this world.

Comparison Chart (Fig. 9)

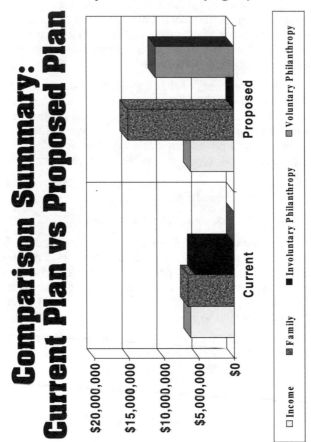

Comparison Summary: Current Plan vs Proposed Plan